TO STRIVE AND NOT TO YIELD

First edition, published in 2002 by

WOODFIELD PUBLISHING
Woodfield House, Babsham Lane, Bognor Regis
West Sussex PO21 5EL, England.

ISBN 1-873203-95-0

To Strive and Not to Yield

No.626 Squadron
RAF Bomber Command
& the Battle of Berlin

Dennis West

Woodfield Publishing

To those who flew
in the 626 Squadron Lancasters:
those who came back and those who did not.
And to the men and women on the ground
who kept them flying.

Contents

Introduction

I have tried to piece together, from many sources and to the best of my knowledge, what happened during the Battle of Berlin and 626 Squadron's part in it. There are already some books on the subject written by professional writers and Squadron members. Much information can be gleaned from the Operational Records Books of 626 Squadron, RAF Wickenby and One Group - held at the Public Records Office.

One has to imagine a room full of over a hundred airmen who have been in combat all night with an Intelligence Officer taking notes of the crews' experiences in a raid quickly by long-hand and later passing the information to a clerk to type in an Operational Records Book. 'To err is human', as someone said once, and consequently typing errors and mistakes have crept into the Official Records, as the Register's own researchers have found out, as well as myself.

I was two years old at the time of the Battle, the young men and women that took part are over seventy years old now, if they are still alive. To cast one's mind back over fifty years or more and actually put one's memories to paper accurately is a lot to ask. I have done much 'detective' work in piecing the text to-gether in the quest for the truth but having done my best over the years, if some is inaccurate, I can only apologise.

Dennis West, 2002

Acknowledgements

I could not have written this book without the help and advice from many of the members of the Wickenby Register, the 12 and 626 Squadrons Association.

In 1986 the then Register Archivist, Jim MacDonald, started me off by telling me where to look in the Public Records Office. Meanwhile Jeff Pitts sent me copies of books that I should read including the Wickenby Register's own publication 'The Woods Are Dark'. I had long telephone conversations with many which produced much information.

Edward Martin kindly loaned me the Register's photographic records and allowed me to copy some of the old wartime photographs.

Denzil Ede sent me the most heartbreaking but no less important information on all the casualties, aircraft and aircrew, of 626 Squadron. Where the Lancasters crashed or were shot down on operations and the fate of their crews.

To get the other side of the story Eric Foinette gave me the address in Germany of an ex-night-fighter pilot, the result being a long letter from Herbert Thomas in Bochum relating the history of the Night-fighter Arm of the Luftwaffe.

The fascinating story of the genesis of the 626 Squadron badge was given to me in a long letter by Bill Newman. Since it was copied from a Greek vase over 2400 years old in the British Museum, Dr Veronica Tatton-Brown of that establishment wrote inviting me to photograph and see it for myself, which I did.

Roger Bacon was the editor of the Wickenby Register Newsletter and researches 12 squadron and RAF Wickenby as well as

626 Squadron. Living in Derbyshire he has found it difficult in the past to visit the Public Records Office. Being a frequent visitor some years ago he and I swapped information quite often. He supplied a lot of the details of the old airfield as well as some of the activities of the Squadron.

Other people that took time to write to me were Bill Lamb, John Wilkin, Geoff Monk, Frank Faulkner, Jeff Pitts and Jack Cannon. The author Jack Currie, who also wrote a book about 626 Squadron, sent me a note of encouragement for my book and wished me well with it.

Three ground crew gave me their view of 626 Squadron and a great deal of knowledge of working on the Lancasters, Tom Hughes, Sid Field and Mr E.G. England.

Three former WAAFs told me what life was like for them at Wickenby, Dorothy Stillwell, Paddy Groves and Jean Hawkins.

All of the above I hold in gratitude for advice, information, and their memories of over fifty years ago.

Last but not at all least, ex-Flight Engineer Ted Groom. I interviewed Ted in Truro in 1993 and he has been a firm family friend ever since. Nearing eighty, he still plays a game of golf, drives his BMW keenly, an aircraft enthusiast and a member of the Wickenby Register. Over the years he has given me much advice and encouragement, his enthusiasm for the book being as much as mine. Without the time and financial backing of a professional writer, the last few years of the twelve I have spent writing have been difficult, especially as I was working abroad. Many times I have thought of giving up but on returning home every six months Ted always gave me the impetus to carry on. Mere words cannot thank Ted enough, for without his inspiration the story of 626 Squadron in the bitter Winter of 1943/44 might never have been written. **Dennis West**

About The Author

Dennis West was born two years before the Battle of Berlin under the kitchen table in his Grandmother's house in the middle of an air raid at Pitsea, Essex. His interest in aircraft began at an early age when the family moved to Gosport in Hampshire near the Royal Navy air station there. After being educated in Southsea he joined the Royal Navy as an aircraft apprentice but after four years terminated the apprenticeship and joined the Royal Air Force in the Avionics trade on a twelve-year engagement. He served in Wiltshire, Northern Ireland, Scotland, Yorkshire, Bahrain and Sharjar in The Middle East, Hampshire and finally Thorny Island in Sussex.

It was while at RAF Leuchars in Scotland that he met his wife, who was in the WRAF, and married her four years later. He was stationed in Yorkshire at RAF Lindholme, a name familiar to many wartime bomber crews, in 1965 on The Bomber Command Bombing School. This qualified him to become a life member of the Bomber Command Association. He left the RAF in 1973 as a Corporal Avionics Technician.

After a brief spell in the Licensed Trade he went back to aircraft servicing at Boscombe Down for eighteen months and on the BAC Lightning contract in Saudi Arabia for six years. On return to the UK he worked in Quality Control in a factory that made mainly aircraft components. After two years of being bored with the factory environment, he found employment at the Army Air Corps Centre at Middle Wallop with Bristow Helicopters, working mainly on the TOW anti-tank guided missile system on the Army's Lynx Helicopters.

To finance a move from Wiltshire to Cornwall and eventual retirement, he joined the British Aerospace contract in Saudi Arabia in 1991, working on the Royal Saudi Air Force Tornado squadrons at Khamis Mushayt in the Avionics field.

His home is now near Falmouth where he retired from a lifetime with and around aircraft in 2001, sharing it with his wife Elizabeth who he met in the RAF in 1964.

1. Bomber Command

After four years of war the Royal Air Force, particularly Bomber Command, was on the offensive. The second front was fast becoming a reality with the build-up of materials from America and the Dominions. Britain was also host to many 'Free' forces waiting to go back to liberate their own lands. But German industry, armed forces, communications and oil supply had to be dealt with first as when the time came of going back across the Channel the Allies did not want a repeat of Dieppe on a larger scale. The British Isles, mainly Eastern England, became one vast 'Aircraft Carrier' off the coast of Europe whereby the USAAF carried out the offensive by day and RAF Bomber Command repeated it at night.

By the autumn of 1943, Bomber Command aircraft had flown over Germany and Occupied Europe nearly every night, setting fire to factories and the workers' houses alike. Railway centres, ports, oil refineries and chemical works were also on the target list at the Command H.Q. at High Wycombe. These targets were being set ablaze by sometimes as many as 800 to 1000 bombers a night. The new Avro Lancaster made its debut in the beginning of 1942, firstly in small numbers raiding Essen, Cologne and in mine-laying duties with other aircraft of the Command. It was not until April 17th of that year that a full squadron attack was made, against the Augsburg U-Boat engine factory, in daylight.

The Pathfinder Force had been formed into No.8 Group in the autumn of 1943 by the ace pilot and navigator Donald Bennett to guide the bombers to their target. Meanwhile, on 23rd of November 1943, No. 100 (Special Duties) Group was formed to support the command in the electronic intelligence and countermeasures role.

Bomber Command's leader was Air Chief Marshal Sir Arthur Harris, 'Bert' to his friends, 'Butch' to his crews and 'Bomber' to the media. On 3rd November 1943 he wrote to Churchill: "We can wreck Berlin from end to end if the United States Army Air Force would come in on it. It will cost 400-500 aircraft. It will cost Germany the War." He underestimated the first part of the statement, overestimated the second part and due to the lack of long range escort fighters, the Americans did not "come in on it" until right at the end of what was later to be known as The Battle of Berlin. His theory for the solution of ending the War, and Germany's eventual surrender, included new and more 'tools' for the job. These were consequently ordered in the form of new bomber squadrons and airfields.

At one time Lincolnshire had 29 main and satellite airfields and these, along with airfields in Yorkshire, formed the nucleus of the Command's front line. In late 1941, land was acquired and construction started on an airfield near the village of Wickenby, ten miles north-east of Lincoln, When completed, Wellingtons of 12 Squadron moved there from RAF Binbrook and began operations. In November 1942 this Squadron converted to Lancasters and with 626 Squadron forming a year later, Wickenby was to remain a Lancaster station for the remainder of the war. Besides 626 Squadron, six more were formed, all in the '600' series during 1943/1944. The first was 617 Squadron, later to become the famous 'Dambusters', the others being 619 (formed

April 1943), 622 (December 1943), 625 (October 1943), 630 (November 1943) and 635 (March 1944). All were disbanded at the end of the War, except 617, which is still operational today.

The severe winter of 1943/44 was one of the worst of the War years, and ground crews worked out in the open enduring appalling conditions. RAF Binbrook in Lincolnshire was cut off for three weeks, and food had to be parachuted in as the snow was three feet deep with 16ft drifts in some places, making the surrounding country roads impassable for supply vehicles.

A bomber station was the home and workplace for about 2,500 men and women. During 24 hours a day, seven days a week, somebody, somewhere was always working, keeping about 32 bombers airworthy and to enable roughly 250 aircrew to do their job of carrying the offensive to the enemy. A typical raid in the winter of 1943/44 would aim to be airborne just as it was getting dark, but preparation would start much earlier in the day, sometimes before the dawn…

In the bomb-dump on a remote part of the aerodrome, men would be rolling giant 4,000lb 'Blockbuster' bombs (as yet unfused) onto special trolleys or packing 4lb and 30lb incendiaries into their containers, while others would be gathering flares and general-purpose (GP) blast bombs of 1,000lbs and 500lbs each. Heavy work. If, as at Wickenby, the station had two squadrons, putting 20 to 30 Lancasters into the air for each operation, that meant 150 to 185 tons of high explosive had to be, for the most part, manhandled and hoisted from the bomb-dumps to the bomb-bays. It would take till the early afternoon to prepare the average 14,000lb load for each Lancaster. Lunch would be a hastily eaten sandwich – a 'wad' – and a cup of tea. Meanwhile other armourers elsewhere would be sweating it out against the clock, as always, to prepare 14,000 rounds of belted .303 calibre ammunition for each Lancaster's set of eight machine-guns.

If a maximum fuel load was needed for a deep penetration raid, flying a long 'dogleg' course over Europe, every Lancaster required 2,154 gallons of 100-octane petrol to fill the six wing tanks. There was no pressure-feeding as on today's modern aircraft. At the squadron dispersal points round the airfield, ground crews would be meticulously carrying out inspections prior to

An unknown 626 Squadron aircrew with a 4,000-pound 'Blockbuster' or 'Cookie' high-explosive bomb.[1]

the pre-flight ground test, engine fitters, airframe fitters, electricians, instruments, radio and radar specialists. More often than not some 'snag' would be found and had to be put right, always working against time, with the job not being done till the inevi-

---

[1] Photo courtesy E. Parker.

table paperwork was completed. All this feverish activity was carried out in the open and in all weathers.

As with most aircraft engines, the Rolls-Royce Merlins fitted to the Lancaster had two separate ignition systems and consequently two sparking plugs per cylinder. With twelve cylinders per engine, that meant ninety-six plugs per Lancaster. When pre-flight testing the engines, each ignition system was cut off by

Wickenby 1944. Aircrews awaiting 'the off' outside air traffic control cluster round the Hillman 'Tilly' crew truck.[2]

the flight engineer in turn and if the revs dropped by more than 150rpm, it indicated that the set of plugs in use were dirty and they had to be changed. In driving snow, sleet, rain, or just plain freezing cold, it required two fitters to complete this task, working perhaps ten feet up on a stand. One fitter worked the plug-spanner, the other ready to take over when his mate's fin-

[2] Photo courtesy J. Clark.

gers were too numb to do the job – and the winter of 1943/44 was to prove one of the coldest of the War.

Other sections of the station were a hive of activity. In the air-crew locker rooms, safety equipment, flying clothing, helmets and escape kits all had to be sorted and issued to each individual airmen. Up to 15 articles, from electrically-heated air-gunners flying suits to minute compasses in the escape kits had to be checked and given out. WAAFs in the kitchens were busily making up packs of food, fruit, sweets, chewing gum and thermos flasks of coffee for everyone on 'ops' that night. All this work was against the clock, by everyone from the newest 'erk' to the Group Captain, working as a team for the benefit of about ten percent of the station personnel – the aircrews – and the aircraft they flew.

2.   The Target

The Battle of Berlin was Bomber Command's biggest offensive and started in earnest with a raid on 18th November 1943. There had been previous raids as recent as the last week in August 1943. These raids were not considered successful, there being many abortive sorties to begin with, and many aircraft posted missing after the raid, over seven percent on the night of August 31st alone. This was one of the last raids to Berlin in which the Stirling took part – 16 percent of their number failing to return. The September 3rd raid yielded better results on the target, but still not a complete overall success. It was however an all Lancaster main force that night. But come Autumn and Winter, the nights would be longer and deeper raids to the eastern part of Germany including Berlin could be flown with a greater chance of survival for the crews and aircraft.

As well as being the German Capital and home of the seat of government, the Reichstag, Berlin also possessed a vast industrial wealth. Ten percent of the country's aero-engines, machine tools and precision instruments were manufactured there, while 23 percent of the tanks and other armoured fighting vehicles were made at Alkett, in the west of the city. One third of Germany's electrical engineering industry, including the giant Seimens complex, was within its boundaries, in fact Siemenstadt was a town in itself built around the factories.

A straight in-and-out trip to 'The Big City', as the aircrews called it, was about six-and-half hours duration, needing a fuel load of about 1,860 gallons of petrol.

Flight Sergeant Edward Groom was the Flight Engineer of P/O Wellham's crew who mainly flew aircraft LM393 and JB595 during the Battle of Berlin.

'1 Group carried more bombs than any other Group in Bomber Command. We were overloaded and they cut back on petrol. One Group had more people ditched and landed away (from base) through lack of fuel than any other reason. Many used to dump their 4,000lber in the North Sea until the modification with the photo-flash circuit. But our crew use to say 'if you don't take the cookie it's not worth going'.

Over Berlin on a clear night you could see all sorts of things happening as you approached, that is if you were not in the first wave, the first wave being for the most experienced crews. When you got to the target, the Pathfinders were dropping Parramata or Wanganui flares, or something like that, and if you were in the third or fourth wave, the whole place would be on fire. You could pick out all the markers going off in the sky, and other pyrotechnic displays and, of course, as regards to the flak, by the fourth wave they had got your height, there was no doubt about it, but you had to go on. When the flak stopped, you knew the night-fighters were there'.

Because of the great distance the American Eighth Army Air Force did not participate in the Battle until towards the end when the superb Merlin-engined North American P-51 Mustang came into service, and was employed to escort the American B-17 and B-24 bombers to the far distant targets. Even then their B-17 bomber, for example, could only carry a 4,000lb bomb-load to Berlin, less than a third of the Lancaster's payload. Royal Air Force Mosquitos of the Light Night Striking Force flew this pay-load there on many a night, sometimes twice. They flew so fast and so high that hardly an aircraft in the Luftwaffe could catch them.

The Battle was fought for just over four months, the sixteenth raid on the Capital concluding the conflict on the night of 24/25th March 1944. Interspersed between the sixteen raids were attacks on Frankfurt, Leipzig, Stetin, Braunschweig, Magdeburg, Stuttgart, Schweinfurt and V-1 flying-bomb sites.

Berlin was an aggressive, burning cauldron of a target, fed with bombs, incendiaries and burning bombers. Because the battle took place in the Winter and early Spring, crews saw the city only occasionally through broken cloud, sometimes not at all. Individual targets were hard to find by the Pathfinders, for unlike targets such as Hamburg or Stettin, Berlin did not stand out well on the 10cm-wavelength radar that was in service in November 1943. Only later on, when about six of the newly de-veloped 3cm-wavelength sets were fitted to Pathfinder Lan-casters, did matters improve and the lakes and wooded areas of Berlin stood out better on the radar screens. However, like most things new they had their share of teething troubles and on some raids only one or two of the special Lancasters would reach the target to be of some use, the others aborting with equipment failures.

Over the target there was a profusion of colour with the fires contrasting with the bright ground and sky-markers dropped by Eight Group Lancaster and Halifax aircraft. The target fires were so bright that crews saw other bombers above them, and even into the gaping bomb-bays as their load dropped to stoke up the destruction below. Above all the noise, the muffled explosions of hundreds of anti-aircraft shells bursting all around. Sometimes running the risk of being shot down themselves, the *nachjagders*, Luftwaffe night-fighters, whose Swastika could clearly be seen by the bomber crews when they flew too close for comfort. Flight Sergeant Groom's experiences again:

> "We flew on the heading on what we were told to bomb on when looking for the markers. Everybody's eyes would be all over the place except the bomb-aimer, Sgt Bill Lamb, who would be looking down at the target. No-one else could look down at the fires, because you would lose your night vision. We would be looking all around the sky and of course one of the gunners, with impatience, would say "Come on Bill!". It would seem ages until letting them [the bombs] go. The wireless operator would check that the 'cookie' had gone with the photoflash. Incendiary canisters could be seen coming out of the bomber above you, and sometimes they used to hit your aircraft. We used to try and pick a path out between the flak, which was hopeless really. The worst part was the searchlights because if they got on to you it was a hell of a job to get out of it, but we use to keep the nose down over the target and go like hell!"

The defences of the city were formidable; Berlin was probably the most heavily defended city in occupied Europe equal, if not better than, the Ruhr industrial area. The area occupied by flak batteries was about forty miles across and the searchlight belt extended ten miles beyond that: hence the reason for calling it the 'Big City'. While London and Coventry were being blitzed in 1940, Hitler's Arms Minister Albert Speer had the foresight to prepare the city for the retaliation to come. There was an outer and inner belt of anti-aircraft guns (flak) but the most impressive were the three huge flak towers in the centre of the city, at the Zoo Gardens, Frieddrichain Park and Humboldehain Park. On top of every ten-storey concrete and steel tower were eight Bor-sigwerke 128mm guns in pairs that, when fired together, put up a salvo every ninety seconds to a maximum height of 45,000 feet, creating a lethal 'box', nearly 300 yards wide.

Having been built by slave labour, the towers were self-contained, having their own electricity-generating plant deep in the foundations along with an air-conditioning system, a hospital and an air-raid shelter. The one in the Zoo Park was the depository of Germany's art treasures. Due to its thick reinforced concrete and steel construction, it was thought it was the best place for them.

Each battery required about 900 rounds of ammunition for a night's work, taking all the next day to refill the magazines. Barrel changes due to wear were very frequent as they were working so hard. Crews were issued with asbestos gloves to load and work the guns as they became so hot. At the lower levels of the towers were 20 and 37mm guns for defence against low fliers. Next to the tower in the Zoo Park was the Control Centre, having its own tower with Giant Wurzburg and Freye radars which controlled the laying of the guns. Deep down on the lower floors were the control rooms for all the Capital's guns and searchlights.

It chills the imagination to think of the experiences of the men that went up against the Berlin defences. The bomb aimer would lie prone in the nose of the aircraft holding the release switch and guiding the pilot on the run up to the target. The bomber would be flying straight and level for what seemed an eternity, searchlights probing and seeking by the hundred, flak so thick 'you could get out and walk on it' according to some. All this time the bomb aimer had to keep calm, watching the target indicator run down the sight glass of the illuminated gratical of the bombsight, sweating, in pure fear of the shell that could blow him and his fellow crewmembers to pieces. After the bombs had been dropped it still was not over, as the bomber had to fly straight and level for the downward pointing camera to record the impact point of the bombs and the damage they caused. The camera lens was open for thirty seconds after bomb release, the 250lb photoflash bomb exploding at a preset height above the target to take the photograph. Those thirty seconds would seem like eternity. While all this was happening there was the ever-present danger of collision with another bomber of the stream, which sometimes tragically occurred. As always, there were night-fighters and, as if all this was not enough, there were special units such as I/Kg7 and III/Kg3 equipped with the FW200 Condor and JU88. These aircraft flew above the city and dropped parachute flares to aid the non-radar-equipped night-fighters.

Bill Lamb was a Flight Sergeant Bomb Aimer who flew with 626 Squadron from the beginning of the Battle until he was posted to 18 Operational Training Unit on 22nd February 1944, having finished his operational tour with the rest of P/O Wellham's crew.

"The actual flying on operations was purely mechanical. One got use to the dangers, or as they used to say, one got 'flak happy'. Fear was never far away, but it's surprising how one gets used to it. Take-off for me was the most nerve-wracking. Once airborne I had work to do, everyone in the crew had the rituals of checking, settling down and watching out. Sometimes, half-way across the North Sea, you would see flak coming up as one of our aircraft would maybe dump his bombs, invariably near one of our convoys and they would put up their ten pennyworth. Getting near the enemy coast you could see the anti-aircraft puffs against the background of searchlights, a fearsome sight. Never a dull moment. Going into the searchlight belt, which stretched from Denmark down the coast as far as one could see,

about forty miles deep, no way round, straight through and no point in dodging or weaving, spotting the odd kite catching it, it always happened to someone else!

Fighters always became troublesome over the target or on the way home. Targets about this time were in Berlin and of the many times I paid them a visit I never saw the ground detail once, 10/10 clouds and blinded by searchlights. We bombed on sky-markers or target indicators, photo-flash pictures, when developed, showing a maze of fire-tracts. I know things were rough, nerve-wracking and fearsome at times but in retrospect a bit of air discipline would have been preferable to the continual returning to the same target time after time. There were enough bombs dropped to wipe Germany off the map. From the enemy coast inwards to the target you didn't need maps, you could track to the target by the trail of incendiaries and bomb bursts. Enemy flak was mobile, on the way in it was a broad belt forty miles wide and narrower on the way home. That was when the 'fun' started, fighters galore and flares lighting up the sky. The reaction after the action over the target was shattering. We always seem to be off track by up to twenty miles at times. It was too much to ask a navigator to keep an accurate track when the aircraft was dodging and weaving all over the sky.

The danger of collision was always with us and did happen to some. The weather at that time of the year was unpredictable at the target, cloud and more cloud, and it was the same on the way home and landing at base. I can recall once, coming back across the coast, I noted aircraft burning on the ground all the way in from the sea to East Yorkshire and on to Lincolnshire. The casualties of the fog and weather were more than over the target! As I remember, we lost over thirty, four-engined aircraft that night due to the weather. It was bad enough enduring the hardship of flying over enemy territory, but I am firmly convinced that if a lot more consideration, planning and discipline were about we would have done better and perhaps saved more lives. A lot of lives were lost through sheer bloody-mindedness of the Commanders and their back-ups."

Bill Lamb was probably remembering the raid to Berlin on December 16th 1943 when 25 Lancasters were actually lost due to flak and night-fighters but thirty-four crashed, collided or were abandoned by their crews over England due to the appalling weather conditions.

3. The Aircraft

The two squadrons at Wickenby operated the Lancaster Mk I or Mk III which was designed by Avro's brilliant designer Roy Chadwick. The Mk I had British manufactured Rolls-Royce 'Merlin' engines, which also powered the famous Spitfire, Mosquito and later the American Mustang long-range fighter. The Mk III had Merlin engines built by the Packard Motor Company of Detroit, as earlier on in the War as it was feared that German bombing could disrupt production in British factories. The American version was much favoured by RAF ground crew fitters, as a superb, comprehensive toolkit was supplied by the Detroit company. The Merlin was, and still is, reliable and for its size, very powerful. This was one of the major contributing factors to the Lancaster being the finest heavy bomber operating in the European Theatre. It could carry a heavier bomb-load over a greater distance than any other aircraft flying over The Third Reich. Roy Chadwick had designed the Lancaster to be constructed in large sections by a relatively unskilled workforce with the minimum of training and manufacturing experience. Most of them were women, former housewives, office workers etc. who elected to do this work rather that join the Forces, work the land or make ammunition in a factory.

The sections were bolted, pinned and shackled together with a piece of doped linen over the join making it easier for major component changes and battle damage repair. This was just as well as on a typical Lincolnshire airfield, like Wickenby, only major repairs and long routine inspections were carried out in a hanger. All other tasks, including most engine changes, were accomplished out in the open and in all weathers.

An engine change could be done in three hours, a feat not matched by some of our modern jet aircraft of today. Lancasters carried a variety of loads throughout their life from propaganda leaflets to the 24,000-pound Grand-Slam bomb, while out over the oceans in Coastal Command they carried lifeboats and at the very end of the War repatriated POWs from Germany and soldiers of the 8th Army in Italy. The bouncing bomb used by 617 Squadron to breach the Dams is now a legend. Incredibly, Lancasters dropped 608,612 bombs in WW2 and 51,513,106 incendiaries, this equating to 63.8% of Bomber Command's total. Bomb loads varied from raid to raid but it was usual to carry a 4,000 pound 'cookie', four or five 1,000 pound high explosive bombs and enough incendiaries to make up a total load of about 14,000 pounds, over six tons.

Falling on a typical Berlin block of flats, the 4,000-pounders blasted the roof tiles off, also the windows and doors out of the dwellings near the impact point. That left a way clear for a good draught so the incendiaries could get to work. Dropping from about 20,000 feet, the thirty-pound type, with their eleven pounds of phosphorus, penetrated at least two floors and the roof, setting alight the lower part of the building. Meanwhile, the smaller four-pounders cascaded through the roof, setting alight everything on the top floors. With no window panes or doors and plenty of draught, the block of flats would be ablaze within minutes. All very scientifically thought out. This worked extremely well in some of Germany's older cities whereby buildings were made of part wood, like Lubeck, Rostock, Hamburg and at the end of the war, Dresden.

Minelaying, or 'gardening' as it was known by the crews, around the coasts of enemy occupied Europe was carried out extensively by Lancasters. These sorties were sometimes flown by new crews yet to experience combat and considered a 'milk-run' compared to an attack on a mainland city although many flew to a watery grave. Each Lancaster could carry six 1500-pound sea-mines (known as 'vegetables' by the aircrews). Of the 47,307 that were laid by Bomber Command aircraft, 12,733 fell from the bomb-bays of Lancasters, and according to records captured after the War, 842 enemy ships were estimated to have been sunk by this means. Flying 2,929 sorties in all and calling for precision navigation, never was there a richer 'harvest' than that gathered in after 'gardening'.

If the Lancaster had a weakness it was in its defence, the calibre of the machine guns being considered by many as being too light, .303-inch. A better weapon would have been the .5-inch Browning, as used by the Americans flying the B17 and B24 on daylight raids. A German night-fighter could stand off a 1000 yards from a Lancaster's tail and score fatal hits with its 20mm multiple cannon, well out of the range of the Lancaster's rear guns, that is, if it could be seen on a pitch-black night at that distance. A few Lancasters of 101 and 106 Squadrons were equipped in late 1944 with .5 calibre tail guns made by the Gainsbough firm Rose Rice Brothers. Although effective, it was all too little and too late.

There were eight guns, two at the nose, two in a dorsal (mid-upper) turret and four in the tail. Over half of the 14,000 rounds of ammunition were for 'Tail-End-Charlie', where most of the attacks came from. Underneath there was no room for a belly turret because of the very long bomb-bay and later the H2S radar scanner. Although a turret in that position was tried as an experiment during development, it was never included on production aircraft, which were totally unprotected from underneath; many a Lancaster met its fate from that quarter.

The rear gunner had a cold, lonely and most dangerous position. His turret was cramped and difficult to vacate in an emergency. There was no room for a parachute, which was kept on a

The rear turret of a Wickenby Lancaster, with much of the Perspex removed (an unofficial modification) to improve the rear-gunners all-round vision.[3]

---

[3] Photo: H.S.G. Rich.

rack inside the rear fuselage. If bailing out he had to manoeuvre the turret fore and aft, open the door, grab the parachute and put it on. He then had to move the turret round to the side again, by hand if the hydraulics were gone, and then fall out backwards through the doorway as he went. It all took time, and many did not make it and died fighting not only time but flames and the G-forces of a falling, spiralling bomber. Lancasters were seen plummeting to earth in a mass of flame with the rear gunner still blazing away at the attacking night-fighter in a last defiant act of courage. The perspex in front of the gunsight was usually re-moved for better vision (an unofficial modification). The tem-perature over Germany in the winter was -30 to -45 degrees C at about 20,000 feet. Bare flesh, such as fingers, stuck to freezing metal.

The crew also had a navigator, a radio operator, a bomb-aimer/front gunner and unlike earlier twin-engined bombers the Lancaster carried a flight engineer to manage the aircraft's sys-tems and to assist the pilot. Flight engineers could and often did in an emergency, fly and land the aircraft, being taught by the pilot, unofficially, just in case he was dead or wounded and inca-pable. The pilot, irrespective of rank, was always the captain.

4. 626 Squadron is Formed

At Wickenby, in the heart of Lincolnshire 'bomber country', the 7th November 1943 dawned with fair weather, not much wind or cloud to mar the day. But today the weather was not on the mind of Wing Commander Haines, who had just been posted in from 1656 Heavy Conversion Unit. He was to be the new CO of Bomber Command's latest Lancaster unit – 626 Squadron. His orders were to form No.626 into two flights of eight aircraft each with four in reserve, in accordance with Group Admin Instruction 46, dated 31st October 1943 to Order WAR/BC/362.

The first eight Lancasters came from Wickenby's 12 Squadron's 'C' Flight to form 626 Squadron's 'A' Flight, with Squadron Leader Roden as Flight Commander. With the aircraft came their air and ground crews and in the coming weeks many more personnel would be posted in from other squadrons and training units. In the weeks to follow, more Lancasters were to form 'B' Flight, arriving from the factories and other units. Over 110 Lancasters were to see service on 626 Squadron by the time it was disbanded, replacements being brought forward as aircraft crashed, were transferred to other units or 'failed to return'.

Although the Squadron was eager to get 'stuck in' right away, operations planned for the night of 7th November were cancelled at 21:30hrs that evening. For the next two days the weather was too bad to allow the new squadron to make its mark over Germany; low cloud, drizzle, fog and bad visibility in the evenings called a halt to flying. The eight Lancasters were brought up to readiness on both days by the ground crews, but although operations were ordered, they were cancelled again in the evening.

Meanwhile, the Squadron began to get itself organized in the enforced layoff. The Squadron identification code was 'UM' and this was painted with the individual aircraft's callsign in large red letters down the side of the fuselage behind the wings.

By this time the CO had appointed leaders to head the various aircrew factions. F/Lt Hay had the important job of Bombing Leader while his colleague F/Lt Whitehouse had the equally important task of Gunnery Leader. F/Lt Whitehouse had already completed two operational tours but 'kept his hand in' flying with the Flight Commander about once a month. He wore the ribbon of the Distinguished Flying Cross. The task of these two officers would be mainly training and keeping their crewmembers up to scratch with flights to the bombing ranges, air-to-air firing with towed targets or fighter affiliation exercises with Spitfires. F/O Cappi was no less important; he was Navigation Leader. To get to Berlin and back, a round trip of over 1,000 miles, bombing the target precisely to the minute, was no easy feat with the limited navigational aids and systems available in those days. New sergeant pilots and experienced aircrew alike would go on long navigational exercises all over the country, both by day and night between operations. Bombing a target is one thing; doing so at the right time to the minute and at the right place over a city that is fighting back, is something else. F/O Cappi carried a lot of responsibility on his young shoulders.

F/O Wood covered all aspects of signals with the radio operators. The H2S radar had not come to 626 Squadron yet, in fact they were not to see it till well after the Battle of Berlin. The flight engineers came under the responsibility of F/Lt Phillips.

One person of note was F/O Bill Newman. He was an ex-12 Squadron bomb aimer and thought it was right and proper that the new 626 Squadron should have a badge and motto, so he took it upon himself to bring this about and give the Squadron an identity. The inspiration for the badge and motto came from Bill's schooldays and his interest in museums and art. Tennyson's poem 'Ulysses' had stuck in his mind and the last line seemed to be what he was looking for. After a slight alteration so that it would fit on the space provided on an RAF badge, "To strive, to seek, to find and not to yield" was altered by Bill to read "To Strive and not to Yield". Tennyson's poem had other appropriate connections. The poet was born in Lincolnshire in 1809 at Someraby and later lived at Mablethorpe, receiving an education at Louth Grammar School. Mablethorpe, as we shall hear later, is where the bombers of No.1 Group often crossed the English coast on their way to Germany and occupied Europe. There were two searchlight beams pointing skywards and crossing at about 5,000 feet above Mablethorpe as a navigational fix on the way out and as a welcome beacon on the way home.

The next part was the badge itself and here Bill's knowledge of museums came into play. Keeping with the theme of the motto, he paid a visit to the British Museum to find out about Greek galleys of the type Ulysses would have sailed, according to mythology. At this time in 1943 the Museum exhibits were long removed to a safe place to escape the blitz, but help was at hand in the form of Mr Norman Keyte of the department of Greek and Roman Antiquities. He had photographed every one of the pieces in his charge before placing them in safe custody. After sifting through volumes of catalogues and photographs, Bill came across what he was looking for: a picture of a vase made in 460 BC, with Ulysses and his ship painted on the side. The painting on the curvature on the vase suited the format of the RAF badge and with a little adaptation Bill's idea became a reality. 626 Squadron had a badge.

Approved

George R.I.

College of Arms,
October. 1944.

J.D.Heaton-Armstrong

Chester Herald
and Inspector of Royal
Air Force Badges.

The original 626 Squadron crest, which was stolen
from the Officers' Mess at the end of the war..

Two more people now enter the story. There was a wealth of talent in the wartime RAF, and the Station Assistant Adjutant told Bill of a Leading Aircraftman Hargreaves who had been a coach painter before the war but was now painting hangar doors. Bill soon had him off that job to help with the design and painting of the 626 Squadron badge, a task more appropriate to his skills.

It is significant that the galley on the badge is travelling from right to left, or east to west, as depicted on the vase; this was to signify a return home from a successful raid in Europe. Furthermore, the Lancaster was crewed by seven free men, the same as Ulysses's Greek galley, if counting the oars in the picture. Ro-

man galleys at the same time had oars pulled by slaves chained to the decks for what little life they had after capture. However, the rules of the College of Arms stipulated that the design should not include the human form, so Ulysses and his crew had to go. The badge was submitted to Wing Commander Haynes and the Station Commander for approval and duly to the College of Arms. Thanks to a Flying Officer, a Leading Aircraftman, a Lincolnshire Poet Laureate and

Greek urn in the British Museum, upon which the design for the 626 Squadron crest was based..

an unknown Greek painter of pots, 626 Squadron had, to quote Bill "a peg to hang its identity on". Unfortunately there is a sad ending to the story. The original badge that bore the Royal Assent by King George VI was stolen from the Officers' Mess at Wickenby at the end of the War, never to be seen again.

5.   The First Operation

The 10th November 1943 began with low cloud and rain with visibility so bad that one could not see from one side of the airfield to the other. It looked as though operations would be put off again for the Wickenby Lancasters, but as the day progressed it brightened, with only a slight wind blowing.

As with most flying units in the Command, 626 Squadron had its fair share of airmen from the Dominions and the Commonwealth. W/O Welham joined from Australia with his crew that day, likewise Sgt Kindt from Canada, who had trained with his crew at 1656 Heavy Conversion Unit. They Joined S/Ldr Neilson from New Zealand, posted in from the same unit the previous day.

At long last, operations were 'on' for that night and stayed on as the weather improved. The target was the western entrance of the Montcenis tunnel near Modane in the French Alps. The tunnel carried the railway from Grenoble to Turin in Northern Italy, transporting most of Germany's war supplies to the Axis southern flank. Crews were briefed to bomb at about one o'clock the following morning, having flown across France and the Alps at 18-20,000 feet. Since destruction by blast was the object, each of the seven Lancasters of 626 Squadron was loaded up with a 4,000lb 'cookie' and five 1,000lb general-purpose blast bombs.

When a new crew joined the squadron from a training unit, it was the practice in Bomber Command for the new crew's captain, irrespective of rank, to fly one mission with an experienced crew before taking his own aircraft into action. On this particular night, W/Cdr Haynes, the Commanding Officer, flew in ED424 with F/Lt Mclaughlin, an old hand from 12 Squadron.

Flying south over France, the Lancasters did not meet any night-fighters, in fact F/Lt Mclaughlin thought it quite a boring trip compared to raids on German cities. The tunnel opened out into a valley, where the only defence appeared to be two field guns, which blasted away ineffectively. He was over the target just after one o'clock and bombed on the target indicators dropped by the Pathfinders, observing a very concentrated attack overall. Most captains praised the Pathfinders for getting the markers right on target. F/Lt Weeks in JB540 saw many bombs hitting the railway line itself even from 20,000 feet, but with so much explosive used on this raid he found it difficult to assess the damage to the railway tunnel and lines, however, this was later confirmed. No trains passed that way for some time after the 313 bombers of the attacking force had returned to their airfields. The French Resistance later blew up an ammunition train that stopped in the tunnel because of the rock fall in the bombed entrance, this being later reported by intelligence sources.

The seven Lancasters of 626 Squadron made the return trip over France in the latter part of the moonlit night. P/O Curry in ED133 reported clearly seeing the winter majesty of Mont Blanc over forty miles away at one point. The moonlit flight did not last however; over England the bomber force encountered low cloud due to a heavy weather front. All seven aircraft returned safely to Wickenby, but it could have been a different story for ED133. Half way across France their oxygen supply ran out and they had to fly low and below the cloud base at about 2,000 feet. While being tossed about in the turbulence they almost collided with a Mosquito travelling in the opposite direction, which missed them by only a few feet.

26

6. The Battle of Berlin

That raid in the moonlight to the tunnel was relatively easy, but to have attempted a raid on a major German city under the same conditions would have been suicide for the crews of the Command. During a clear full moon period the squadrons flew to minor targets and carried out training at home. For the next week, while not on operations, 626 Squadron air and ground crews were far from idle. Crews were still being posted in to form the new 'B' Flight, such as F/Sgts West, Usher and Australian F/Sgt Scott, all from 103 Squadron. Others came from the Heavy Conversion Units. Celebrations were in order as F/Lts Weeks, Wood and Mclaughlin were each awarded the Distinguished Flying Cross. Flying continued over the next four days with cross-country training flights and fighter affiliation exercises on 13th and 14th November; this was where Spitfires of the Bomber Defence Training Flight attacked the Lancasters in mock battle, using gun cameras to later show up mistakes or to apportion praise, as the case may be.

On 16th November, operations were ordered but later cancelled, most likely due to weather conditions, which had been bad for some days. The previous day saw the first snow of winter falling. There was still training for those not flying, the various Leaders organising lectures. On the 13th the flight engineers, who had to know all the systems of their aircraft, were taught the complexities of the Mk.XIV bombsight.

On 17th November the weather was cloudy with wintry showers all day but not bad enough to prevent more training. Bombing on the ranges, air firing and cross-country flights were carried out. Airmen were still being posted in, adding more strength to the Squadron. W/O Gallagher came from 103 Squadron with his crew while F/Sgt Lone and the men under his command from 1662 Heavy Conversion Unit followed by F/O Wilkinson and his crew the next day from the same unit.

On the opening night of what historians would later call the Battle of Berlin – 18th November 1943 – 440 of the Command's Lancasters set out for the 'big city'. Only nine aircraft were not to return, a low casualty figure of just two percent. This may have been due to a simultaneous diversion raid to the much-bombed city of Mannheim and the suburb town of Ludwig-shafen-on-Rhine by other Lancasters, Halifaxes and the older Stirlings to draw away the night-fighters. Also, the night-fighter airfields in Northern Germany, which lay right in the path of the attacking bombers, had a lot of their aircraft, mainly ME110s, dispersed away. They had been defending an airfield near Oslo, which had been attacked by an American bomber force earlier on in the day. That left only about 120 night-fighters divided between the two simultaneous raids.

The route out to Berlin was straight over Northern Holland and almost direct to the German Capital. After bombing, the stream was to sweep south, passing Leipzig to port and Cologne to starboard, heading due west over Central Belgium and Northern France, leaving the enemy coast at the River Somme estuary.

At Wickenby, the day was mainly cloudy and it rained from time to time, hampering the ground crews preparing the Lancasters for the night's operation. Naturally they did not know the target, that was a secret, but many a fitter could make an educated guess by weighing up the fuel and bomb loads of his charge. If the petrol tanks were full, it was a fair bet that the aircraft were going to a target in Eastern Germany like Stettin,

Leipzig or Dresden. This night the tanks were full to the filler caps located on top of the wings. The target was Berlin. Twelve aircraft were made ready for the raid, take off being around five o'clock in the early evening.

For two airmen this raid was something special, the last of their operational tours. F/Lt Weeks in DV171, who had been awarded his DFC only two days previously, was setting out on his 30th and last mission while W/O Smith was doing the same, but for the completion of his second tour. They were both captains of their aircraft. Flying with W/O Smith was F/O Bill Newman (who created the Squadron badge and motto) on his first trip with 626 Squadron. This was the first of eight missions he would fly with 626 to complete his tour before being posted to No.30 OTU for a rest from operations. As bomb aimer in DV177, he dropped his load on the red and green target indicators at 21:00hrs from 21,000 feet. He and the rest of the crew observed that the attack appeared to be scattered. This was probably due to the poor vertical visibility and the Pathfinders not being consistent this night. On the way back DV177 had problems with the starboard outer engine and the flight engineer had to feather its propeller. To shorten their route they crossed the French coast at Dunkerque, well to the north of the planned track but landed safely at Wickenby.

Ten minutes after the bombs of DV177 had fallen, F/O Wright came in at 21,000 feet, flying W4967 to bomb the target identified by the green target indicators cascading into the clouds. Red and green flares were also seen but they were ignored as they were seen to be scattered.

P/O Hutchinson, captain of JB599, was not quite so lucky. Having bombed eight minutes after DV177 from 22,000 feet, his Lancaster set course for home by turning south and a little later southwest as per the flight plan to leave Cologne and the Ruhr to starboard. At ten minutes past eleven, while at 24,000 feet, a night-fighter found them near Aachen and on attacking knocked out one of the port engines. This area of the Third Reich was defended jointly by Nachjagdgeschwaders One and Four with bases at Venlo in Holland and Florennes in Belgium, danger-ously near the flight path of JB599. Further damage rendered the direct reading (standby) compass useless and holed the fuselage extensively, although injuring none of the crew. The aircraft wandered south of track but was not spotted again by night-fighters or hindered by flak on its way to the enemy coast, cross-ing it at Westcaplle. Limping across the Channel on three en-gines the Lancaster made the coast of Southern England whereby it was decided to land at the fighter airfield at West Mal-ling in Kent. Their troubles were not over, however, as on land-ing at nearly two o'clock in the morning a burst tyre caused the Lancaster to crash as soon as the wheels touched the runway. But luck smiled at them. Apart from a few knocks and bruises, all seven walked away unharmed from the wrecked Lancaster.

F/Lt Weeks, ending his first operational tour in DV171, found the trip not quite so eventful. An hour and 130 miles to go to the target, he flew over a dummy target laid out by the Germans near Celle just north of Hanover consisting of red spot indicators, They were very scattered and ignored, as Bomber Command was not using that type this night. The bomb aimer, F/Sgt Baines, bombed the correct target at eight minutes past nine as best he could. Not forecast by the meteorological staff in Command Headquarters was the 10/10ths cloud over Berlin that night. Path-finder target indicators were going straight through the cloud which extended to 10,000-12,000 feet. The crew saw a very large yellow explosion six minutes after they bombed, perhaps as a result of their own efforts or of some other crew.

The attack was very scattered due to problems aiming through the unpredicted cloud and very few Pathfinders finding the town of Brandenburg thirty-five miles west of Berlin. Bomber Command's plan was for the Pathfinders to locate this town by radar and on a timed run from it, pinpoint the target. Unfortunately, the Lancasters equipped with the new and improved H2S Mk.III radar had problems with the sets before reaching this important waypoint and had to resort to marking the target by conventional means through the murk shrouding Berlin below. Out of the twenty-six blind marker Pathfinder aircraft only eight dropped their flares on the aiming point, consequently, bombs were scattered all over the city with very little damage to show for their effort. Only 169 houses were burnt out with some minor factories and under 150 people killed. The route marker aircraft were using yellow target indicators this night and DV171's navigator, Sgt Michell, found them most useful in the flight home across occupied Europe. As dawn appeared on the Lincolnshire airfield all crews were safe after their first raid on the enemy capital.

For the next three days the weather was bad for flying, Lincolnshire experiencing low cloud rain and fog. All flying training was cancelled and a stand down was ordered. People from the training units were still being posted in, individuals and whole crews like P/O Breckenridge with his men from 1662 Heavy Conversion Unit, a crew whose exploits will be written about later.

On 22nd November, RAF Wickenby awoke to a cold day of cloudy skies with an early fog that when it dispersed by mid morning it was soon followed by drizzle. As the day wore on it became fine and a clear night was forecast. On 626 Squadron, flight line ground crews were preparing eleven Lancasters for another raid on Berlin. When the raid details were received on the Operations Room teleprinter, it was headed with the code 'Goodwood', which demanded a maximum effort by all in the Command. The weather was to be clear for take-off and landing the next morning and Berlin would have only broken cloud at the time of target zero hour, two minutes to eight when the first markers were due to go down just east of the City centre. The route over Europe out and back would have cloud and fog, hindering night-fighter operations but there would be no diversions or doglegs, straight in and out as quick as possible.

The Pathfinders promised four Lancasters with the new H2S Mk.III radar sets but when the time came for take-off five actually thundered down the runways of 8 Group's airfields. Due to technical problems, the new radar was hardly out of the development stage, three of the Lancasters turned back but not before bombing the island of Texel bristling with flak guns off the coast of Holland. This was standard practice with aircraft turning back with problems having got as far as the enemy coast. The eleven crews were briefed for the raid at 626 Squadron Operations, for some it was their first sortie with the new unit, for others their first ever time on operations. F/Lt McLaughlin was taking along W/O Rew in his aircraft while F/O Belford was flying with F/Lt Wood's crew. It was practice for new captains to fly their first operational trip with an experienced crew. This was not always popular with the flight engineer who had to give up his position next to the pilot for most of the time. The engineer's panel included the gauges, switches and controls of the aircraft's many systems.

At around five o'clock the eleven Lancasters took off, armed with a 4,000lb 'cookie' blast bomb and 1286 incendiaries in canisters apiece and headed for the Lincolnshire coast and the North Sea. Just over fifty miles out over the sea from Mablethorpe, F/Sgt Usher, captain of JB646, became ill after one hour of flying. The 'cookie' and four canisters were dumped into the sea and the aircraft flown back to Wickenby to land just after 19:00hrs. W/O Gallagher was not without his troubles in DV244 having reached the target at 20:19hrs at 21,000 feet as he bombed on the Pathfinders illuminated sky-markers. He came over the burning city at 165 miles-an-hour as directed by his navigator but as the load was dropped a canister of 180 four-pound incendiaries remained hung-up in the bomb bay. As there was so much cloud and fog over the occupied countries and Germany, it was left up to the radar controlled flak batteries to defend the Capital.

It was flak that damaged F/Sgt West's Lancaster JB141 in the wings and fuselage. He flew his aircraft in at 22,000 feet to bomb through 10/10 cloud, his bomb aimer seeking out the sky-markers. The crew noticed the glow of many fires below the clouds when only about eighteen minutes into the raid while on the bomb run at 8:16pm. But as with DV244, a canister of ninety four-pound incendiaries hung up in the bomb bay. S/Ldr Neilson, a long way from home, being a member of the Royal New Zealand Air Force, was captain of JB599 that night and took off with his crew a little before 5:00pm. His navigator picked up the route markers laid by the Pathfinders and arrived over the target at 20,000 feet, dropping the bombs at 8:10pm. At twenty past, the tail gunner reported a huge explosion just to the south-east of the centre of the city, which was later identified as the Neukollen gas works. The crew observed a gradual spreading of the fireglow below and feared that the attack was scattered. P/O Curry, captain of EE133, took along Sgt Jackson, who had arrived on the Squadron with his crew from 1656 Heavy Conversion Unit only fourteen days previously. All went well except that the pitot head iced up after leaving the target but cleared itself in time for a safe landing back at Wickenby. For three hours they flew over enemy-occupied Europe and the North Sea with no indication of airspeed till right to the end of the mission. Without airspeed indication, navigation was impaired and they were nearly caught when the aircraft strayed too near the Hanover flak defences.

A new method of marking was being tried by the 8 Group Pathfinders this night which depended heavily on the target being initially pinpointed by the two H2S Radar Mk.III carrying Lancasters. The sets of these two aircraft worked brilliantly as they each released their four red and four yellow target indicators with sixteen sky-markers, the target indicators falling straight through the 10,000 feet or so of cloud. They were quickly followed by the nine blind marker aircraft, which dropped seventy-nine target indicators and sixty-eight sky-markers between them for the duration of the raid. Even though only two of the five Lancasters fitted with the new radar reached Berlin, it was enough, as the load came down right on the aiming point with credit also going to the blind markers that carried on throughout the raid. After the target was illuminated it was then up to the Mainforce to capitalise on it, which they did which such élan that it was to be the most successful of the sixteen raids of the Battle of Berlin.

W/O Gallagher in DV244 still had problems. When the aircraft was some eighty miles into the homeward flight from Berlin the two port engines cut out without warning; fuel lines damaged by flak being the suspected cause. With only 350-400 gallons of petrol left in the tanks, flight engineer Sgt Dixon wrestled with the engines and fuel system and managed to get them going again. Their position now desperate, the navigator plotted a track for the shortest route home to the English coast and safety. This took them just to the north of Rotterdam and out over the North Sea. Thanks to cloud cover and a lot of luck, they successfully ran the gauntlet of the Dutch seaport's flak guns and the area covered by the crack Nachjagdgeschwader No.1 night-fighter Division. The problem of the hung up incendiary canister was solved twenty-five miles out from the enemy coast when at 10:30pm the bomb aimer managed to jettison it from 20,000 feet. If it had come loose on a bumpy landing the crew and air-craft could all have ended up as one big funeral pyre. Fuel short-age was still a problem; even by direct flight DV244 still had over 180 miles to go to Wickenby. After covering nearly 100 miles after dumping the canister, it was decided to land at Coltishall in Norfolk. On landing at just after 11pm it was found that there were only 80 gallons of petrol left in the six wing tanks.

F/Sgt West in JB141 decided to take the hung-up canister back, not bothering to dump it. On the way home JB141 experienced considerable icing problems but landed safely at Wickenby, although with a lot of holes, at seven minutes past midnight. S/Ldr Neilson, flying JB599 encountered no such problems, his route home being uneventful, but no route marker was seen by any of the crew. After flying for a little over seven hours JB599 touched down at Wickenby four minutes after JB141.

This was the first truly successful raid on the city of Berlin. The weather had been dry for the time of year and the buildings set on fire by the incendiaries were hard to control. Over 3,000 dwellings were destroyed making over 12,000 people homeless with twenty-three industrial complexes completely gutted and flattened. Several thousand other businesses were damaged. Buildings severely damaged included five factories of the Siemens Electrical Group and the Alkett tank factory, which had only just moved from the industrial area of the Ruhr. Nearly seven hundred bombers reached the target, dropping over 2,500 tons of high explosive and incendiaries, the largest force yet. Twenty-six bombers were posted as missing in action. About 2,000 Berliners lost their lives in the 22-minute raid.

In the early hours of the morning, while the crews were being de-briefed and tucking into their aircrew breakfast of bacon and eggs, the Lancasters were in the capable hands of the ground crews for damage assessment and repair and the routine after-flight inspection. Dawn came some hours later to reveal another cloudy winter day with drizzle to annoy the technicians working on repairs and re-arming. They had orders of what was required by mid-morning as 'ops were on' that night, an assessment having been made regarding which aircraft could be repaired and recovered in time. By mid-afternoon on 23rd November, 11 Lancasters had been rearmed, ground-tested, inspected and were on the flight-line ready to go.

For eight of the crews it would be the second night out in a row but for three, W/O Rew, F/O Belford and Sgt Jackson it was the first time out with their own crews, having flown their initiation trip the night before. To the astonishment of the crews, as they filed into the briefing room, the red ribbon of the route across the huge operational map of Europe had not moved from the position of the previous night! The route to Berlin was to be the same, straight in and straight out, but unknown to them the total bomber force was to be just over half the strength of the night before. Even the Meteorological Officer had nothing more to add to the weather forecast and conditions over the target or for landing the next morning. The target would have to be found through the cloud by the radar-equipped Pathfinders again. Two raids in 48 hours was very taxing on aircraft and crews alike but much credit must go to the ground crews who managed to get the aircraft on the flight-line for the second raid where repairs, fuelling, bombing-up and re-arming had to be carried out in the cold and rainy day to follow.

In the late afternoon, the crews boarded the crew transport, usually a Hillman Tilly and went out to the Lancasters to be met by the NCO in charge of the aircraft and its ground crew, nearly always a sergeant in the airframes trade. Having accepted their aircraft by signing the Aircraft Form 700, the ground crews cleared the Lancasters for starting. On hearing the mighty roar of the engines of 12 Squadron's aircraft and the forty-four Rolls-Royce Merlins of 626 Squadron, the surrounding villages and farms soon knew that an operation was 'on' for that night. The din they made on take-off caused many a cup to rattle as children just home from school were having their tea at about five o'clock in the afternoon.

Sgt Jackson had flown the previous night with P/O Currie for his initial raid over enemy occupied Europe but tonight he was the captain of his own Lancaster, JB646; it was his crew's first operational flight. JB646 took off at four minutes past five and flew the straight route to Berlin as briefed, picking up the green route markers on the way. The raid was to be between 19:58 and 20:15 hrs, their Lancaster arriving over the target in Berlin at five past eight, flying at 21,000 feet. Immediately the bomb aimer, Sgt Fox, found the cloud cover was up to 3,000 feet thick in some places. This night the two available H2S Mk.III radar equipped Pathfinder Lancasters were forced to turn back with faulty equipment, but the other Pathfinders marked accurately enough for Sgt Jackson's aircraft and the rest of Mainforce to drop nearly 1,400 tons of high explosive and incendiaries into about the same area as the previous night. It was noticed that the red target indicators were scattered but the others were quite concentrated. On their arrival, fires appeared to be burning from the night before, as there was a red glow below the cloudbase. Having finished the bomb run, Sgt Jackson turned JB646 to fly an approximate reciprocal route to the outbound flight, landing at Wickenby just after midnight, their first mission over. S/Ldr Nielson had a similar experience flying JB599, not only seeing fires from the previous night but also he reported observing the fire glow over the target from at least a hundred miles away. He navigated back, finding the green target indicator route markers effective, unlike some others, landing his Lancaster at seventeen minutes past midnight having flown for seven hours forty minutes.

P/O Sergeant, flying JA922, had icing problems not long after take off, and his Lancaster could only climb at a rate of 1,000 feet in twenty-five minutes and then only to a maximum height of 10,000 feet. Faced with this dilemma, his bomb aimer dropped the 4,000lb 'cookie' into the North Sea about fifty miles off the Norfolk coast at sixteen minutes past six to lighten the aircraft. Even then JA922 could only cross the enemy coast at 12,000 feet, dangerously low for flying into Europe, but as the fuel was used up on the route in they managed to achieve a height of 18,000 feet for bombing the Berlin target at a quarter past eight.

P/O Currie got EE133 off the runway just after a quarter past five to head out to the North Sea with the rest of Squadron but with one problem. Not long after take-off, the pitot-tube heater became inoperative, allowing the slipstream to freeze up the vital probe feeding the pilot's and navigator's airspeed indicators. P/O Currie decided to fly on, but as a precaution against stalling the aircraft he set the throttles a little more forward than usual. Picking up the route-markers on time, EE133 bombed the target two minutes after the first target indicators went down from 21,500 feet, a remarkable feat of airmanship by navigator and pilot, considering they had no real speed indication. On the way back, unlike the previous night, the Hanover defences did not give them any trouble, but somewhere else did... As it was flying through thick cloud at 20,000 feet, the Lancaster was hit in the fuselage by obviously radar-controlled flak from one of the batteries on the Dutch Frisian Islands.

The weather became worse and the Lancaster flew through severe turbulence in the thick cloud so a decent to about 1,500 feet was made. They still had a problem; the pitot tube was not de-icing, even at lower altitude, and P/O Currie had to face the prospect of landing without airspeed indication. Help was at hand, however, in the form of the rear gunner, Sgt Lanham, who had completed over twenty operations on Lancasters, plus many training flights. He said he could judge the speed of the aircraft by the sound of the slipstream passing his turret. They had nothing to lose, so the idea was given a try and with that, and the pilot's guesswork, EE133 came in to a good landing at Wickenby at thirteen minutes past eleven.

Lancaster W4990 carried F/O Belford and his crew aloft for their first operation on 626 Squadron but like JA922 they found it difficult to climb to height at any appreciable speed. Twenty-five miles south of Oldenburg in Northern Germany, it was decided to drop a canister of 56 thirty-pound incendiaries. Afterwards, altitude was eventually gained on reaching Berlin and the target. There were other problems too, the hydraulic pressure had failed, serving the rear and mid-upper turrets for about an hour, making it difficult for airgunners Sgt Mewburn and Sgt James, who had to manoeuvre them manually. Arriving at the target to find 9/10 cloud cover, this very new crew, undaunted by their problems, found the Pathfinder target indicators and bombed from 20,000 feet at a quarter past eight, right at the end of the raid. No more difficulties were encountered and they landed safely back at Wickenby at about midnight. Their first ordeal was over, but as will be seen later, it was not to be their last...

In the night battles over Germany Bomber Command alone lost 55,375 killed (72.53% of the 76,342 RAF aircrew lost worldwide in WW2). During the Berlin raids of the winter of 1943/44, 2,938 aircrew were to perish, including the Commanding Officer and 55 other aircrew belonging to 626 Squadron. Danger was ever present from flak, night-fighters, collisions, engine or vital airframe failure and from the elements themselves such as fog, low cloud and the icing-up of wings and flying controls. But one of the greatest fears was of oneself. Fear that one would not perform well in front of comrades. Fear that one would not survive the conflict. Fear of 'cracking-up' and letting down the rest of the crew. Seeing the empty spaces at the breakfast table and at the debriefings after raids, sometimes two or three times a week, every aircrew member of the Command must at sometime, if not many times, in their private thoughts, have speculated how long their luck would hold and when it would be their turn for 'the chop'. During the Battle of Berlin the Command's losses were appalling; not only was the German capital attacked sixteen times but also other cities, including Leipzig and Frankfurt twice and Stuttgart three times. The aircrews were not insensitive, they knew what was going on and that their chances of completing a thirty-raid operational tour were slim. Yet with seemingly immeasurable courage they carried on night after night. Some historians have called the Battle of Berlin the 'Paschendale of the Air'. In other wars, certainly the First World War and before, dazed soldiers walked away from the guns, carnage, noise and filth of the trenches, to be caught and in some cases shot for 'cowardice in the face of the enemy'. We now know, because the advancement of medical science and psychology, more about the phenomenon of shell-shock and battle fatigue.

It perhaps could be said that it took more courage to admit to one's crew and comrades that one could not go on, to give up, to refuse to fly than to go on the raids themselves. And so it was with the captain of DV388 this night, for as with the raid the night before he declared himself ill while flying, dumped the bombs in the North Sea and returned to Wickenby within a couple of hours. Within twenty-four hours he had been taken off flying duties and posted from Wickenby. Stripped of his rank and other badges he was declared 'LMF' (Lack of Moral Fibre). Many who were categorized LMF had just come to the end of their tether and could not take the fear and pressure any more. Such airmen were sent to rehabilitate in RAF psychiatric hospitals such as the Rockside Hydro at Matlock in Derbyshire. Not much sympathy was given and the plain blue uniformed 'patients' were generally treated as malingerers and cowards. Suicides were not unknown and most were remustered to the Army or sent to work down the coalmines.

At this early point in the battle, Bomber Command Headquarters took stock of a few things that were going wrong. 1,447 sorties had been flown until then but although only fifty-one bombers had been lost, not counting those that crash-landed on reaching home, many more were badly damaged on reaching their airfields. To send the Stirling against the overwhelming defences of Berlin and the Luftwaffe night-fighters, for this bomber flying at its best height of about 15,000 feet, it was considered suicidal, so they were withdrawn from the order of battle. The Stirling's new role was no less important, as glider tugs, minelayers and dropping secret agents in France and the Low Countries. The Lancasters of Mainforce were loaded to the full with bombs and fuel so much so that sometimes they could not fly at their best height and speed. Some crews began dropping the 4,000lb blast bombs deliberately over the North Sea on the way out for better performance. Command brought out a modification to the bomb release circuit so the photoflash was only dropped automatically when the 4,000-pound 'cookie' went with the rest of the load. This tended to stop the dumping.

The morning of the 24th November was a fine but windy day, which eventually brought rain to Wickenby and the ground crews working on the Lancasters. Six were being made ready for cross-country and fighter affiliation training flights, which took place later that day to hone the skills of the air-gunners and navigators. The next day a raid was scheduled for Frankfurt but cancelled for all 1 Group aircraft. Only 236 aircraft of 4 and 6 Group Halifaxes of Bomber Command took part, being led to the target by 26 Lancasters of the Pathfinder 8 Group. Twelve aircraft failed to return and at the target area cloud masking Frankfurt caused the bombing to be scattered with less than half the force even hitting the city.

On 26th November, the rested 1 Group, including the Wickenby Squadrons, was ready to get back into the battle. The teleprinters that morning revealed to Squadron Operations staff that the target was Berlin for the fourth time. The route was via the

English Channel to France, crossing the French coast near the Somme Estuary then due east to a point just north of Frankfurt, where a force of mainly Halifaxes with 21 Lancaster Pathfinders was to break off and fly south to raid Stuttgart as a diversion. The main force would turn north-east and with a small dogleg near Magdeburg, fly on to Berlin, then with a long turn to port, fly back over Northern Germany, Holland the North Sea and home via the Norfolk coast.

626 Squadron was to put up eleven Lancasters this night, led by the Commanding Officer, Wg/Cdr Haynes in J8599. P/O Sergeant in JA922 would be taking along P/O Cuthill for his initiation flight before starting operations with his own crew. Likewise F/O Wilkinson would fly with F/Lt Wood in LM362 for the first time over enemy-occupied Europe; it was nearly his last...

In the early evening, aircrews were taken to their aircraft scattered around Wickenby's perimeter track dispersal pans. Full of apprehension, the airmen climbed into their crew positions to carry out last minute checks before starting the engines. Navigators would be arranging maps and pencils while gunners inspected the widows of their turrets. A smudge of oil or a speck of dust could look like a night-fighter under certain conditions on a dark night over Germany. Private thoughts were put aside by all at about 5pm, when ground crews plugged in the 'trolley-accs' (accumulators) a set of powerful batteries, to turn the starter motors of the Merlin engines. Once started they were set to run at 1,200 rpm to warm up, the external power being disconnected when all engines were running and turning the aircraft's own generators, which supplemented the power supplied by onboard batteries. When all engines were running and any last minute problems were swiftly rectified by ground crews, the Lancasters would move out onto the perimeter track. To avoid running into each other, strict discipline in following the light signals of ground crew and air traffic control was as essential as radio silence at this point was in force. Flight Engineer Ted Groom takes up the story:

> "Because so much happened when you were flying, you did not have much time to think about fear. The worst part was waiting for take-off and getting the wheels up and airborne. You would be waiting your turn with about twenty-eight other aircraft on the perimeter track. On a hot night in summer you can just imagine what it was like with engine temperatures rising. You could be taxiing down wind and could see the engines getting hot and on seeing an empty dispersal, turn into it, face into wind and run your engines quite a fair whack to cool them down, but you would loose your place in the queue for take-off. Someone would probably let you in and you would eventually go up to the end of the runway. You would get your 'green' (light), as the pilot would be standing on the brakes and revving the engines up. You (the engineer) would be watching everything to get full power because the aircraft would be about 63,000 pounds on take-off, which was quite a lot for a Lanc."

The Squadron aircraft started to take off down Wickenby's runway not long after five o'clock and one by one climbed over Lincolnshire to head south towards the English Channel. W/O Welham, piloting JB595, did not get far, for at 7,000 feet, while climbing to operational height, his starboard outer engine spluttered to a stop with magneto trouble. The Lancaster could not go on with only three engines, so turning eastwards, the 4,000lb 'cookie' was dumped by bomb-aimer Sgt Bill Lamb in the North Sea, thirty-five miles off Grimsby, from 12,000 feet. (The landing weight of the Lancaster had to be less than 55,000 pounds for safety.) JB595 returned at nearly half-past-six.

The bomber stream passed over the Channel, across Northern France, through Belgium and into Germany heading for a point just north of Frankfurt. German night-fighter controllers obviously thought the target was Frankfurt and Me110 and Do217 night-fighters of 1/NJG6, based at the nearby Mainz Finthen airfield were up and waiting. The controllers were so convinced that Frankfurt was the target that even the crack NJG1 had flown in from Holland to defend it. Five bombers were shot down, but much to the German's surprise, many of the force flew on towards the north-east. Meanwhile, to add to the confusion, 157 Halifaxes and 21 Pathfinder Lancasters turned south to bomb Stuttgart, about 100 miles away. The diversion was working, as those on the ground switched their attention to what they now thought to be the Main Force heading for Stuttgart, keeping the bulk of the night-fighters in the Frankfurt/Stuttgart area.

F/Lt Wood in LM362 and W/O Rew in EE133 reported quite a lot of fighters in that vicinity. F/Lt Wood's navigator, P/O Kirby, set a new course ten degrees further north to avoid them. Although the crew saw the night-fighters, they were lucky and did not attract the attention of their cannons. As the bombers flew the long dogleg north-east, the controllers at Oberbefehlshaber-Mitte Main Control Centre in the middle of Berlin realised it was too late. As the bomber-stream approached, frantic orders were given to get the night-fighters to come to the aid of the German capital, but most were low on fuel and too far away to the west, only a few being in the right place at the right time to meet the attacking Lancasters. NJG5, whose airfields were dotted around Berlin, were far away to the south and out of reach.

The bomber crews were told that Berlin would be covered in low cloud, but it cleared some miles to the west of the city, giving an advantage to the searchlight operators and flak gunners.

When the lead Pathfinders reached the city, one Lancaster dropped its markers about nine miles to the north-west of the real aiming point. Another crew, heading for the target straight and on time, were put off by the intensity of the searchlights and flak. Not knowing if they were over the target because of the confusion, they dropped their 'cookie' only because they did not want to mark the wrong place. But all was not lost; coming up at the rear at about at 21:15hrs were the 'blind markers' to rain down their red target indicators, although a little short of the intended aiming point. Following them were the 'backers-up', putting down green markers, still five miles short of the aiming point, but within the city boundaries.

Sgt Cuthill had left his crew behind to fly with P/O Sergeant on his first initiation flight over Germany as second pilot in JA922. The flight for them to Berlin was uneventful, but they found the city devoid of cloud when over the green target indicators and Wanganui sky-markers at 21:24hrs at 21,000 feet. Although the predicted cloud was gone, sky-markers were still used. These burst hundreds of feet above the target to be carried by the wind. If bombing through cloud they were the only way to mark the target. Probably because of the target indicators on the ground and the drifting sky-markers, P/O Sergeant reported the target marking to be very scattered, as did other crews that night. On their way back, only one route marker was observed and used by the navigator P/O Oliver. On their return, the crew encountered what all bomber crews dreaded after a long trip, fog and low cloud over England. Just about all airfields south of Yorkshire were closed, bombers being told to divert to others further north. As instructed, by Ground Control, P/O Sergeant turned JA922 towards RAF Dalton, but landed at Middleton St George by mistake, although safe.

Nearly all the aircraft landed away from Wickenby, the Commanding Officer, W/Cdr Haynes, in JB599 at RAF Dalton, likewise P/O Hutchinson in, DV177, arriving just after twenty past nine. On bombing from 24,000 feet through thin cirrus cloud, his crew saw large areas on fire with Pathfinder markers well concentrated by the time the bomb-aimer let go the cookie and incendiaries to add to the inferno below. F/O Belford in W4990 landed at RAF Leeming, while Sgt Jackson in JB646 flew to RAF Skipton.

F/Lt Wood, captain of LM362, when bombing the target from 22,000 feet, saw none of the cirrus cloud P/O Hutchinson reported. His bomb-aimer and namesake, F/Sgt Wood, found the target at 21:16hrs and bombed it three minutes later, having seen the target indicators and Wanganui sky-markers together. This was all keenly observed by F/O Wilkinson, flying 'second-dickey' on his inaugural trip. Now it was time to turn the long arc to port and back home over Northern Germany between Bremen and Hanover, across Holland and the North Sea. On approaching Lincolnshire and Wickenby the weather was found to have clamped in, but this was F/Lt Wood's last mission on his operational tour and he was determined to land at his home airfield. As pilot he brought the Lancaster round carefully, lining up with Wickenby's runway, flying in from the east. The checklist for landing had been gone through, autopilot disengaged, superchargers were in low 'M' ratio, brake pressure was checked at over 250psi, flaps brought down from twenty-five degrees when first in circuit to now fully down, undercarriage down and locked and the engines at 2,800rpm or so to give the Lancaster about 110 mph flying speed for landing. Due to the weather, F/Lt Wood was using the radio aid Beam Approach Landing System. Unfortunately, unknown to him, it was off calibration. The first thing he knew about it was when the aircraft touched down in the middle of the WAAF site, just north of the village of Holton and about half a mile short of the airfield boundary. One wing came within a foot of one of the huts, the other narrowly missing a haystack. Further on the bomber and luck separated. Slithering at about a hundred miles an hour across the fields, ditches and fences quickly took the undercarriage legs clean off and the nose parted from the body of the 24-ton bomber. LM326 had flown its last flight and was a complete write-off, but miraculously the crew walked away from the wreck with no serious injury.

To the south, in rural Norfolk, at RAF Marham, F/Sgt Windus tried to bring Lancaster DV295 in to land. Whether he was wounded, tired or the aircraft was shot up and hard to handle will never be known... He overshot the runway and crashed at 1:14 in the morning; he and all his crew were killed.

F/Sgt Kindt took off with the rest of the Squadron at 1723Hrs in DV388 and was never to return. All crewmembers were killed when their Lancaster was shot down either by flak or a nightfighter near Finow, about 20 miles northeast of Berlin. They must have bombed the target but been caught as they turned to port and westwards to start the flight home.

These were 626 Squadron's first casualties. Seven airmen were lucky to be alive and fourteen had paid the ultimate price. Forty-two other squadron members in the coming months of the Battle of Berlin would make the same supreme sacrifice.

The markers had fallen five miles short of the aiming point, but the size of Berlin meant that damage had still been inflicted on important industrial areas to the north-east of the city centre in the areas of Reinickendorf, Siemenstadt and Tegel. Thirty-eight factories that produced war materials such as electrical components were destroyed, along with the gun factories of

Borsig. Some bombs dropped on Berlin Zoo, allowing some of the frightened and dangerous animals to escape, which had to be hunted down and shot. Many workers houses and flats were destroyed, civilian casualties for the raid being about 750.

No. 626 Squadron was stood down for the next three days. Although the weather was not conducive to operations at Wickenby, Mosquitoes of the Command carried out minor raids on industrial centres and mines were laid off the coast of France. Meanwhile at Wickenby, on 30th November and 1st December operations were ordered but cancelled later although cross-country flying training flights were flown day and night.

Regrettably, DV390 crashed at RAF Coltishall in Norfolk and written off. On the last night of November 1943, the inaugural flights of the newly-formed 200 Group took place. Their role was radio and radar countermeasures in jamming and deceiving the German defence transmissions on the ground as well as in the air. Starting with a flight of four Wellingtons they would later have Lancasters and American B-17 Fortresses in their Squadrons, their contribution to Bomber Command's efforts in the coming months being immeasurable.

The posting in of airmen to establish the new Squadron was at an end, although there were always new crews arriving to take the place of those who failed to return. What impression did Wickenby make on new airmen, ground or aircrew, having come from other units or training establishments? Of course opinions varied, as one might expect with a station of over 2,000 servicemen and women, who each have a different tale to tell according to 'their lot'.

A former 12 Squadron Pilot Officer navigator who was transferred to 626 Squadron on its formation in early November recalls that throughout the Battle of Berlin morale was high,

Wickenby being run by 'an intelligent and efficient leadership'. Most of the aircrew that flew with him were in their very early twenties, not many having attachments to wives, children or long-term girlfriends.

> *"They were highly motivated in the support of the other members of their crew and not to let them down. One tended to socialise with the other six members of one's own crew in off-duty hours, and although friendly towards perhaps another couple of crews of equal experience, the rest of the Squadron were kept as passing acquaintances. If one did not know a crew that was missing at the breakfast table the next morning the overall effect on morale was less severe."*

On the other hand, here are some comments from a Sergeant bomb-aimer who was posted in from 460 Squadron RAAF at RAF Binbrook about the same time:

> *"In contrast to Binbrook, Wickenby was a shambles, the addition of the extra load thrust upon the already overworked ground crew led to a lot of ill-feeling, conflict and confusion. The phrase 'not being able to organise a booze-up in a brewery' must have stemmed from Wickenby. It was thus so in the first few months, the Battle of Berlin was in full swing, crews were being pushed to the limit. One of the saddest things I recall was a crew of Canadians that arrived on the Squadron. They did not have time to unpack, were on 'ops' that night and did not return. That was by no means unusual. Contrary to what has been written by various writers with a view to glamorising events and personalities of the time, life for us was one long nightmare. The saying that where there is no sense there is no feeling is not quite accurate; those of us at that period from November 1943*

to March 1944 were punch-drunk. The new non-entities in control were hopeless and useless.

I can remember on return from a rather shaky-do from Berlin in January 1944, about fifteen NCO aircrew from 626 were left outside the debriefing room waiting for transport to our Sergeant's Mess situated about five miles away up a muddy lane. Snow on the ground, freezing cold, it was at least ninety minutes before transport arrived. The sergeant cook had thought we had bought it, all fifteen of us, and had dished up our 'flying' breakfast to his pals. A plate of cold sausage and mash was all we got. That was typical of the cock-ups during that period. I have nothing good to recall about Wickenby, I was just lucky I survived, that was the main thing".

When 626 Squadron was formed some of the ground crew personnel were transferred from 12 Squadron along with their aircraft, but many more were posted in from other units. Here is an opinion from an armourer on arrival at Wickenby in the winter of 1943/44:

The first impressions one got was mud everywhere, the drabness of the buildings, such as they were, consisting of Nissen huts or corrugated roofed concrete buildings and big black aircraft hangers out on the airfield perimeter. Every place, except the hangars, was in wartime camouflage and seemed to be scattered anywhere in no particular order. But although the accommodation and administration sites lacked order, the dispersals where the Lancasters were serviced and parked were better situated, at the far side of the airfield away from the main buildings. Thankfully, trees sheltered the aircraft and ground crews from the bitterly cold winter winds which swept across the Lincolnshire Wolds.

As time wore on, I grew to like Wickenby, but we had our fair share of problems. Living in one of the Nissen huts it was always difficult to keep warm in winter and even more of a problem finding enough fuel for the stove. It was quite common to have to go on scavenging parties in the middle of the night to purloin coal and coke from the boiler house and where other hoards were kept, as the official ration was never enough.

The local pub and the most popular being only a mile away, was The White Hart at Lissington. The bicycle was the only means of transport for just about all ground crew, very few aircrew SNCDs and officers even had cars and of course there was petrol rationing in those days. The pubs were always crowded with airman from all over the Empire as well as our own, WAAFs, girls from nearby farms and soldiers from the local Army camp at Wragby. Everybody got on very well, considering the eager competition for the attention of the best looking girls!

Friendships were struck up between ground crews and aircrews of the Lancasters, but a lot of aircrews didn't even last ten sorties. It was even more sad when they failed to come back with only a few trips to go to the end of their tour or even on the very last sortie, which happened sometimes. There would be long faces around the flight-line for a few days until another Lancaster and its crew arrived and the whole process would begin again. After take-off a few men would always stay behind to see the Lancaster in and greet the aircrew on their return some hours later – perhaps sooner if the flight was aborted for some reason.

When the aircraft came back from a raid, a bomb symbol would be painted on the left side just below cockpit. Some Lancasters survived over 100 raids and there was stiff rivalry among the *ground crews as to whose 'kite' had been on the most trips. If the crew managed to finish their 30-raid operational tour, they would take the ground crew for a night out in one of the more select pubs in Lincoln, such as the Saracen's Head or maybe the George in nearby Market Rasen. Aircrew would come and go, some tragically, some cheerfully at the end of their tour. Working conditions outside were appalling in winter but in the end many would not have missed the experience for anything."*

The second day of the last month of 1943 started with rain and cloud, not very promising, but in the afternoon it started to clear up and things looked better. Meanwhile, ten of 626 Squadron's Lancasters were being prepared for a raid on Berlin again. That night the route was straight in and out, like the night of 22nd of November, but with a slight variation. After bombing the target, the bomber stream would turn North for about twenty miles, then completing the triangle turn again to rejoin the same route as the outward trip. They would pass between Bremen and Hanover westwards, then across Holland, the North Sea and home.

After a three-night stand-down, followed by two nights when raids were cancelled, there was just enough time to get two more raids in before the 'no moon' period ended.

Towards the end of the afternoon and early evening, the rain returned, bringing in fog as well. Zero hour over the target was set for just after eight o'clock, so take-off time for 626 Squadron's Lancasters had to be between four-thirty and five in the late afternoon, before the weather clamped in. Indeed, a lot of squadrons to the north, in Yorkshire, didn't get off the ground at all due to fog. The weather was going to be a big problem for many this night, particularly as a large cloud front was building up near the Dutch coast. The bombers had to climb through this and some were to experience icing problems. Many were to turn back due to various other difficulties.

One of the two Lancasters from 626 Squadron that turned back was JB595 captained by W/O Welham. This was the second time in a row that this aircraft had let its crew down; on the raid of 26th November to Berlin JB595 had to abort due to magneto trouble on the starboard-outer engine. Tonight the problem was to be the exhaust system on the same engine and only within an hour's flying time from Wickenby, just twenty miles off the Norfolk coast. To decrease the all-up weight for a safe landing, as they could not go on, 1236 incendiaries were dropped in the North Sea before heading for home. Needless to say, the Flight Engineer was not too happy about the performance of this particular Lancaster!

"We took the same aircraft out again and got it up to about 14,000 feet, then shoved the superchargers into 'S' gear. I was watching this engine (starboard-outer) because we were not very happy as it wasn't performing as it should – its temperatures were different to all the others. As it got darker, flames from the exhaust could be seen going over the wing leading edge between three and four feet long, just like a blowlamp! The shield over the exhaust stubs had fallen off. The petrol pipes to the engines were very near to the leading edge of the wing, so the pilot said "What do you think?"

I said, "Two chances. Drop the cookie, feather the prop and go on with three engines or drop the cookie and return to base".

The pilot was not happy with the first choice so we returned to base. We went into interrogation with the Winco, we were the only ones there that night, and on asking what was wrong, we told them. The Skipper said, "I am not taking that plane again, it's best you put a new engine in it."

The engineering officer was there and replied, "There was nothing wrong with the engine, I went up with your aircraft during the day."

My answer to that was, "Tell you what... we will go on the next trip if you will come with us."

He was a Flight Lieutenant and I was only a Sergeant at the time and he said "That's asking a bit much!"

I said "That's what you've got to think of, if you want us to go. Look if we are not flying (on operations) you come up with us at night with the plane."

He still argued "I don't know, there is nothing wrong with the engine, its alright."

But we didn't fly it again and they gave us LM393.

W4967, with W/O Rew as captain, made it all the way to twenty-two miles north-east of Hanover before running into trouble and having to turn back. The port inner engine lost oil pressure while the starboard inner was overheating. To make matters worse, the vital rear turret would not work. At just after seven-thirty and two-and-half flying hours from Wickenby, W4967 was found losing height and descending through the 17,000 feet level, so the crew had no alternative but to drop the bomb load and head for home . A Lancaster with only two engines, even with half fuel and no bomb load could only just maintain 10,000 feet, so flying on was out of the question. The engines also supplied various aircraft services essential to the mission. The port inner engine had a compressor that supplied the air driven gyros of the Mark IV Autopilot and the Mark XIV Bombsight Computer. A vacuum pump on each inner engine supplied the gyroscopic instruments of the cockpit.

Turning back, alone now and out of the protective bomber stream, the Lancaster passed no less than four night-fighter bases on the way west before reaching the Dutch coast. Crossing the North Sea was uneventful but after making landfall on the Lincolnshire coast the crew's ordeal was not over as W/O Rew prepared to land. The two inner engines, apart from items already mentioned, also powered 1500-watt generators for the many electrical services and the hydraulic pumps to drive the undercarriage and flaps down for landing. Since this was an emergency, the flight engineer had to use compressed air from charged bottles, so introducing air into the hydraulic oil lines and 'blowing' the wheels and flaps down. This later would present no small problem to the ground crew technicians to 'bleed' the hydraulic oil lines of this unwanted air, but this was not on the mind of W/O Rew at the time as he landed W4967 safely at half past eleven, having flown for more than six-and-half hours.

When Lancasters approached their home airfield, or due to bad weather diverted elsewhere, they would have to 'stack' at 500 foot intervals, awaiting landing instructions from air traffic control. The lower aircraft would be first to land, or 'pancake' as was the radio instruction code. The rest would land in turn, sometimes having to wait up to an hour while flying in a circle many feet above the airfield, dropping down 500 feet every time somebody below had instructions to land. If a returning bomber was shot up or had wounded aboard, naturally this aircraft would have priority to land, the rest waiting even longer. After flying for six or seven hours in combat conditions, crews would be tired, hungry and impatient. Under these conditions mistakes could be made and sometimes were.

Only one Lancaster was allowed on the runway at a time, but if its radio was not working or if the tired pilot forgot to transmit to air traffic control that he had landed and was clear of the runway, there was an obvious problem. Observers in the control tower could not see a taxiing aircraft in the pitch dark, three-quarters of a mile away at the western end of Wickenby's 4,000-ft main runway. More delay for the weary crews above. The solution to the problem was to post a man with a field telephone about halfway down the duty runway, so the tower was better informed of runway activity. Extra lamps were put on the last part of the runway to advise the pilot he could slow down at the last possible but safe moment, therefore using the runway to land in the minimum of time. With these innovations the Lancasters were able to land at less than two minute intervals.

Like W4967, JB646 this night only just reached the Hanover area. On the way out and crossing the Dutch coast, it was noticed that the oxygen system contents gauge only read five-eighths full. Either the gauge was not reading correctly or the vital oxygen was leaking out somewhere. The captain, Sgt Jackson, told the navigator to monitor the supply and tell him when there was only half left. When the critical indication was reached, the aircraft still had 150 miles to go to the Berlin target and get back home afterwards. Realising the supply would not last the duration, a suitable target was sought for the bomb load. A concentration of searchlights near Hanover came into the bombsight graticle so the bombs were let go, just as the red target indicator route markers, dropped by the Pathfinders, were seen about five miles to the north. After this, W4967 headed for home, the crew not entirely dissatisfied with their night's work.

There were, however, those who managed to get to the target in Berlin, or it would seem so, as it shall be seen. F/O Wilkinson, captain of JB599 and F/Lt McLaughlin flying ED424, both thought the target fires were well concentrated, the Pathfinders having done a good job, except for the route markers on the way home, which were thought to be rather scattered. P/O Sargent in JA922 and P/O Hutchinson piloting DV177, had the same comment to make but at eighteen minutes past eight, when JA922 bombed the target, the stratus cloud had started to build up over the city to obscure the aiming point. F/Sgt Belford, flying LM391, came across a dummy target on the way in, and on reaching the real target about ten minutes after JA922, found the cloud cover at 6-8/10ths. The Berlin defences gave the night-fighters priority so most of the flak guns were silent. Although all crews reported seeing many fighters on the way there and back, none saw them over the city.

Not so fortunate was S/Ldr Roden, the 'A' flight commander and captain of JA864. His Lancaster took off at 16:57 hrs with nearly five tons of high explosive and incendiaries but was never heard of again. JA864, it was revealed later, was shot down at Gleinicke on the outskirts of Berlin.

Sgt Cuthill, who had flown on his familiarisation trip to Berlin in JA922 on the previous raid a week previously, was tonight with his own crew on their first operational sortie in DV244. After take-off and with the English countryside being left behind, they flew over the North Sea where the gunners went through the routine of testing the guns. Crossing the enemy coast of Holland, DV244 was met by a hail of fire from a flak battery. One shell burst very near the aircraft, stunning the new crew, but not near enough to do any real damage or slow their progress eastwards. Cloud was encountered, giving the gunners a rest from their vigil of watching for the dark silhouette of a night-fighter against a slightly less dark sky. When they eventually came out of the cloud there was a dark shape only feet above them, but it wasn't the shape of a night-fighter, it was the massive form of another Lancaster! The rear gunner, Sgt Smith, gave the warning and by quick reaction of the pilot, DV244 dived to another part of the sky.

DV244 approached the Berlin target about twenty minutes into the attack at 22,000 feet and was one of the last aircraft to drop its bomb load. By this time, haze and cloud was building, to affect vertical visibility. The attack and the resulting fires were scattered over twenty miles, not concentrated, as they should have been by this time. The wind and weather had played their part, blowing the Pathfinders and Mainforce south of the track they should have been flying along. Many of the Pathfinders were late marking what they thought was the target. The Pathfinders should have gone in following a line of three towns picked out by radar, Stendal, Rathenow and Neuen. The winds had blown the Pathfinder aircraft south of track. Unknown to them, coming in from the west, the on-board radar had displayed three similar images, the towns of Gethin, Brandenburg and the Berlin southwestern suburb of Potsdam. After a timed run from what they thought was the last real reference waypoint, the 'target' was reached and down came the green target indicators fifteen miles south of the real objective, the arms factories to the north of the city.

Turning for home, after dropping the bomb load, DV244 headed westwards but the fickle winds affected them once more. In ignorance, the Lancaster drifted over the heavily defended and dangerous Ruhr industrial area, just over a couple of hours later. Cloud was with them all the way but without warning the

Lancaster was caught by flak for the second time this night, shrapnel hitting it from all sides. In desperation, the pilot changed height and weaved all over the sky to throw the flak guns and their radar guidance off the mark. Shrapnel tore a large hole in the starboard fin and punctured the petrol tank in the port wing. Until the self-sealing action of the tank material got to work, precious fuel streamed past the rear gunner's turret. The starboard outer engine stopped suddenly, the propeller having to be feathered by the flight engineer. Then the rear turret ceased to move under power and had to be trained fore and aft by hand to reduce drag. Just as the crew reached what seemed to be the pinnacle of noise and flying metal, they were out of it, only to find the port inner engine loosing power. All the way to the North Sea coast this engine coughed and sometimes stopped altogether, but kept on restarting again. The coast was crossed twenty miles north of Antwerp, but at this point the direct reading compass failed, adding to their catalogue of problems. Having left one enemy behind, two more now came into play – time and gravity.

When the English coast came into sight at last, DV244 was down to 4,000 feet with very little petrol left in the tanks. RAF Woodbridge, on the Suffolk coast, was the nearest airfield, so when permission was granted by air traffic control to land, Sgt Cuthill flew his aircraft straight in. On approach, the undercarriage was selected down but there was no visible sign of it being locked in position on the undercarriage indicator in front of the pilot. Then the port inner engine stopped after running rough for many miles. The Lancaster landed on the Woodbridge runway very hard, the undercarriage collapsing straight away, causing the stricken bomber to career down the tarmac in a shower of sparks and flying metal from the screeching underbelly. Fortunately, because it landed on its last dregs of fuel, it didn't catch fire, and eventually came to a halt, spinning broadside to the runway. Miraculously, all the crew members were able to make their escape successfully, to be met by an ambulance and the Station Wing Commander in his jeep.

After staying the night at Woodbridge, the crew went back to the airfield. On seeing their aircraft in daylight, they marvelled at the amount of damage it had sustained and still got them safely back. Then, still in flying kit, they made their way back to Wickenby on the train. Although it looked it then, DV244 was not a write-off. It was repaired and flew again, finally going missing on a raid to Karlsruhe in April 1944.

The raid was not judged a total success. The bombs were aimed at a point fifteen miles south of where they should have been, many falling in open country to the south of the city. Only two important places were hit but only slightly damaged, the Henschel aircraft factory and the Daimler-Benz complex. The wind blew many bombers off track and out of the protection of the 'window' radar countermeasures, the night-fighters and flak accounting for forty aircraft shot down, nearly nine percent. Some 626 Squadron Lancasters were scattered at diversion airfields, just four out of the nine that made it back to England landed at Wickenby. Of those four, only two crews and one aircraft were fit to take part in the next raid the following night.

The moon was waxing more and more each night but there was just time to go on one more raid before too much light at night made it dangerous for Bomber Command to put on a large scale operation. No sooner had JB595 had its exhaust system repaired, then it was prepared for a pre-raid test flight by its ground crew in the fog and drizzle that persisted throughout the morning. This was to be the eleventh major raid in nine nights for the

Command's bomber crews and on this night it was back to Berlin again. There were five Lancasters of 626 Squadron available for the raid, involving only two crews that flew the previous night to the German capital. By the time all five aircraft had had their ground test, the target had been changed to no less a deep penetration into Germany, Leipzig, roughly ninety miles south-west of Berlin.

Leipzig had been the site of a pre-war World Fair Exhibition Centre. One of the halls of this magnificent venue occupied 170,000 square feet of floor space over which was a 320 feet span of unsupported roof. Intelligence reports revealed that this and other spacious buildings of the complex were being used to repair Junkers aircraft engines and airframes.

The flight path of the attacking force was to go straight for Berlin as on the previous night, but eighty miles from the capital, and just north of Magdeburg, the stream would turn south and head for the industrial heart of Leipzig. Nine Mosquitos flying with the main force of 307 Lancasters and 220 Halifaxes would fly straight on to drop target indicators on Berlin in a decoy raid to draw off the night-fighters. For the first time, tonight three Lancasters of the Pathfinder Force with their superior H2S Mk.III radar, were to go on a raid other than Berlin. The route flying home was a long dogleg over Southern Germany and Northern France.

The take-off time for 626 Squadron aircraft was to be a late one, around midnight, to be at the target 600 miles away at four o'clock the following morning. It will be remembered that W/O Wellham's crew complained about the engine performance of JH595, the aircraft that let them down in two succesive raids. They were given another aircraft, LM393 for this trip and, hoping for better luck, they took off at ten minutes to midnight with a 4,000lb cookie and 1286 incendiaries. The Pathfinders laid down route markers accurately and effectively as commented by most crews as they flew across enemy occupied Europe. There was 10/10ths layered stratocumulus cloud between 3,000 and 6,000 feet on the way there but the vertical visibility at 21,000 feet over the target was good enough for LM393's bomb aimer, Sgt Lamb, to see the green target indicators on the Lancaster's bombing run at four o'clock. They were one of the first at the target and as yet could not see any fires taking hold. Of the three special Pathfinder Lancasters, with the new radar, two put their markers right on top of the target. No fighters were encountered over Leipzig; the nine Mosquitos that went on to drop target in-dicators on Berlin had completely misled the night-fighter con-trollers into thinking that the capital was the target. All night-fighters were directed to Berlin to find, too late, nothing to shoot at. Using their high speed and altitude to avoid trouble, all the Mosquitos returned safely home.

The other four aircraft of 626 Squadron followed LM393 within the next fifteen minutes to bomb the target. By the time W4990, with F/Sgt Welford as captain, bombed at six minutes past four, the fires below were well concentrated and taking hold. Cloud was now gathering steadily over the city but the Pathfind-ers were still able to rain down ground and sky-markers to take the place of those extinguished, the target now being bombed through the cloud cover. Sgt Jackson's crew in JB461 observed a large fire track running from north to south across Leipzig when they got there and two columns of thick black smoke rising to 7,000 feet.

All the attacking force bombed the target flying in from the north across Leipzig, but now it was time to turn onto a long route home, first south, then westward. After losing three aircraft to flak over the target area, many bombers wandered too far south and into the Frankfurt air defences, perhaps due to the navigator's old adversary, the wind and the mystery of its fickle speed and direction. About a dozen bombers were shot down here to mar the satisfaction with the good work done around one-and-half hours previously. Fortunately, five of 626 Squadron's Lancasters made it past this point to arrive back in England safely but not without problems along the way for one of them.

On board JB59S, the two gunners, facing rearwards for most of the time, saw the glow of the fires at Leipzig through the clouds many miles after leaving the target. Due to the unpredicted northerly winds they drifted with many others into the Frankfurt area. Here Sgt Higgs piloted the Lancaster through flak and the threat of night-fighters unscathed. On reaching the English Channel he was attacked once again by the coastal flak batteries. Out over the English Channel they were unsure of their position and short on fuel, the only thing known was that they were heading in the right general direction. Flying on, the situation was getting desperate but along the way a Gee navigational fix was found, and as fuel was critically low, a direct route to the English coast was worked out by the navigator, Sgt Chase. Still their ordeal was not over; on crossing the Kent coast an anti-aircraft battery opened up on them! Fortunately, they were not accurate, and at 07:47 JB595 managed to land at RAF West Malling, a Fighter Command station southeast of London.

Leipzig had not been attacked for some considerable time and being a large and important centre for aircraft production and repair with other key industries, it was long overdue for a raid. With reports from the bomber crews and the next day's reconnaissance flight photographs, it was assessed that the raid had been a success. The former World Fair complex used to repair

Luftwaffe aircraft, and many other industrial buildings had been hit. Over forty-per-cent of the city's housing was destroyed or damaged in some way. Twenty-four bombers, nine Lancasters and fifteen Halifaxes, did not come back out of the 527 strong force that set out.

The Command stood down from operations for two weeks after the Leipzig raid as the moon was too bright during that period. Only minor raids were carried out, these by fast Mosquitos of the Light Night Striking Force to Germany's industrial areas, 109 sorties in all with only the loss of one over Essen. Such was the high speed and altitude capability of these magnificent aircraft that they could fly anywhere over enemy-occupied Europe with near impunity.

626 Squadron took a rest for the next few days, low cloud and fog putting a stop to flying anyway. S/Ldr Spiller took charge of 'A' Flight replacing S/Ldr Roden who had been killed in the last Berlin raid. The lack of operational flying was used to advantage to brush up on skills and knowledge. From 8th December training flights across country and bombing practice were carried out day and night. There was always maintenance work under way and afterwards the mandatory air test to be flown if a major inspection had been done. There were two days of flying against the Spitfires of the Fighter Affiliation Flight at RAF Kirton-in-Lindsay to give the gunners some practice, swapping live ammunition for gun cameras. There were lectures to attend. All aircrew went to a demonstration and talk on the bright yellow survival dinghy carried in the Lancaster's starboard wing root. 1 Group formed all its airfields into three station 'bases'. Ludford Magna became No.14 Base Station with Wickenby and Faldingworth as sub-stations. S/Ldr Roden was awarded the Distinguished Flying Cross posthumously.

7. Black Thursday

The 16th December was just another winter's day to the farmers in Lincolnshire, but at Wickenby there was a hive of activity around the Lancasters. Visibility was three miles down the runways, 'ops were on' and Berlin was again the target.

626 Squadron pilots in the briefing room before the Berlin raid of 16/17th December. *From left to right*: W/O J.F.V. Butcher, W/O A.H. Rew, S/Ldr J.L. Spiller, S/Ldr J.A. Neilson RNZAF, F/Sgt S. Jacques (taken POW Feb 44), F/O R.E. Wellham RAAF, F/O J.P. Hutchinson RAAF (killed Schweinfurt, 25.2.44 in LL 797).[4]

It was to be an early raid, time on target between 1958hrs and 2012hrs that evening. A three-quarter moon was due to rise later on, and to miss it, the 483-strong Lancaster main force and Path-

---

[4] Photo: W Whitehouse.

finders had to take off at around four in the afternoon. Five Mosquitos were to drop decoy fighter flares south of Berlin. The route out was to be straight east from the Dutch coast to Berlin. After the attack the escape was to be northwest to the Baltic then west over Denmark and the North Sea. It was predicted that there would be fog and low cloud over the German night-fighter airfields and perhaps Eastern England around midnight. This was the time when, almost certainly, tired crews with perhaps damaged aircraft low on fuel, would be attempting to land. The risk was there but the gamble was taken.

Fourteen Lancasters of 626 Squadron took off for the raid on Berlin in the late afternoon. After taking off from Wickenby at 1621hrs, Sgt Cuthill, piloting DV177, had to abandon the mission due to the overheating of the two outer engines. The bomb aimer dumped the 'cookie' and some of the incendiaries in the North Sea about fifty miles from Den Helder off the Dutch coast at 1800hrs, the Lancaster turning for home to land at Wickenby one-and-quarter hours later. At about the same time DV177 was dumping its load halfway across the North Sea, the crew of JB774 were experiencing trouble. Their mid-upper gunner, Sgt Smith, was feeling ill and could not concentrate on his vigil. Although only at 12,000 feet and still climbing, his oxygen supply control was turned to the 30,000ft setting but on reaching the Dutch coast at 18,000 feet, he was still unwell. It was no good carrying on with effectively only half the defences operational so the captain, F/Sgt West, turned the Lancaster around and headed back to Wickenby, dumping the cookie and half the incendiaries in the North Sea on the way.

The Lancaster's three turrets were moved by hydraulic pressure from pumps on three of the engines, for example, the starboard inner engine hydraulic pump powered the front turret. On

LM393, oil from a leaking hydraulic pipe serving the front turret was being thrown back onto the cockpit windscreen, making it difficult for the pilot, P/O Wellham, to see forward. There wasn't much the flight engineer, Sgt Groom, could do about it and since the night-fighter threat nearly always came from the rear it was decided to carry on with the mission.

626 Squadron's remaining dozen aircraft, led by New Zealander S/Ldr Neilson in JB599, flew on across Holland and Germany. The moon had yet to rise and it was noted by most crews that it was exceptionally dark. As predicted, the clouds were stacked up to between 10,000 and 17,000 feet. From the ground, flying conditions looked appalling for the Luftwaffe night-fighter force, but their best and most experienced crews were alerted and ordered to make the effort. Between fifty and sixty night-fighters climbed into the fog and cloud, at least one crashing. This was probably due to icing problems in the cold air. High flying German aircraft dropped fighter flares to aid the defending force all the way from the Dutch coast to the vicinity of Hanover. Fourteen bombers were thought to be shot down on this part of the route.

All 626 Squadron's crews escaped the attention of the night-fighters, many reporting flying through continuous cloud all the way to Berlin. P/O Curry, captain of EE133, took along Sgt Elkington for his initial raid experience flight but he didn't see or learn anything of note as there wasn't much to observe through the murk. The Pathfinders still dropped route markers, which was seen by some as they dangled on their small parachutes before disappearing through the cloud.

The bombers went straight for Berlin as planned but the German fighter controllers did not guess that this was their intention at the time. Thinking that the Berlin approach was a feint, they expected the attacking force to turn off suddenly and head for the real target, as had happened before. But the bombers didn't turn, leaving the defending fighters assembled over Brandenburg thirty-five miles to the west of the target, in the wrong place at the wrong time.

As the Lancasters neared Berlin, the conditions were almost ideal, searchlights could not penetrate the thick cloud and there were no night-fighters to contend with. The Pathfinder Force had four of the newly equipped H2S Mk.III Lancasters flying this night, the target appearing to be effectively pinpointed by sky and ground markers in the opening stages of the raid.

Despite oil all over the windscreen, LM393 arrived over the target on time at 22,000 feet, seeing the red and green target indicators disappearing through the cloud tops 5,000 feet below. Fire glow was not seen through the cloud cover, the only evidence of their visit being the ascending smoke seen above the cloud by Australian rear gunner, F/Sgt Atherton, as LM393 left the city below heading north. JB595 was over the target at eight o'clock, F/Sgt Torrance, another Australian, as captain: The crew saw nothing of the city below, just endless banks of cloud. His bomb aimer, Sgt Fox, waited till there was a cascading green target indicator in the bombsight gratical and let the 10,600 pounds of high explosive and incendiaries go. The crew, like those of LM393, saw no evidence of fires except the smoke coming up through the cloud.

Only when they realised their mistake did the fighter controllers direct the Luftwaffe on to the raid now taking place. By this time they were a spent force being that they were low on fuel from orbiting Brandenburg waiting for a decision. Only a token attempt was made to defend the City, only one Lancaster was shot down over the Capital. F/Lt Wright, captain of W4967, thought the target marking scattered but bombed on time. A Lancaster, with a twin-engined night-fighter close on its tail passed right in front of his aircraft at high speed, banking steeply to avoid the defender's cannon. As F/Lt Wright's Lancaster left the German capital behind, due to an unknown fault the rear turret ceased to work but the worst was now over.

Because the target marking was scattered, bombs were dropped onto individual clusters of target indicators as they came into the bombsight gratical of the attacking Lancasters. What the bomb-aimer looked at was the cluster of target indicators through a circle of light, the gratical, projected onto piece of glass held in a frame. After inputs of airspeed, height, aircraft drift, aircraft heading and a setting for the particular bombs to be dropped, the bombsight computer worked out the bombing angle sight-line and then motored a small light projector to position the gratical on the glass. A gyroscope further stabilised the sight glass to compensate for aircraft pitch and roll in flight irrespective of how well the pilot flew the aircraft straight and level on the bomb run.

The fires that were first produced by the incendiaries were not concentrated; consequently large fires did not develop until later on in the raid, as reported by Sgt Higgs flying W4990. Between him and his flight engineer, Sgt Fowler, they could not get the Lancaster above 17,000 feet, even after dumping a canister of incendiaries on the way. W4990 arrived over the target half-an-hour late, low in altitude and about alone as one can be as the raid finished twenty minutes earlier. By this time fires were at long last getting a hold, so since he had no target indicators to aim at Sgt Keatings, the bomb aimer, dropped the load in the largest concentration of fires he could find. Like the rest before it, the Lancaster quickly sped away to make its escape as the three-quarter moon was beginning to rise over Northern Germany and the Baltic.

The route home was to head for the Baltic, over Denmark, the North Sea and on to Wickenby. The night-fighters did not follow or intercept; with fog, low cloud and casualties of their own, they were unable to put up any more of a fight. Twenty-five Lancasters had been lost in the attack up to this point. The bombs had fallen to the east and west of the aiming point as revealed much later in the month. Due to the thick cloud cover, no photographs were brought back that night. There was no widespread damage due to the lack of concentrated fire and an insufficient total weight of incendiaries dropped, only 848 tons. The greatest damage was to the Berlin railway system, many loads falling in the Ostbahnhof marshalling yards, two important stations and the office of the State Railways. The National Theatre in the centre of the City was totally destroyed, along with the country's military and political archives in another building. No industrial premises of importance were damaged but a lot of housing and flats were hit, causing over 700 deaths.

All this was behind the bombers as they flew homeward towards the English coast, but one of the greatest tragedies of Bomber Command was about to unfold. One of the greatest fears of any pilot, even today with modern electronic aids, apart from being shot at, is to try and land an aircraft in low cloud and fog, especially at night. The Lancaster crews had been flying for over seven hours, at least half of that time in combat approaching and at the target. The crews were tired and in some cases flying damaged aircraft with wounded on board. Their East Anglia, Lincolnshire and Yorkshire airfields were shrouded in the same low cloud and fog that had hampered their adversaries a few hours before. Being low on fuel, diverting to clear airfields in the

West Country and Scotland was out of the question. Faced with this terrible dilemma, crews had to decide whether to risk all and attempt a landing or point the aircraft towards the sea and bale out, hopefully over land. Four crews did just that, jumping into the cloud and not knowing for sure what was below them. Six airmen were never seen again, presumably lost in the icy North Sea. Twenty-nine Lancasters crashed while trying to land, plus a Stirling that had been minelaying around the enemy coast, more than the total shot down by the German night-fighters and flak that night. 127 airmen were killed and thirty-four were injured when their bombers tried to land, the equivalent of twenty-three complete crews. One Group lost fifteen aircraft all together, more than any other. Throughout Bomber Command, December 16th 1943 became known as 'Black Thursday'.

Somehow, all of 626 Squadron's aircraft brought their crews home safely. P/O Breckenridge, piloting 626 Squadron's LM391, managed to belly-land his aircraft at Kelstern rather than risk landing on a damaged undercarriage, all seven crew surviving. LM391 was repaired and flew again on operations in less than three weeks.

After the tragic events of the night before it was with much relief that the Command stood down, fog persisting throughout the day of the 17th December. However the visibility, although bad for flying, was good enough to hold a football match between 626 Squadron's A and B flights. The next two days at Wickenby improved a little weather-wise although sometimes it rained. On the night of the 19th it became fine and fit for flying, navigation training routes being flown well into the evening towards midnight. Earlier on in the day, fighter affiliation flights were flown to give the air gunners valuable practise.

On 20th December, thirteen 626 Squadron Lancasters were made ready for a raid on Mannheim that evening, take-off being around four-thirty in the afternoon. Fortunately, for the technicians and armament load crews, the weather was fair for most of the day. Only fifty-four Lancasters and Mosquitoes from One and Eight (Pathfinder) Groups were to take part, as this was to be a diversionary raid in support of an attack of Frankfurt by another 650 of the Command's aircraft, the idea being to draw the night-fighters away from the main operation. Mannheim is about 45 miles south of the large industrial target of Frankfurt. What was of concern was the night-fighter base of Mainz-Finthen near Weisbaden, thirty-two miles north-east of Mannheim. This airfield was home of I/NJG6 with radar-equipped Me110 and Do217 aircraft.

Wing Commander Haynes led his Squadron in Lancaster JB599, taking off at four-thirty with the other dozen aircraft. W4967, with F/Sgt Lone as captain, ran into trouble forty minutes after leaving Wickenby. Having got as far as just to the north of the Wash at 16,000 feet, it was found that the rear turret would not move due to a hydraulic failure and the direct reading compass was not working correctly. This instrument had repeaters in the cockpit and at the navigator's station, and was essential for navigating the aircraft. It was decided to turn back, but not before dumping the 'cookie' and incendiaries in the North Sea, 100 miles to the east of Mablethorpe. W4967 flew back to Wickenby to land at just after seven-thirty.

W4967 was not the only aircraft in trouble. Sgt Elkington could not get his Lancaster, DV177, to climb above 14,500 feet. The 4,000lb 'cookie' was dumped sixty miles east of Orfordness in the open sea after which the Lancaster flew on, climbing steadily to operational height of 20,000 feet.

The Squadron's Commanding Officer and his crew in JB599, the crew of DV177, DV171 captained by Sgt Cuthill and the rest of the Squadron all bombed the target around 7:25pm. All crews observed that there wasn't much cloud about, visibility being generally good, 3/10ths cloud in some places. Unfortunately, the Pathfinder target marking, red target indicators, were scattered and consequently so were the resulting fires over the target area. The opportunity to use the good visibility was missed by the defenders as all the attacking force came away from Mannheim safe and almost intact. P/O Curry, captain of JA922, saw fires getting a good hold when leaving, so did the crew of JB599, the Squadron Commander's aircraft; one very large fire was seen by the tail gunner of DV171, Sgt Smith, when heading homeward.

From 20,000 feet and forty miles away, the main attack on Frankfurt was seen to be going well but the diversion raid to Mannheim had not worked as planned by Bomber Command Operations. The main force was tracked correctly by German Air Force fighter controllers all the way in from the North Sea coast, the Command losing forty-one bombers out of the 650 sent out. No attention was paid to the Mannheim-bound Lancasters and Mosquitoes.

How many of the 41 casualties were shot down by fighters or by flak is not clear. A lumbering Lancaster or Halifax flying at 160mph, full of fuel and explosives, was easy prey even for a single-engined night-fighter, which did not have the benefit of onboard air interception radar. The bombers were unfairly outgunned, outranged and outmanoeuvred. This night, Major Wilhelm Herget of I/NJG4 alone shot down eight of them. I/NJG4 was based at Florennes in Belgium but in the December was detached to Brandis airfield outside Leipzig to serve alongside III/NJGS that flew Me110s.

The lack of night-fighters hindering the Mannheim force spelt luck for DV177 and its crew. The starboard outer engine gave trouble with 'flames shooting out from the very start', according to the Squadron Record Book, from the exhausts, a beacon for any roaming night-fighter. Sgt Elkington, under the circumstances, had every reason to turn back, but with much courage on the part of the crew they lightened the load and pressed on to the target. Thankfully DV177 came home undetected to land at Wickenby about eleven-fifteen. Luck was also with JB646 this night as on landing at eleven-thirteen, the captain, F/Sgt Torrance, and his crew found a hole in the wing caused by flak in number three petrol tank.

When P/O Curry landed JA922 at eighteen minutes passed eleven, his tail gunner, F/Sgt Lanham, had completed his tour of thirty operations. Twenty-one had been with the present crew and nine more in Wellingtons. (Many crews and airmen didn't even reach ten missions in the fight over Germany.) For two-and-half years he had been in England, 12,000 miles away from his native Australia. He was typical of the many airman who came to our shores unselfishly to fight Nazi Germany from all parts of the Empire.

All the Wickenby force, thirteen from 626 Squadron and fifteen from 12 Squadron came back safely, as did the rest of the aircraft belonging to One Group. No raid into enemy occupied Europe was easy but this one, for One Group, went smoother than most with no attacks by night-fighters and very little flak damage to the aircraft.

Fourteen crews on the 23rd December, 98 airmen, of 626 Squadron filed into the Squadron Operations room for the briefing of that night's raid. Patiently they sat down at the long tables and waited for the briefing officers to take the stage at the front and inform them of the route, weather expected on the trip and the latest intelligence on the enemy defences. Individual branch officers were also to give information and advice about gunnery, radio procedures and frequencies, bomb aiming etc. One officer on 626 Squadron's Intelligence staff was F/O Michael Bentine, who was to become a well-known radio scriptwriter and broadcaster of 'Goon Show' fame a decade later. Conversations may have varied, but the most popular topic, no doubt, was the target that lay hidden behind the cloth covering the large operational map at the end of the room facing them.

The crews had been rested after the last operation on Mannheim. On the 21st and 22nd there was an official stand-down from operations for most of the Command's squadrons. Christmas was in a couple of days time and already the festive spirit was being felt. There had been a party hosted by the WAAF at the station in one of the larger recreational buildings. The prospect of operations on Christmas Eve and Christmas Day, of killing Germans and perhaps being killed oneself on these two sacred days, seemed diabolical. Only minor operations had been carried out in the previous 48 hours, the largest being as few as 51 aircraft attacking flying-bomb sites in between Abbeville and Amiens. The weather was typical for December, rain showers and cloud but on the day before it cleared up so cross-country navigation training was carried out. On the morning of the 23rd it started cloudy but became fine in the afternoon.

At long last the Commanding Officer came into the room and as military protocol demanded, the crews were called to attention. After being placed at ease again the target was revealed ... Berlin. Originally, when the attack was planed it called for an early evening take-off but it was forecast that the weather would be bad for crews starting out in Yorkshire and Lincolnshire. Take-off time was therefore put back to just after midnight, the first few minutes of Christmas Eve, but it meant that landings would take place in daylight about eight hours later. The fateful December 16th was still in the minds of the planners.

After crossing the enemy coast at the Rhine estuary in Holland, the red ribbon on the map showed a southern route to the German capital. Flying south-east from the coast, the bomber-stream would fly across northern Belgium until the German border was reached, then east, below the Ruhr industrial area and over the top of Frankfurt. On reaching eastern Germany the force would skirt Leipzig, leaving it to port and head north to arrive at Berlin about four o'clock in the morning. It was hoped that the fighter controllers would think the raid would be on one of the southern industrial cities, there being plenty to choose from along the route, Karlsruhe, Mannheim and Frankfurt again, Nuremberg, Augsburg, Munich or Leipzig. A route marker was to be dropped by the Pathfinders as a turning point a little to the east of Leipzig. Eight Mosquitoes were to conduct a spoof raid on this city at this point in the raid. After the attack, Berlin was to be left heading north for about fifty miles then turning west, fly a long dogleg across the North German Plain between Bremen and Hanover, the last leg being flown across Holland, the North Sea and home. Another route marker was to be dropped north of Hanover. (The Command gave up this practise of route markers later on in the Battle as it was found that enemy night-fighters were also using the markers to find the bomber stream's path.)

Near to midnight, 626 Squadron's fourteen crews boarded their Lancasters to take off in the first few minutes of Christmas Eve. Unfortunately, while taxiing, two of 12 Squadron's aircraft collided in the dark. Although one was even cut in half, no crew member was injured. This probably caused the delay of at least two of 626 Squadron's aircraft. ED424 took off sixteen minutes after midnight piloted by F/Lt McLaughlin. This was to be the last and thirtieth operation of his tour, likewise for the Flight Engineer of DV177, Sgt Rawlinson, who was airborne nine minutes later.

The aircraft made their way to Mablethorpe and out over the North Sea, heading south-east for the Dutch coast. F/Sgt West, flying JB748, was soon in trouble with the engine-driven generators overcharging, which had to be taken off line. Each inboard engine drove a DC generator, both being connected electrically in parallel to charge the aircraft batteries, so it was probably a problem of voltage regulation. All electrical systems were now running on draining battery power, so any that were not essential were closed down. These included the radio and power for the bombsight and gun sights. The situation made it futile to go on, so the 4,000lb 'cookie' was dumped along with the incendiaries sixty-five miles east of Spurn Head from 10,000 feet. With the mission abandoned JB748 landed back at Wickenby at twenty minutes to three.

F/O Wilkinson, flying JB599, took off late but still headed for the Dutch coast hoping to catch the bomber stream. Realising that this could not be achieved, JB599's mission was also aborted. Not wanting to waste the bombs, at two o'clock they were dropped from 16,000 feet onto Haamsteide airfield on Schouwen Island, after which a large fire with smoke rising to 2,000 feet was seen. JB599 touched down safely at Wickenby just over one-and-quarter hours later. The third abortive Lancaster was DV190 with a defective rear turret, the main defensive armament. The 'cookie' and 120 incendiaries were dumped fifty-five miles east of Great Yarmouth after which F/Sgt Butcher flew the Lancaster back to base to land at two-thirty in the morning.

ED424 left the Wickenby runway at sixteen minutes past midnight with F/Lt McLaughlin at the controls for the last time. An uneventful two hours later saw the Lancaster' over enemy occupied Europe, flying along the top of Belgium. The cloud cover over Western Europe at the time was between five and nine-tenths, which gave problems for the Luftwaffe night-fighter force. It was the same weather that would have hampered the bombers if an early takeoff time had been called, and was now effecting the operational performance of the defenders seven hours later. Few night-fighters were able to attack the bomber force on the southern route to the target because of the bad weather at their airfields and the severe icing conditions in the clouds on gaining operational height. Another factor was that the eventual location of the target was not known and was confusing the controllers, consequently the Luftwaffenhelferinnen (the women communication auxiliaries who were in radio communication with the fighter pilots) could not tell them where to go. It was estimated that only five or six bombers were shot down on the southern leg of the route to Berlin. The route marker was picked up near Brandis outside Leipzig but F/Lt McLaughlin's crew also noticed dummy red and green target indicators nearby, supposedly planted by the Germans. They lacked the brilliance of the real thing, which gave them away.

Heading north now, the attacking force encountered eight to ten/tenths cloud as it approached Berlin. The Luftwaffe were now in no doubt of the target, but it was too late. Only a small number of night-fighters was seen over the target, even though the Beleeuchter Steffeln flare dropping units were dropping fighter flares to aid them. Time on target was between two minutes to four and twelve minutes past and just before this JA922, captained by F/Sgt Stewart, was having problems. At the crucial moment of the bomb run it was attacked by a Fw190 'Wilde Sau' (Wild Boar) night-fighter – a single-engined night-fighter without radar. Bombs were dropped a little late at 04:21, with the mid-upper gun turret not working and the four rear guns jammed. The FW190 made three attacks hitting the Lancaster in several places but not fatally. With the flying skill of F/Sgt Stewart and the cool nerve of his crew, the guns were working again within fifteen minutes, after which the FW190 was shaken off. (the Focke Wulf 190 was one of the fastest and most manoeuvrable fighters in the Luftwaffe inventory).

Twenty-thousand or so feet below, because of the cloud, the Wanganui method of sky-marking was being employed by the Pathfinder Force this night. Most Main Force crews on 626 Squadron reported the markers were concentrated, but in reality they were scattered mostly over the south-eastern part of the city suburbs, the bombs following not doing much damage as hoped. Four crews even dropped their load on Erkner, a township fifteen miles south-east of the aiming point; quite by accident they seriously damaged an important ball-bearing factory. At ten minutes past four, 626 Squadron crews saw a huge red explosion; this would have been the Neukolln Gas Works.

It was only at the end of the 14-minute 'bombing window', by all accounts, that the night-fighters appeared in force. Only four bombers were shot down over the city. The first phase of the route home involved flying north to a turning point fifty miles away, near the town of Templin and another place that was going to etch its name in history – Ravensbruck. All along this section, fighter flares were dropped to illuminate the bombers speeding home across the North German Plain. Another batch of route markers were dropped just north of Hanover. A little further on, over Osnabruch, F/O Breckenbridge's aircraft, W4990, suffered icing in the carburettor of the starboard outer engine lowering its performance for some minutes and giving the crew some anxious moments.

The round trip on this raid was one of the longest, eight hours for some but all 626 Squadron aircraft made it back to the enemy coast and over the North Sea, although not without some worried crews. JA922 was holed by a night-fighter, W4990 with de-icing problems on one engine, plus splinter damage from a heavy Flak shell.

Sgt Henty's Lancaster, JB595, was so short of petrol it had to make an emergency landing at Coltishall on the north-east Norfolk coast. One advantage of the late timing of the raid was that all aircraft landed safely in daylight.

In all, 379 aircraft had taken part in the operation; sixteen did not return, a low figure compared to recent raids on Berlin. It was thought that this was mainly due to the weather conditions being against the defending force, the chosen route and the diversion spoof raid on Leipzig by eight Mosquitos deceiving the German fighter controllers. Although there were favourable conditions for the Pathfinder and Main Force on arrival at the target, very little searchlight activity, hardly any night-fighters, a light wind and no high cloud, the opportunity to hit a relatively new target area of Berlin was thought to have been missed. Berlin targets were always difficult to mark as mentioned before. Many of the Pathfinders were equipped with the old H2S radar of which quite a lot were unserviceable by the time it came to find and mark the target. Only five Lancasters had the new Mk.III H2S sets on board and even one of them dropped its eleven target indicators six miles away from the Aiming Point. In short, the

Main Force did not have much to aim at but sparse and scattered sky-markers. The Neukolln Gas Works, the Frankfurter Allee Goods Station and Tempelhof Airport were the only places of note that were hit anywhere near the target area plus the ball-bearing factory in Erkner miles away. 600 people were made homeless and 178 were killed. The attack cost sixteen Lancasters shot down, a toll of 4.2% of the 390 dispatched, one of the lightest losses of the Battle. 1,265 tons of high explosive and incendiaries were dropped.

Eleven of 626 Squadron's Lancasters landed at Wickenby in time for breakfast, some shot up but safe, with a little cloud about but otherwise a fine day, and it was Christmas Eve.

After the Lancasters landed, the aircrew went to debrief and a well earned breakfast after flying for about eight hours. The ground crews assessed and got on with the battle damage of the aircraft as well as the routine servicing and rectification of faulty systems. The work of Bomber Command did not stop just because it was Christmas, although there was an official stand down from bombing operations that day. For the ground crews working outside the weather was cold but fine with some cloud. In the various messes later on in the day and evening, there were the usual Christmas Eve celebrations with anticipation of more to come the next day, operations permitting. The only operation flew this hallowed night was carried out by thirty-five Halifaxes which laid mines off the Frisian Islands, after which all got back safely.

Christmas Day dawned with thick fog, improving later on into fine haze with cloud later. To the disgust of 626 Squadron's air and ground crews alike, they were warned of a possible operation that night and put on standby. Fortunately, plans were cancelled in the middle of the morning and the Command stood down officially at a quarter to ten, in good time for Christmas day lunch, not that it was lavish what with wartime rationing in force. In the afternoon, a football match was played between the two Wickenby Squadrons in which 626 Squadron beat Twelve Squadron and won a cup, presented by the Station Commander. Boxing Day came and went whereby a Twelve Squadron member was heard to comment that due to the previous days festivities there were more Lancasters serviceable than aircrew to fly them. It was just as well that fog persisted throughout the day. The next day was better and work was resumed with flying training carried out in the morning. The fog came back to Lincolnshire the next day resulting in another stand down but minor operations by a small number of Mosquitos were flown from other stations to Düsseldorf, Duisburg and Cologne with no losses.

With just three days left of 1943, Wickenby awoke to another morning of fog and another day of inactivity was expected. As the day wore on the weather improved and the signal came through from Command that operations were on for that night. The 29th December was to stage the last major attack for that year by 626 Squadron, the target for the eighth time since the Battle started, Berlin. Nearly twice as many of the Command's bombers were to take part this time compared to the last operation against Berlin which was to include thirteen Lancasters of 626 Squadron. This time it was to be an early evening take off for an attack with a time on target between two minutes to eight and eighteen minutes past, all aircraft landing back about midnight. All of the Command's aircraft would converge at a point over the North Sea about forty miles west of the Dutch Frisian Islands, then fly in a direct line to a turning point twenty miles north of Leipzig. A unique feature of this operation was two 'Spoof' raids along the way by eight Mosquitos to Magdeburg, which, to the night-fighter controllers, was meant to look like a 'Spoof' raid. The other diversion was to look like the beginning of the real thing and to be carried out by another flight of Mosquitos to Leipzig, so drawing off the fighters while the Pathfinder and Main Forces pressed on to the north-east for Berlin. To add further confusion there was to be a third minor operation to Düsseldorf, in the centre of the Ruhr industrial region. The route back was to be a similar dogleg to the previous attack before Christmas, ending by flying out over the North Sea above the Frisian Islands.

Between four-fifteen and five o'clock in the late afternoon the thirteen Lancasters of 626 Squadron took to the air with, unlike the last time, no incident or delay. Arriving at the Dutch coast it was found that the Continent was covered with thick cloud. At the night-fighter airfields the defenders had to contend with low cloud and rain, where it was decided that only the most experienced crews with twin-engine, radar-equipped fighters were to take off, 66 of them in all. Confused, the controllers ordered the fighters to Magdeburg, then realising they had been deceived by the Mosquitos, directed them to Berlin. But the defending force was too few and too late, arriving at the end of the 20-minute attack giving the Lancasters and Halifaxes only the flak to get through.

The crews did not see anything of the ground, only the fires reflected on the underneath of the 10/10ths cloud. F/Lt Wright's crew, flying in W4967, observed two large red explosions in the target area. F/Sgt Annersly, the bomb aimer of ND324, was concentrating on the bomb run and looking for the sky-markers when a Halifax, taking evasive action, missed the Lancaster by a very small margin.

Flying back from the target was uneventful for most of 626 Squadron's crews although the wind blew quite a few south of the intended route. The forth route marker was not seen by many on the way back and the third one dropped by the Pathfinders was reported to be scattered by nearly everyone. At least two Lancasters strayed about sixty-five miles south from where they should have been when coming back over Holland. F/Lt Wright piloted W4967 passing Amsterdam five miles to the south on three engines. The starboard outer had a coolant leak and had to be stopped with the propeller 'Feathered' by the Flight Engineer. Half-past-ten found F/Sgt Higgs flying JB595 at 21,000 feet over Amsterdam, having also been blown south of track. Already the starboard inner engine had been damaged by debris when another aircraft exploded right in front of JB595 earlier on. Now, to add to their plight, a flak battery managed to target the Lancaster but luckily only with a near miss, causing damage to the bomb doors.

All of 626 Squadron's Lancasters landed safely around midnight, although once again, some with battle damage. 487 Lancasters took part in the raid and for the first time in a month, 252 of the Halifax force. Twenty aircraft were lost, 2.8'/. of the force. It was known that two of them were shot down by Oberleutnant Heinz-Wolfgang Schnaufer, who was later to be the Luftwaffe's most decorated night-fighter pilot. His Messerschmitt Me110 aircraft was captured in the allied advance at the end of the War. Painted on the tailfin is a score of 121 RAF Roundels, each representing a bomber shot down, and can be seen in the Imperial War Museum in London.

Like the last operation against Berlin, the marking by the Pathfinder Force was not as good as it should have been considering the conditions. Damage was spread over a large area instead of being concentrated at the target, the bombs dropping on mainly to the south-east of the city once again. No serious devastation was caused to any industry of note, 388 ordinary dwellings being destroyed and over 10,500 made homeless. Of course the failure was not realised at the time as no bombing photographs of the ground beneath the bombers were brought back due the cloud cover. The results came later when the photographic reconnaissance aircraft, usually Mosquitos again, were able to fly over Berlin on a clear day, which was rare for that time of the year. Everything seemed to be in the attacking force's favour. The defending force was confused and did not know where the target was until too late, the diversion attacks worked and although there was cloud the conditions were once again near perfect for sky-marking. There appears to be no reason why the operation was not more successful.

The last days of 1943 were spent in inactivity with a stand down and bad weather cancelling flying on operational and training flights alike. On New Year's Eve an operation was called for but cancelled, probably due to the fog that night over Eastern England.

Since November 18th, when the Battle proper had been started, there had been eight attacks on the German Capital, some less successful than others. Because of the continuous winter cloud cover over the target the crews rarely saw what they were aiming at. Only occasionally could the photographic reconnaissance Mosquitos bring back any evidence of the bomb damage for the same reason. Overall morale never flagged in Bomber Command but crews were getting tired physically and mentally, especially with no photographic confirmation of their hard work and the sacrifice of so many young crews night after night. Air Chief Marshal Harris knew that in the New Year that

Bomber Command would be required to switch from attacking German industrial targets to disrupting French communications and the defences of Hitler's 'Atlantic Wall' in the lead up to the Normandy Invasion. The time left to 'Wreck Berlin from end to end' was getting short, although a lot of damage to the German war effort, contributed by this city, had been done up to this point, the end of 1943.

Many neutral countries still traded with Germany and maintained embassies and consulates in Berlin to serve their interests as before the war. The Swiss Embassy's intelligence section was keeping very much in touch with the destruction of Germany's war industries and reporting to their government. Because of the many factories destroyed and the loss of irreplaceable machine tools, the Swiss reported that by the end of 1943 Berlin factories had uncompleted arms contracts worth 300 million Reichmarks. By December 31st, over fifty-three factories were totally destroyed or damaged so much so that only a very low output was possible. Also on the list that the diligent Swiss had compiled were the railway marshalling yards, rolling stock and important main line stations destroyed or heavily damaged. Electricity and gas production was severely disrupted, The Berlin Central Telephone Exchange was destroyed on November 26th and Albert Speer's private office and War Industries Ministry on November 22nd. The list went on to include the Erkner ball bearing factory, next most important to the factories in Schweinfurt, which was very severely damaged on 23rd December. The Swiss had the opinion that the Battle of Berlin was the beginning of the end for Germany. Much of Berlin's manufacturing potential was either totally destroyed or severally damaged with many of its workers either killed or wounded and unable to work. It must be noted that the Swiss were not spying for the Allies. They were selling

Germany all kinds of war materials and they wanted the information for themselves. They considered that there was no point in selling to a defeated neighbour if the bill could not be paid.

8.   New Year, Same Targets

Saturday 1st January1944 started with cloud and rain but by the evening it became fine with good visibility down the length of Wickenby's 4,000ft main runway. Earlier on in the day, ninety-one 626 squadron airmen had been briefed and were now ready with their thirteen Lancasters for another raid on Berlin. This time the command put up an all Lancaster force with 421 aircraft dispatched. The original take off time was earlier but now it was amended to around midnight because of the weather. The inbound route was also changed for the same reason. Instead of going north over Denmark and the Baltic they would now take a more direct route over Frisland and Northern Germany. A 'Spoof' raid was to be carried out by fifteen Mosquitos to Hamburg on the way. The wind was going to be behind the Lancasters so a time on target was set for between two minutes to three in the following morning and twelve minutes past. The way back was a long flog against the wind heading south and after rounding Leipzig to starboard, flying west across Central Germany avoiding the Ruhr area to the north, then across Belgium, Picardy and the English Channel to make a landfall at Beachy Head in Sussex.

Eight of 626 Squadron's Lancasters got into the air on time, five being left behind due to an obstruction holding up the 'queue', making them too late and therefore missing the time slot. The Merlin is a liquid cooled engine which is difficult to keep from overheating on the ground, unlike in the air where a 150 MPH plus draft through the radiator would keep the temperature down. As the temperatures rose this night, some Lancasters had to detach themselves from the 'queue' and face into wind to get more vital cooling air through the radiators. By the time temperatures were stable again it was too late.

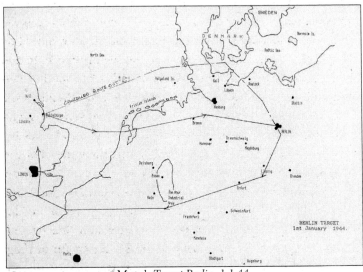

Map 1. Target Berlin, 1.1.44.

Wickenby's bombers headed south-east out over the North Sea to rendezvous with the rest of the bomber stream at a point about forty miles west of Den Helder. On the way out, over the sea, a large, multi-coloured explosion was seen by many aircraft. It was thought that a Pathfinder aircraft full of target indicators and fuel had collided with another bomber. Once again, thick cloud covered Europe from the coast inwards at 12,000ft, the tops getting higher as the attack progressed, with aircraft skimming in and out of the cloud tops at 18,000-20,000ft.

Despite the speed of the bombers, enhanced by a 40-50 mph tailwind and the cloud cover, the German fighter controllers had no difficulty in tracking the stream. There was a lot of fighter activity between the two yellow target indicators dropped by the

Pathfinders as route markers on the way to the target. No notice was taken of the Mosquito feint attack on Hamburg.

DV177 sped down the Wickenby runway at five minutes past midnight, a young F/Sgt Stewart at the controls, the crew on the third operation of their tour. The flight was uneventful across the North Sea and into Europe except for the steadily mounting cloud before them, although the crew did see the concentration of yellow target markers that was route marker 'P'. Shortly afterwards, at about thirty-five miles south-west of Bremen, the mid-upper gunner, Sgt Smith, spotted a single-engine nightfighter through the haze of the cloud tops. It was 700 yards behind, 200 feet up and diving in fast. Immediately the pilot was warned, his training coming into play now as he instinctively pulled on the control column and turned it to the right to execute a climb sharply to starboard. Meanwhile, Sgt Smith fired his guns at just under 400 yards range as tracer from the fighter's cannon whipped under the belly of the Lancaster. All of F/Sgt Stewart's crew were more than alert now; this was an uneven fight – a 400mph Messerschmidt 109 or Focke Wulf 190 against a 150mph Lancaster where the fighter had 20mm canon and the bomber had .303 machine guns. Round the night-fighter came again, this time keenly seen by the rear-gunner, Sgt Vigar. Up from the port quarter it came to be met by Sgt Vigar's four machine guns at 500 yards range. Sgt Smith in the upper turret, eager to have another go, could not bring his guns to bear as the Lancaster dived to port with all four Merlins screaming and tracer once again flashing harmlessly underneath and out into the night. Straightening out, the pilot started to weave the big bomber to give both gunners a better chance of seeing below and to the rear. Not put off by the fierce defence, the fighter hauled round for a third attack on the Lancaster. This time both gunners saw it, the rear-gunner opening fire at 600 yards, the mid-upper a split second later but the enemy aircraft did not reply and broke away in a dive to port. Meanwhile, in reaction to the gunners' report, F/Sgt Stewart pulled the control column over, the bomber turning into a starboard 'corkscrew' manoeuvre. Three attacks and three evasions where not a single cannon shell had penetrated DV177's skin, and it must be remembered that this was only the crew's third operational mission. There still seemed to be some fight left in the enemy aircraft as it came in again a few minutes later from dead astern, aiming straight for Sgt Vigar in his rear turret. Quite unexpectedly, from 300 yards out it broke off the attack, diving under the Lancaster to port and on fire. Down it went, followed by Sgt Vigar's sharp eyes as he turned his turret to port, plummeting straight through the tops of the clouds. Seconds later the glow of a violent explosion was seen by Sgt Vigar, Flight Engineer Sgt Wilson and Wireless Operator Sgt Williams. The ordeal was over, but there was still 160 miles to go to the target and then the long southerly flight home against the wind. Vigilance of course was still kept up, but there were no more encounters with night-fighters for the rest of the mission for this relatively inexperienced crew.

Not very far away was EE133 with P/O Currie in the cockpit, who along with Australian P/O Cassidy were on their 24th operation, with six more to reach the end of their tour. In the rear turret was F/Sgt Bretell nearing the end of his second tour. EE133 was held up on take off by the taxiway obstruction and only got off in time before it was too late to catch up with the rest. The Enemy coast was crossed at Zandvoort with 10/10ths cloud below. Further on the Lancaster wandered south of route near the city of Hanover due to a small navigational error but was soon back on track although at the rear of the stream now. A hundred miles short of the target another dilemma beset them but more serious this time. The rear gunner's oxygen partially failed due to ice in the tube leading to his mask. Even in his semi-conscious state F/Sgt Bretell still had a sense of duty and refused to leave the turret, even after many efforts by the wireless operator, a qualified air-gunner himself, to relieve him. It was also found that his electrically heated flying-suit was not keeping him warm which meant the risk of exposure in the cold temperatures of 20,000 feet. The symptoms of anoxia, lack of oxygen, is much the same as being drunk, one thinks one can do things but one can't. There was no way of getting him out of the turret so he was left but watched, in the hope he would be alright and they would not be attacked.

Sgt Berry was posted in from 1667 Conversion Unit having been trained as a pilot, the rest of his crew following the next day from the same unit, like him, all young sergeants. On the 16th December and after a period of training and familiarisation with the activities of the Squadron, Sgt Berry flew as second pilot with P/O Sargent in JA922 to Berlin, as was the practise with new captains. A week later, on 23rd December, he took his own crew into combat for the first time, again to Berlin. The operation flown on 1st/2nd January, was the third for this crew where they took off at sixteen minutes past midnight flying in DV190. About eighty to ninety miles west of Berlin the aircraft was shot down crashing near the town of Gardelegen, whether by flak or night-fighter it is not known. The sole survivor of the crew was the navigator, Sgt Edwards, who was taken prisoner of war. All the other crew members perished and are laid to rest in The British War Cemetery in the Grunewald Forrest in Charlottenburg, West Berlin. There are 3576 graves here where over four out of every five are of RAF airmen. Over 2000 of them are aircrew who died in the Battle of Berlin including thirty-six members of 626 Squadron.

Sixteen Lancasters were known to be shot down on the way to the target, most of them by night-fighters, a large proportion of them being Pathfinders in the van of the bomber stream. When the target was reached eight Pathfinders were already lost, with one more taking a direct hit on its marking-run. Over Berlin there was cloud with 18,000 foot tops and the same strong wind that pushed the bombers to the city giving them a speed over the ground of e nearly 200 M.P.H. Target marking this night was a mix of green target indicators and parachuted sky-markers, the methods known as respectively as Wanganui and Paramatta. The green target indicators went straight through the clouds making them of little or no use, the sky-markers were blown across the target by the wind.

F/Lt Belford, flying JB748 at 20,000 feet, reached the target at a quarter past three. His Bomb Aimer, Sgt Lee, saw only five flares that were dispersed over a wide area at the beginning of his bomb-run but eventually dropped the load in the estimated centre of some glowing sky-markers as they disappeared into the cloud. No fire glow was seen by the crew at that time. However, a few minutes earlier the crew of DV177 did see some results of the bombers' efforts with fire below when Bomb Aimer Sgt Wilson dropped the incendiaries and bombs. He also had to aim at a cluster of vanishing sky-markers, one of many that were scattered.

After leaving Berlin, the bombers made their escape heading south-west to skirt Leipzig to starboard and then west over Central Germany, Belgium and the Northern tip of France. Route-markers of green flares were placed at the Leipzig turning and near Neuweld, a town south of Bonn, by the remaining Pathfinders, but 626 Squadron crews saw little of them because of the cloud.

F/Sgt Bretell was still alive but cold in the rear turret of EE133 so it was thought that oxygen was still getting through the partially blocked tube. Fifty miles from the Enemy coast Pilot P/O Curry started a slow decent to give the rear gunner a better chance against the cold and lack of oxygen. After a short flight across The English Channel the Lancasters made their way up Eastern England as it was just getting light, 626 Squadron Lancasters landing around eight o'clock in light flurries of snow. One of the first to land was EE133 having been given special clearance as P/O Curry told the control tower that F/Sgt Bretell was suffering from cold, possible frostbite and anoxia. The aircraft was met at the flight line by an ambulance where he was whisked away to Wickenby's Station Sick Quarters.

Once again the attack was not really successful, bombs being scattered all over the south of Berlin from Kopenick to the wooded area of Grunewald. The thick cloud and high wind carrying away the sky-markers prevented concentration of bombs on the target. There were gaps also in, what should have been, the continuous marking as over 11% of the Pathfinders were lost before and during the marking procedure. Accuracy was also impaired because the H2S Radar equipped Lancasters were still not reliable.

There was no extensive damage by fire and no major destruction but bombs fell on two railway goods yards, the main offices of the Army Ministry, the Main Post Office and the Rhienmetall-Borzig arms factory. The only significant damage done was when a high explosive bomb fell on a lock-gate, stepping traffic on an important canal for several days. For the movement of goods, in German industrial cities, canals were just as well used as roads and railways.

Twenty-eight Lancasters did not return from this operation. One 12 Squadron aircraft from Wickenby ran out of fuel over Germany, the crew parachuting out before it crashed. 168 airman were killed and thirty-four taken as prisoners of war, some would say a high price to pay for so little achieved.

The crews were debriefed after the night's operation and then having been transported the their respective Messes, went down to the aircrew breakfast of bacon and eggs. Meanwhile, outside it was snowing and many thoughts were on sleep for the rest of the day as it was thought that no way were the Lancaster-s going to take off that night along a runway deep in snow. Now in the Royal Air Force there is the legend of 'Murphy's Law' which states that, apart from other things along the same lines, "If something cannot possibly go wrong, somehow in the due course of time it will". While the airmen slept, the snow stopped! Shovels were issued to everyone on the Station from Group Captain Crummy down and runway snow clearing commenced. The only people excused were the ground crews that were preparing the Lancasters for the next operation which, unknown to the sleeping aircrews, was that night. As Stations throughout Bomber Command informed their Group Headquarters that the runways were being cleared the details of the night's operation came back. At ten minutes to two o'clock in the afternoon of 2nd January Wickenby's Operations Room teleprinter clattered out the message. Date/Time group: 2/44 021350, SECRET, Target: Berlin. This was the forth attack in a row on the German Capital out of ten so far into the Battle. But the crews did not know that - yet. They were still asleep. The ground crews, out in the open it must be remembered, pre-flight inspected, refuelled and armed the

Lancasters. Meanwhile anyone that could move snow with a shovel cleared Wickenby's 4000 foot runway, completing the task before it was dark. At about three o'clock the aircrew were woken up with the shock that they were on an operation that night. After the evening meal they had an even greater shock at the briefing when, with dismay, the target was known and called for another midnight take off. This night 626 Squadron fielded 14 Lancasters, one more than the previous night, an outstanding feat on the part of the ground crews considering the weather and the conditions they had to work in. Overall, the Command had fifty-nine Lancasters less on the flight lines than the night before.

The route was more or less straight in and out with small dog-legs before and after the target. The Pathfinders and Mainforce would approach Berlin from the north-west from seventy miles out, having turned at the large lake of Muritzsee which was chosen because it could be clearly-seen on the H2S radar screens and the bombers would also have the advantage of a eighty miles an hour tailwind for a fast run in. There were to be no tactical diversions to elsewhere to deceive the German Luftwaffe controllers. Route markers were to be placed just below Bremen (P) and Muritzsee (Q) going in and coming home one at twenty-five miles east of Magdeburg (R), the last one being dropped twenty-five miles south of Hanover (S). To try and confuse the German radar operator each bomber was issued with 306 bundles of 'Window'. These aluminium strips, cut to a correct size to the frequency they were meant to disrupt, however did not effect the new night-fighter radar Lichenstein SN-2. This was not found out until long after the Battle when in the Summer of 1944 a Junkers Ju88G-6 landed at RAF Woodbridge in Suffolk due to a navigational error.

Between half-past eleven o'clock and midnight the fourteen Lancasters of 626 Squadron took off down the cleared runway illuminated with flares as the usual Drem lighting was still under the heaped snow.

```
                        SECRET
2/44.  021350.

Mablethorpe. 5245/0330 - 5250/0850 - 5325/1240 -
TARGET-5210/1310 - 5150/1030 - 5230/0820 - 5245/0330 -
Mablethorpe.

ZH 0245.
Section 1 ZH +3. 4 from 626.
Section 2 ZH +3 to +7. 4 from 626.
Section 3 ZH +7 to +11. All remaining Lancs of 1 Group.
15 A/C from 101.
Section 1 manned by best crews.

Window 306 bundles from each A/C.
Start 5245/0344.5309/1255.5205/1230.
Stop 5245/0344.

Route Markers.
Out. P 5255/0850. Q 5322/1243.
Flares green with yellow stars.
Home. R 5208/1209 S 5202/0950.
Flares green with yellow stars.

Attack open with Red TI dropped in target area. Aiming
point will be marked with Green TI. In addition, the
release point will be marked with bundles of flares, Red
with Green stars thoughout the attack. Mainforce aim at
all Green TIs visible NOT Reds. If TI not visible they
are to aim at the centre of flares Red with Green stars
on exact heading 168M in this case with usual Wanganui
settings.

2 X 103 Sqn, 2 X 460 Sqn and 2 X 100 Sqn are to fly in
sect 1 and TX wind to Groups laid down by Group Nav
Staff. No TX at ZH. Winds apply at 20000'.

Tactics - Climb on track and rondezvous @ 5245/0330
18/20000'. Cross enemy coast at 19/22000'. Bomb between
19/22000'. Maintain that height until cross enemy coast.
```

Document 1 Bomber Command Battle order.[5]

The bombing 'window' was between 02:43 and 02:56 A.M. but not all aircraft were to drop their loads at the same time. To lessen the risk of collision it was common practise for the stream to bomb in three or four waves, the most experienced and best

[5] From Air 25-11. 1 Group Operational Records. Public Records Office.

crews in the first wave. Four Lancaster crews from 626 Squadron were detailed to bomb in the first wave and another four in the second, the rest coming up behind a few minutes later in the third and last.

At the same time, but unknown to the 1 Group crews heading out over the North Sea, there were eight Wellingtons of 1 Group minelaying off the Bay of Biscay U-Boat bases. At sixteen minutes passed midnight a signal was sent on a 1 Group frequency to re-call them and to divert to land at Exeter in Devon. To use the same frequency and code as the bomber force heading for Ger-many was a mistake as fifteen bombers took it as face value and landed back in England two to three hours later after dumping part of their loads in the North Sea. Four of them were from 626 Squadron. The rest of the force took the signal as a mistake, which was verified an hour later.

The Pathfinders and Mainforce flew on towards the Dutch coast crossing it just below Den Helder the same as the night before. The route to the target was well worn and the German controllers were able to track the stream from very early into their flight once they crossed Holland. When within 110 miles to the target the Luftwaffe night-fighter controllers guessed right that the target was to be their Capital again. Prior to this many night-fighters were told to make a holding pattern centred around a radio beacon, code named 'Marie', near Bremen. By mistake, they were not released until the bomber stream had gone past, a good opportunity for them missed. Many night-fighter airfields were closed due to bad weather but nearly 200 single and twin-engine aircraft were able to take off and defend Berlin.

Originally, fifty Pathfinders from 8 Group had taken off from England but eight had turned back due to various problems. On reaching the target, apart from being a depleted force, the Path-finders were once again met by 10/10ths cloud up to 16,000 feet and at the height they were flying, an eighty miles an hour tail-wind. As soon as the sky-markers left the bomb-bays and deployed their parachutes, they were blown quite some way downwind. To help the night-fighters the flak gunners set the shells to explode no more than 21,000 feet and aircraft of III/KG3 were detailed to drop fighter flares over the target to illuminate the attacking force.

S/Ldr Spiller, flying JB599, found good visibility above the target when his Lancaster arrived in the first wave some minutes before three o'clock. It was too early to find fire glow below the clouds but having found the red markers with green stars his bomb-aimer, P/O O'Dea, aimed the load at them. Also in the first wave was P/O Currie, captain of EE133, nearing the end of his tour. However, his new bomb-aimer was just beginning his, having spent a long time as an instructor in Training Command. The only way he knew how to aim the bombs was 'by the book' and this he attempted to do even so far as to request going round again to get the aiming perfect.

Needless to say, he was told, in no uncertain terms that no one lingers over a 'Big City' target and to drop the bombs irrespective as it was not a precision target that had to be hit with deadly accuracy. By this time, nearly a quarter past three, smoke was seen to rise from the ground up to 18,000 feet with a lot of fire glow below the clouds. JB599, flown by F/Sgt Welford, experienced icing problems over the North Sea and at eleven minutes to one o'clock had to dump the 4,000lb 'cookie' 155 miles north-east of Lowestoft to gain operational height. On arriving over the target the bomb-aimer only saw one sky-marker, then a whole cluster appeared a great distance away. This could be evidence of the scattered marking, and to be seen later, the poor bombing results. JB599 flew on to bomb the most significant cluster of sky-markers, the crew also noticing the fire glow below the clouds.

The crew of ED424 were flying in the third wave and captained by F/Sgt Lone. The aircraft was flying at 21,000 feet over Berlin just after three o'clock with an unserviceable airspeed indicator, probably due to an iced-up pitot tube. It was usual for the wireless operator to be stationed, when not operating his set, in the astrodome looking out for fighters. The astrodome was a clear dome of Plexiglas used by the navigator to take star shots with an aeronautical version of a sextant. The Berlin searchlights were deliberately plying on the underside of the clouds to silhouette the bombers as seen from on high. ED424's crew also saw the fighter flares as mentioned before.

Many fighters were about and the wireless operator, F/Sgt Nosworthy, saw one of them, a Messerschmitt 109E single engined 'Wild Boar', diving towards the Lancaster's port side from 800 yards to the rear. From 700 yards range he ordered F/Sgt Lone to 'Corkscrew' the Lancaster to port, away from the fighter's line of fire. The bomber's two gunners, Sgt Rees and Sgt Begley, opened fire at 600 yards, quite a long range for .303 machine guns. The fighter broke off his attack at 400 yards range after which it was never seen again. Considering that most night-fighters were congregating in the Berlin area, the fighter flares dropped, searchlights active under the clouds and the superior performance of the Me 109E they were very lucky to frighten off the fighter. It is also of note that one of the mid-upper guns had a stoppage after fifty rounds had been fired; not an uncommon occurrence.

Of the twenty-seven Lancasters that were lost on this attack it was thought that most met their fate over the target area. Luftwaffe night-fighter pilot Major Prince Sayn-Wittgenstein flying one of the very latest type of Junkers Ju88, the R2 version, was credited with shooting down six bombers this night alone. He was the Commanding Officer of NJG2 based at Quakenbruck.

After leaving Berlin behind the bomber stream headed west to find route markers R and S; these were laid by the remaining Pathfinder Force where most crews were to comment later that the green with yellow stars type flares were more helpful and visible than the previous two (P and Q) inbound. Pilot F/Sgt Welford had to take JB599 down to about 12,000 feet as the oxygen supply to his mask had failed. This was a dangerous situation to be in as the Lancaster now came within range of the lighter flak weapons that the Germans had. Although they flew through cloud most of the time many of the guns were radar controlled and it was still many miles to the relative safety of the North Sea coast of Holland.

The weather over the home airfields of Lincolnshire and Yorkshire was not good and many bombers had to divert to other clearer airfields such as Eastmoor and Acklington. The ten 626 Squadron Lancasters that did not divert at the beginning went on to bomb the target and all got back safely around eight o'clock in the morning including JB599 after flying low all the way.

Twenty-six Lancasters were posted missing that morning throughout the Command with 168 of their aircrew dead and thirty-one parachuting to safety and POW camps. Later, intelligence reports and photographs were to reveal a poor return for the sacrifice of so many young lives as no significant damage was caused to Berlin industry. Only eighty-two dwellings were destroyed and thirty-six people killed. The bombers' loads were scattered all over the city where the emergency services easily coped with-the fires as soon as they started.

For the crews at Wickenby the day was a stand down from operations but for the ground crews working outside it was carry on as usual hampered by cloud and rain all day long. The next day the stand down continued but at least it was fine weather and welcomed by the ground crews servicing the Lancasters that had just returned from the diversion airfields after the last raid.

The three-week moonless bombing period, where it was deemed relatively safe to fly over Europe, was nearly up but there was just enough time to get in another raid if it was planned carefully with the waxing moon in mind. For the night of the 5th/6th of January the port of Stettin was chosen as the target.

Stettin was Germany's most important Baltic Sea port, it being connected by rail and ship canal to Berlin as well as having excellent communications with the eastern end of the Ruhr industrial area and the northern half of the Russian front offensive. It was just inside the Polish border and forty miles from the mouth of the River Oder. The port was last attacked in April 1943 but most of the damage was in the southern half of the town, which accommodated the docks, shipyards and transport facilities. Reconstruction and repair was undertaken in the months that followed but hardly any to the residential and business areas that were hit on that particular raid. The attack on the 5/6th January was aimed at the civic life of the town, the railways and the small industrial factories to the east of the river. Situated in the northern half of the target area was a large military barracks spread over a hundred acres. The port activity, shown by reconnaissance photographs, was equal to Hamburg and twice that of Bremen. Like other raids, the plan was not only to bomb the industries and communications but to eliminate the working population and their houses as well.

The total Stettin force that night was 358 bombers where 626 Squadron put up eleven Lancasters for the attack. In addition to the Main and Pathfinder Forces, twelve Mosquitos were detailed to fly a 'Spoof' raid to Berlin. Zero hour for the raid was to be a quarter-to-four in the morning, 626 Squadron aircraft getting airborne around midnight to meet this time.

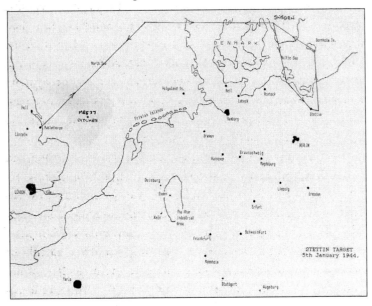

Map 2. Target Stettin, 5.1.44.

Most at the Wickenby briefing thought the raid was going to be 'The Big City' again, Berlin. When the map revealed the long red ribbon across Denmark, Sweden, The Baltic and on to Stettin the crews knew they were in for a cold nine hour flight, particularly the gunners. The rear gunners were especially vulnerable as although they had their heated suits these were prone to failure causing frostbite and hypothermia in the typical temperature of thirty degrees centigrade below zero while flying about 20,000 feet in winter over Northern Europe.

Sgt Henty and his crew in ED623 thought they would never get airborne as they sped down the long runway. With maximum fuel for this long trip plus a bomb load of over 12,000 pounds, the Lancaster needed two attempts to get unstuck from the runway, only just reaching flying speed at the potato field at the end of the runway! Usually, the bombers gained height by circling the airfield so giving the navigators the opportunity to check their systems, find the wind speed and its direction and to reset the GEE set and air position indicator navigation aids. This was rather tedious for the rest of the crew with the aircraft only managing to climb at 500 feet a minute. But on this night, once airborne, the Squadron set coarse across the countryside to Mablethorpe and out over the North Sea.

F/Sgt Arthur Lee, navigator of ME577, would be sorting out navigational problems about then. Although surface wind velocity and its direction was known before take off, from their experience, navigators knew that wind speed and direction could vary while gaining height approaching the enemy coast of Europe. If a wind shift went undetected, a wrong track would be calculated and the aircraft would unknowingly leave the protection of the bomber stream. Finding the aircraft's airspeed, heading or direction to fly and track was achieved by what is known as dead reckoning, which is a process of calculation with two known vectors. The first is the direction and speed that the aircraft is required to fly and the second being the speed and direction of the wind that could be 'Pushing' the bomber sideways off the desired course. The geometrical resultant when worked out would give the navigator the third vector called track, which is the compass heading, and the speed that the aircraft is required to fly. Unless the wind direction was the same or reciprocal to the course required to fly, the aircraft would need to 'Crab' across the sky to compensate for the side-wind.

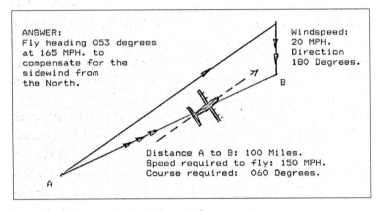

```
ANSWER:                                      Windspeed:
Fly heading 053 degrees                      20 MPH.
at 165 MPH. to                               Direction
compensate for the                           180 Degrees.
sidewind from
the North.                                   B



                    Distance A to B: 100 Miles.
                    Speed required to fly: 150 MPH.
                    Course required:   060 Degrees.

A
```

Figure 1. Side-wind compensation.

The first vector was obtained by looking at the map and knowing the route and airspeed required. In those days the speed was in statute miles per hour, unlike today's instruments that have their displays in nautical miles per hour or knots. All this was not easy as it sounds if the pilot had to take evasive action during which the compass repeater pointer would swing aimlessly when the compass gyroscope toppled. Also, gyroscopes have a natural tendency to drift due to the variation of the earth's magnetic field from one place to another and inevitable small manufacturing errors. Pitot-static instruments that depended on outside atmospheric conditions needed to be corrected for altitude and outside temperature by tables in the navigator's almanac. The second vector was more difficult as this depended on the unpredictable weather conditions at the aircraft's height and the skill of the navigator to interpret them. With all this varying information the navigator had to work fast to find the way to the target and the aircraft's position when required, often working in poorly lit and cramped conditions with nothing more than a pencil, ruler, dividers, slide rule, navigation tables and a good head for mathematics. Often as not he worked on a vibrating surface that occasionally pitched and rolled violently due to aircraft manoeuvring to avoid night-fighters and flak. Only good navigation by all kept the bomber stream together. Being buffeted by the slipstream of another bomber ahead never failed to give the feeling of security, there being safety in numbers.

Two hours out from Wickenby and eighty-two miles off the enemy coast, 626 Squadron's Lancasters turned due east heading for Denmark, The Kaddegat and Sweden. As the Force approached the northern tip of the large Danish island of Sjaelland, with the capital on the eastern shore, the first route marker burst below with a display of a green flares with yellow stars. The 626 Squadron Lancasters were on track and on time even though the navigational aid GEE had long since been rendered useless by German electronic countermeasures halfway across the North Sea. The bombers droned on, probably bringing some comfort to the people below whose country, being occupied, longed for liberation. Over the country of Hans Christian Andersen they flew passing his little mermaid at the entrance to Copenhagen harbour to the south and on to neutral Sweden.

For Sgt Jack Cannon, rear gunner of LM391, this was his forth operation and recalls at the time being quite naive. He and quite a few others just did not think that the British would invade a neutral country's airspace. At the briefing before take off they were told if caught over Sweden it was a 'Navigational error'. Sweden, particularly the town of Landskrona, greeted them with bright lights and intense anti-aircraft fire, which exploded well below them. Some aircrew even reported afterwards seeing Swedish Airforce fighters. A little way into Sweden the Force turned south and out over The Baltic towards the German coast where more route markers were laid down, yellow target indicators this time near Peenemunde. Whether the target indicators were chosen or not to scare the remaining scientists and workers at the secret rocket base it is not known. By now it was some sixty-five miles or twenty-five minutes flying time to Stettin and about 1:00 in the morning.

On approaching the port the Main Force could see the Pathfinders at work dropping sky and ground markers in conditions that were ideal. F/Sgt Arthur Lee navigated his Lancaster, ME577, in at 20,000 feet on a heading of 142 degrees Magnetic as briefed to be on target just after 1:45. The vertical visibility was perfect, the streets clearly seen in contrast to the snow covered buildings, where the bomb aimer, Flt/Sgt J.C. Lee, could easily see the sky markers of brilliant green flares with red stars and the green ground markers. By extraordinary good luck and planning on the part of Bomber Command, the German night-fighters were away to the south, having been deceived with a dummy attack on Berlin by twelve fast Mosquitos. Many Lancaster crews noted that the flak was exploding far too low to be effective, likewise the searchlights found very few bombers. Maybe this was due to the lack of practise.

The incendiaries that were dropped caused many fires in the northern part of the town where the built-up areas were hit the most. The bombs blasted open the doors and windows of the dwellings causing drafts to aid the fires started by the incendiaries, a proven de-housing technique. Smoke rose up to 12,000 feet in places. Two very large red explosions were seen by P/O Wellham and the crew of LM393 at about 4:10am and twenty minutes later Sgt Henty in ED623 observed another dull red explosion which lasted all of three seconds. This could have been ammunition from the army barracks or ships in the naval port.

After dropping their loads, the Lancasters turned round and headed north to pick up the route marker at Bornholm island off the south-east coast of Sweden. Sgt Butcher, piloting 626 Squadron's ME576, thought this marker of not much use as it was seen by his crew as scattered but most of the rest of the Wickenby force had no problems. F/Sgt West, captain of JB599 and P/O Currie of EE133 reported still being able to see the glow of the fires raging in Stettin 110 miles away. Turning north-west at this green and yellow route marker, F/Sgt Torrence's Lancaster, LM391, soon reached the east coast of Sweden again and heading for the Fifty-Six Degrees North latitude line. His rear gunner, Sgt Jack Cannon, was a Canadian in the Royal Air Force and was only sixteen in September 1939 when the 'Blackout' was enforced. He could not help noticing, unlike back in England, that the villages, towns and cities were 'Alive' with bright light. after this attack Sgt Jack Cannon went on to complete his tour of twenty-eight missions with a last trip to Berneville on the night of 3/4th June 1944. He gained a Commission to Officer rank in the summer of that year which came into force while actually flying on his last raid at one minute past midnight on the 4th June. In the recommendation for his Distinguished Service Cross, which he received some time later, the Commanding Officer of 626 Squadron said of him:

Sergeant Cannon as Rear Gunner has carried out 28 operational sorties against the enemy, many of these being against distant and heavily defended targets such as Leipzig, Stettin, Brunswick and Berlin, the latter being the target on six occasions. Throughout this long and successful tour of operations,

Sergeant Cannon has proved himself to be an outstanding Rear Gunner. His technical knowledge and exceptional fearlessness in the face of danger has inspired a confidence in his crew and ensured maximum safety for his aircraft by repelling enemy attacks with cool and skilful direction to his crew and determination in handling his guns.

Sgt Henty, captain of ED623, had problems when his flight engineer, Sgt Fradgley, calculated they did not have enough fuel to reach Wickenby if they kept to the planned route. After rechecking the gauges and a looking at the maps, it was decided to fly due west at Bornholm Island. In doing so the Lancaster would by flying about sixty miles due south and parallel to the bomber stream, rejoining it over the North Sea. This only shortened the route by about forty miles but by also flying slower to conserve fuel even more, ED623 landed at Wickenby at 08:46 having flown for nine hours. Luckily, most of the time ED623 was flying over Europe it was over the Baltic Sea and not Northern Germany, as a lone Lancaster would almost certainly have fallen prey to night-fighters over land.

F/Sgt Lone, the pilot of ED424 and his crew, went through an extraordinary experience. On the way home over the North Sea they all fell asleep! The Lancaster was flying itself on autopilot but for how long the crew had dozed off none of them knew. When they awoke they were in the dilemma of not knowing where the aircraft was, the thought of having overshot England and on their way to Ireland and the Atlantic Ocean was not ruled out. It was generally agreed to head south-west and by good fortune twenty minutes later they flew over the Yorkshire coast near the River Humber.

Things started to go wrong for ME577 and its crew, with F/Lt Belford in command, soon after leaving the target. The navigator found the turning point at Bornholm Island but only after having turned north-west was the actual route marker seen. The Path-finder aircraft were using H2S ground mapping radar to navigate and drop markers so their accuracy and timings were not in question by the navigator F/Sgt Lee. He suspected his Lancaster had turned north too soon after leaving Stettin or the fickle wind had changed direction. So back behind his curtain he went to amend the course. Soon the pilot started complaining about the trim of the aircraft and the difficulty of keeping it on the proper heading. Arriving at fifty-six degrees north, ME577 turned to the west on the pilot's gyro compass repeater, Sweden by this time was covered in cloud. The flight plan then called it to fly 200 miles along this latitude to the North Sea, pick up a GEE fix followed by a long decent south-west to the English coast and home. But fate was to intervene.

Sometime after crossing the coast of Sweden, the mid-upper gunner, Sgt Mewburn, asked the navigator what course was being flown. 'Due west,' came the reply. F/Sgt Lee was then enlightened to the fact that the Pole Star was dead astern! The gyro compass was checked and according to that the aircraft was flying due west but the magnetic compass indicated they were flying south and indeed they were. It must be understood that the pilot, on instructions from the navigator, selected the desired heading on the compass repeater. This selected heading electrically commands the autopilot to fly on it. While the aircraft is trimmed to fly straight and level towards the west the faulty gyro-compass had drifted and was constantly commanding the auto-pilot to turn left. With the continuing alteration by the pilot to correct the flying attitude, the Lancaster was now ninety degrees off track. Now the crew did not know where they were so the aircraft was turned west according to the magnetic compass.

Dawn was coming up and an astro-fix was suggested but by then the stars had disappeared and it was too late. Navigator F/Sgt Arthur Lee did not rate himself too good at it anyway.

The 'Grass' cleared from the GEE screen which told the navigator that they were out over the North Sea and out of the range of the German electronic jamming. The first indication to where the aircraft was was hard to believe but a further two fixes confirmed them that they were in a dangerous position, being within twenty miles of the German end of the Friesian Islands and having passed Helgoland on the way. Eight o'clock in the morning now found them 150 miles south of track and a long way from home flying in broad daylight! To avoid detection by coastal radar, ME577 was flown westwards at fifty foot above the waves with all the crew mentally keeping their fingers crossed. Meanwhile, the flight engineer, Sgt Hill, checked the fuel on board and more importantly how long it was going to last. He estimated that at most there was two hours of fuel left but it was later to prove that it was too optimistic and not enough to reach the English coast. The crew had no option but to fly as far west as possible and ditch the Lancaster in the sea.

At 0845 the wireless operator, Sgt 'Tommy' Trinder, broke radio silence and sent out the distress signal "SOS TGWB V C09 RX6B7". This was picked up by wireless operator Sgt Hicks in LM391 flying at 8000 feet and about thirty miles east of Flambrough Head. The sending of the message eased the tension on board ME577 a little as the captain went through the pre-ditching drill checks with his crew so that every one knew what to do when the time came, which proved to be just before ten o'clock. Another position fix was hastily got off by the wireless operator on the distress frequency after which the Morse key was clamped down so any shore station or friendly ship could get a bearing on their position. The map reference was put on a message and tied to the leg of the aircraft's carrier pigeon and the bird let go.

After the roof hatches were jettisoned, the gunners left their turrets to take up crash positions aft of the main spar in the centre of the fuselage. F/Sgt Lee stuffed the Lancaster's Verey pistol and as many cartridges as he could carry down the front of his uniform tunic, the flight engineer staying up front to help the pilot with the wheels up landing on the water. All braced themselves as pilot F/Lt Belford brought the Lancaster into land on the sea in a near text-book ditching. Nobody was hurt and all seven of the crew got out of the escape hatches to find the rubber dinghy inflating automatically from its stowage compartment in the starboard wing root. Unfortunately, after launching itself, it started to drift away but all except Sgt Mewburn swam for it to climb on board. Sgt Mewburn, being a non-swimmer, was reluctant to leave the dubious safety of the now sinking bomber's tailplane but with encouragement from the rest of the crew he plunged into the cold water as the dinghy drifted nearby and was hauled on board.

In sizing up the situation, the dinghy was half full of water, the sea rough and by estimation at least 100 miles east of Grimsby. On the good side, a distress signal had been sent, there was over six hours of daylight left, and the dinghy had rations, water and an extra Verey pistol on board. The gunners had their warm Taylor-suits on and bomb-aimer Sgt John Lee had the foresight to bring along a parachute for protection against the elements.

About midday, a Royal Air Force Hudson of Coastal Command found them with the help of navigator F/Sgt Lee's Verey pistol. After releasing a smoke-float to find the wind direction, the Hudson dropped an airborne lifeboat which floated down on its parachutes to splash in the sea about 100 yards from the dinghy. This might as well have been 100 miles, as try as they might it could not be reached by the tired crew, the lifeboat being blown along faster by the wind than the crew could paddle their dinghy. Disappointed, the crew saw the Hudson leave but at least they knew their position was known and rescue could not be far away. The airmen had been awake now for over thirty-six hours since before leaving Wickenby so sleep came easy for some but not for long. Their dozing was interrupted by a flight of low flying Spitfires that came roaring out of the mist to circle and dive on them. Finally, after giving this welcome display, they lined up in line astern at wave-top height and dipping their wings in salute sped off towards the horizon towards the west. It was known that a German rescue seaplane was looking for them too, the Spitfires having been sent to prevent it finding the crew first.

Night came and the crew sang songs to keep awake until about midnight when another aircraft was heard circling them. Full of hope, they fired off red flares and waited. In the darkened sky a light blinked 'GASR' from the unknown aircraft. Overjoyed, they took it to mean 'Grimsby Air Sea Rescue' so the crew shot up more flares, although it could have meant 'German Air Sea Rescue' for all they knew. The still unknown aircraft now dropped brilliant white target indicators to illuminate the scene and much to the crew's relief, Rescue Launch R.M.L.498 hove into view, a voice hailing them in English. Because of the waves the transfer from the dinghy to the launch was not easy but with the strong arms of the rescuers the tired but jubilant survivors were soon on board. Quickly they were dried and wrapped in blankets, given a tot of rum, hot soup and warm bunks to rest and sleep in.

On being wakened some hours later, the airmen were surprised to find they were on board a Royal Navy rescue launch and not a Royal Air Force one. Having put on their now dried clothes they found out from the boat's crew at breakfast time that it was not usual to find a whole crew alive and well. The sailors had been on many searches but more often than not found dead airmen or an empty dinghy. It was debatable who were more excited, the rescued or the rescuers.

Twenty-six hours after their Lancaster ditched in the North Sea the rescue launch docked at Yarmouth, having picked up F/Lt Belford and his crew nearly 100 miles away on the edge of a minefield. After spending a night in a Naval hospital, the sisters thwarting the idea of an evening celebrating in Yarmouth, the crew returned to Wickenby the next day. Group Captain Basil Crummy, Wickenby's Commanding Officer, flew down to the nearby American Army Air Force airfield at Seething in ED623 and took them back himself. Because of their ditching and rescue, the seven crew of ME577 automatically became members of the Royal Air Force 'Goldfish Club'.

Including 626 Squadron's ME577, the Wickenby force lost three Lancasters that night, 12 Squadron loosing ND324 and JB357. Lancaster ND324 crash landed at Kalmar in Sweden but F/O Kroker and his crew survived and were interned by the Swedish authorities. In September 1944 they were eventually repatriated. All the crew of JB357 perished over Poland but what is extraordinary is the story of its wireless operator, Sgt Colin Farrant. He was just seventeen years old when he died having falsified his age when he volunteered to join the Royal Air Force as aircrew two years earlier. He and the other six members of JB357's crew are laid to rest in Poznan Old Garrison Cemetery in Poland.

From the 113 aircraft of Number One Group, to which 626 Squadron belonged, 184 tons of high explosive was dropped on the target, most of it being of the 4000lb blast bomb type. To start the fires, no less that 78,548 incendiaries plummeted down on the port of Stettin. Numbers Five and Six Groups of Bomber Command put up another 155 aircraft while Number Eight (Pathfinder) Group supported the raid with ninety of its Lancasters and Halifaxes.

After the Stettin raid there was a period of moonlit nights making operational flying over Europe dangerous for most of the Command's aircraft. For the next few days the only Command aircraft to fly were the Mosquitos on minor nuisance raids and in a new role for the Stirling, dropping secret agents and supplies in the occupied countries. It was not a time for 626 Squadron's crews to be idle as there was still plenty to do in training. The aircrew were involved in training programs in the air and on the ground with lectures. On the 7th January there was Bulleye and Fighter affiliation practise in the air while on the ground, instruction was given on Operations Procedures, Operations Distress Procedures, Escape and Evasion Tactics, POW Security, Aircraft Recognition and even the diverse subject of Light Naval Forces. To give the air gunners some practise there was clay pigeon shooting on the 12th January.

It was not to be quiet for long. After a week of inactivity over Europe by 626 Squadron, the teleprinters spelt out orders for the next raid, the city of Braunschweig standing about 100 miles west of Berlin, the main target being the railway marshalling yards to the south of the city. Fourteen crews were briefed, their Lancasters ready on the flight line. As the target was not so far away as the previous Berlin raids, bomb loads of over 10,500 pounds had been winched into each Lancaster by the toiling armourers some hours before. Fuel for the trip was 1600 gallons per aircraft, at least that was the official figure given by Wickenby Operations. It was not unusual for the engine fitter, who was responsible for refuelling, to put in an extra 100 gallons or so with a 'Nod and a wink' to the Flight Engineer to make double sure there was enough fuel to get back.

The weather was fine that day for the time of year, although becoming cloudy later on but with good visibility down the runway for a late afternoon takeoff by the Squadron around four-thirty.For P/O Currie and his crew, this was to be their last flight in EE133, the Lancaster that had served them well since 12 Squadron days when it was new. The aircraft was destined to take up a more peaceful role on a training unit after this raid.

Getting a Lancaster started and airborne was not a long job from the crew's point of view but many checks had to be carried out beforehand to ensure that everything worked, after all, their lives depended on it. After the customary 'wetting of the tail wheel' EE133 was inspected and started for the last time by this crew. The Flight Engineer had the most to check compared with the other members of the crew.

On the outside the pitot tube cover was removed and all inspection covers and hatches checked in place and secure. Likewise all security of the control surfaces, radio aerials, bomb doors and anything else the Flight engineer could reach and see. He would also look at any airframe repairs that had been done since the last flight. Engines would be inspected for oil and fuel leaks. Up in the bomb-bay the bomb aimer would be looking at the load for safety and security. Only when the crew was satisfied that everything was secure, safe and in place would the Pilot sign the RAF Form 700 and accept the aircraft from the SNCO in charge of the aircraft's ground crew. The ground crew would have by now plugged in a 28-volt starter trolley, the Wireless Operator would be checking out his sets and the Navigator his instrument systems. Strict radio silence would be observed at all times. There was no H2S radar fitted to 626 Squadron Lancasters. Before climbing into the aircraft, if it was still light enough, crews would often look intently at the airfield and the Lincolnshire countryside; after all, it could be for the last time, only the next few hours would tell.

On the pre-raid ground test previously carried out earlier in the day, the engines would have been seen to have performed well with no lack of power. The Bomb Aimer, P/O Myring, would have checked the equipment connected with his job, the bombsight, the two guns in the nose, any pyrotechnics if carried and bundles of 'Window' for correct stowage and security. A double check for him was to examine the forward escape hatch for locking as well as ease of opening. It was up front in the floor of his compartment and he had to lie prone on it in the bomb run! First aid kits, hand fire extinguishers and portable oxygen bottles were seen to be in place by the Flight Engineer likewise the top escape hatch and rear door safely locked. The pilot meanwhile was checking all his cockpit instruments; switches and control levers for the engines start sequence. The control column and rudder pedals were moved to see that the control surfaces had freedom of movement and in the correct sense from the cockpit side windows.

When all were seated and strapped in the business of starting the engines for takeoff got underway with the booster pumps being tested and the carburettors primed with fuel from a hand pump in the undercarriage nacelles. The starboard inner was started first, followed by the other three engines in turn. Once all the engines were running, the Flight Engineer would cast his eyes over the engine instruments on his panel paying particular attention to temperatures and pressures of the oil and coolant. for each engine. The bomb doors would now be closed and movement of the flaps and turrets checked. While the engines were warming up the navigation lights would be switched on, compass checked with the directional gyroscope set, oxygen and intercom tested and altimeters set to the airfield height above sea level. With all four engines running, magneto switches would be locked on and a brake accumulator pressure of at least 300psi expected.

Still with the engines, Flight Engineer Sgt Walker would be looking for engine oil temperatures of plus fifteen degrees centigrade and coolant temperatures of plus forty degrees on each engine before the next check. Each engine was run-up in turn to zero boost indicated then the propeller pitch mechanism tested for correct operation. At +4psi boost, the supercharger was put into 'S' ratio, if the engine revolutions fell it was OK, then put back into 'M' ratio on the gearbox. 'S' ratio was for flying above 15,000 feet while 'M' ratio was engaged for flying below that and take off. While at +4psi boost the all important magnetos and ignition systems are tested, two systems per engine.

Each was tested individually, if the revolutions dropped by more than 150rpm when one system was switched out it was not good enough and the sortie was aborted. By the time it took to change the twelve plugs and run the engine again for testing the rest of the Squadron would be well on their way.

On this night, for EE133 on its last flight on 626 Squadron, everything was working correctly. By a signal from the air traffic watchtower, usually a green light, permission for the Squadron's aircraft to taxi was given. With throttles held back and P/O Currie's feet holding on the brakes the ground crew was signalled to pull away the wheel chocks and when done, the Lancaster rolled forward to the perimeter track holding point. There the engines were run up for the last time before takeoff for a final look at temperatures and pressures also the opportunity was taken for the directional gyroscope to be reset. While waiting for their turn, Navigator F/O Cassidy informed the Captain the course to take after getting airborne. Shortly afterwards EE133 rolled forward to take its place at the end of the concrete and tarmac runway ahead of them, flaps being set between fifteen and twenty degrees for takeoff.

With a green light from the air traffic runway control van, the throttle levers were pushed all the way forward by pilot P/O Currie holding the aircraft on the brakes until the four Rolls Royce Merlins came on to full song and at about zero boost. After ensuring that the engines responded correctly, throttles were pulled back and the brakes released. Throttles were then pushed forward again by the pilot, but with the port outer leading to counteract the natural swing to port due to the torque of the four engines.

On this cold January night, the Lancaster sped down the runway at Wickenby for the last time on an operation against the enemy; 65,000 pounds of aircraft, fuel, bombs and seven men becoming airborne at about 110mph. It was cold too for the ground crew and anyone else who cared to be there, the girls of WAAF, cooks, drivers and others lining the end of the runway waving and wishing the Lancaster crews good luck and Godspeed. This was a tradition throughout Bomber Command, and unfortunately for some it would be the last time they would see their home base. At about 130mph indicated airspeed and above 500 feet, the undercarriage was retracted and the flaps retracted gradually, the throttles being set to give a climbing speed of around 170mph.

EE133 was heading towards the English coast and on its way.

As the bombers sped across the North Sea, they were detected on German Radar about forty miles out from the English coast. After crossing the German frontier near Bremen, the Luftwaffe night-fighters were vectored into the stream and would harass the bombers right up to the target and back to the Dutch coast on their return. There was no moon and eight-tenths cloud on this route, which was more or less a straight line from the frontier to Berlin, turning short at the last moment to Braunschweig. This tactic did not deceive the German fighter controllers at all and radar equipped night-fighters (codenamed 'Tame Boars') and single-engine types working independently ('Wild Boars') attacked at will throughout the night.

DV171 with F/Sgt Jacques as Captain, had taken off just ten minutes to five, for the first two hours the sortie being uneventful. The next three was to make up for that. While flying east and fifty miles inside Germany the Lancaster was attacked by a Wild Boar night-fighter believed to be a Focke Wulf FW190. Nearby there was the Luftwaffe base at Oldenburg where at the time of the Battle there were units of the original 'Wild Boar' Jagdgeschwader 300 of Nachtjagdgeschwader Six. The unit also fielded the Messerschmitt Me 109G. The stalking enemy fighter was spotted 500 yards out on the starboard beam and 50 feet below with all guns blazing, hitting the rear part of the Lancaster's fuselage. Quickly DV171 took evasive action and was put into a corkscrew manoeuvre to starboard. Both gun turret systems were rendered useless, the hydraulic lines having been shot away. The ammunition tracks to the rear turret were smashed, the exploding rounds setting fire to the spent hydraulic oil. With much courage, the mid-upper gunner, Sgt Holford, quickly got out of his turret and fought the flames until they were out. He now had to operate his turret on manual control, likewise Sgt O'Donnell in the rear turret although with limited ammunition. The fighter came in again a minute later on the port side and below, firing from 400 yards out. Immediately F/Sgt Jacques wrenched the control column to put the Lancaster in a diving turn to port. He had to use his own judgement and instincts as warnings from the gunners were not forthcoming, since all electrical circuits to the turrets were shot away.

The port-outer engine stopped and caught fire under a hail of bullets. This burst of fire also smashed the into the Wireless Operators panel. Miraculously none of the crew was killed or wounded, but it was not all one sided. From 200 yards out, the enemy fighter received punishment from the Lancaster's gunners and hits were seen to be scored. After this pass, the fighter sheared off and was never seen again. Taking stock of the damage and the chances of survival over hostile territory, it was decided to turn back. At the time, they were 25 miles south-west of Bremen. With only three engines, no hydraulic power for the turrets, the damaged ammunition feed to the rear turret, both fins damaged with the rudder trimmers shot away, and the wireless sets shot to pieces, the crew could hardly be blamed for this decision. But there was more to come.

When the bombs were jettisoned the bomb doors fell down of their own accord, but there was no hydraulic power to close them again. Having turned for home, F/Sgt Jacques flew DV171 back via Bremen and Rotterdam to make a landfall on the East Anglian coast at Orfordness. On landing at RAF Gravely at one minute to ten, the undercarriage and flaps had to be blown down by the emergency air system as the hydraulic lines had been damaged in the second attack.

~ ~ ~ ~ ~

After gaining height and testing the guns over the North Sea, EE133 flew on to cross the enemy coast near the Frisian island of Texel off Northern Holland. The islands of Texel, Vlieland and Terschelling had many flak batteries to catch the bombers flying to and from their targets, so wisely the Lancaster flew a little to the north of these hazards. Flying over the rich farmland of Northern Holland and the flat plain of Lower Saxony, EE133 continued eastwards leaving Bremen to the north so avoiding the defences there. That night, the Pathfinder Force, some miles ahead, were dropping yellow route markers and P/O Currie picked these up nearing Hanover.

All of a sudden, there was a terrific explosion only yards ahead of EE133. A profusion of colour erupted as yellow, red, green and white flares cascaded all over the sky, like Guy Fawke's night 22,000 feet up! Target markers and route markers all going off at once amid a ball of fire. Those of the crew facing forward were temporarily blinded but quickly recovered and gained their night vision to see several similar eruptions ahead. Were the Pathfinders being shot out of the sky, were the flak gunners that good with a direct hit every time? If this was true the raid was in serious trouble, as they carried the target markers and sophisticated radar to guide the main force to the target. The crews were the very best of Bomber Command, many with a 30-trip tour already behind them. The Command could ill-afford to loose them. Many theories were aired about this phenomenon during and after the Battle. One is that there was a special flak shell designed to give the imitation of an exploding bomber, the purpose of which was to erode morale, but could all these pyrotechnics be put into an 88-millimetre round weighing just 21 pounds or even the larger 128-millimetre variant? The second theory is more feasible; a rocket was used to carry out the deception. These 'scarecrows', as some of the crews called them, were more likely to be actual hits on aircraft by flak. After the war, German flak gunners were questioned about this and it was disclosed that no special shells or rockets existed to their knowledge. Hanover was one of many places that had a reputation for accurate and concentrated flak, therefore EE133 was flown around the city before turning south-east for the final run to Braunschweig and zero hour at 1915 hours.

The target, as reported by some, was covered in ten-tenths cloud with the tops reaching from 12,000 to 15,000 feet with varying vertical visibility. F/Sgt Henty, flying ED623 and F/Sgt Lone in ED424 reported good Wanganui flares to aim at but no green target indicators. After leaving the city a good fire glow was seen to be building up under the clouds. The bomb aimer of JB464, F/O Poushinsky, was lucky enough to encounter only seven-tenths cloud and actually did see a concentration of four or five red target indicators to bomb. No sky-markers were seen until his aircraft had left the area. P/O Wellham's crew had borrowed JB478 from No.12 Squadron as there usual aircraft was unavailable. Having taken off at 1605 Hrs, the Lancaster arrived over the target a little over three hours later at 22,000 feet where the Bomb Aimer F/Sgt Bill Lamb found that the red and green target indicators he was told to aim for had died away and sky-markers were spread over a large area. S/Ldr Neilson, the New Zealand Captain of JB599 reported that his Lancaster was over the target at twenty-one minutes past seven at 22,000 feet. His bomb aimer found a red target indicator and several red flares with a couple of green stars coming from each. The crew was in considerable doubt to where the actual target was owing to the uncertainty of the weather and if the flares were genuine in the first place and not a decoy put out by the German defences.

The raid was not considered a success, most bombs missing the target and falling to the south. Nearly six per cent of the attacking force was lost including two from 626 Squadron. Very little damage was done for the cost in Lancasters and crews; only twenty people were killed on the ground.

The way out from the target was to the south and then west across lower Germany, the low countries and on to the North Sea, for EE133 the last time dodging night-fighters and flak on the way. On reaching the enemy coast and relative safety the nose was dipped a little to start the decent to the English coast and pick up a bit more speed without the expense of the ever diminishing fuel. The crew relaxed a little but not too much, the gunners P/O Myring and Sgts Protheroe and Brettell still keeping their vigilance. Although a Bomb Aimer, P/O Myring was trained to operate the nose guns. It was not uncommon for long range Junkers Ju88 night-fighters, 'Fernachiagd', to follow the bomber stream back to England and shoot down aircraft over their home airfields. During the winter of 1943/44, a Junkers Ju88 fighter followed a Wickenby Lancaster down the runway approach. The alert runway controller shone a red Aldis signal lamp into its cockpit and on being discovered, it sped off. It was thought afterwards that this was an intruder with lack of fuel and not enough time to hang about waiting for another victim.

EE133 did not come under the guns of any intruder while flying over the familiar Lincolnshire countryside with the last operational crew at its controls. Five-and-half hours after take off saw the Lancaster with flaps down at twenty-five degrees, throttles back and the wheels kissing the runway at one minute past ten.

The next trip it would make would be to the Number One Lancaster finishing School, a training unit.

Sadly, this night 626 Squadron lost its fifth and sixth crews with JB141 and ME576 not coming back. JB141 had an experienced crew, led by F/Sgt West, all being posted in to Wickenby from 103 Squadron on 11th November 1943. No records show where JB141 actually crashed but all the crew are buried at Hanover War Cemetery except Wireless Operator Sgt Wheatstone who was never found. His name is on Panel 240 at the RAF Memorial at Runnymede. All seven of ME576's crew came from 1667 Conversion Unit in early November 1943 and led by Pilot F/Sgt Elkington. The crash site once again not known according to records. All seven are laid to rest in the Berlin 1939/45 War Cemetery.

The raid was not a success to weigh against the sacrifice of thirty-eight Lancasters and their crews, eleven of them being Pathfinders. Most of the bombs fell well to the south of the city in the countryside or on the town of Wolfenbuttel and its surrounding villages six to eight miles off target. The Germans considered it a light raid with only ten houses destroyed and fourteen people killed from the bombs that fell within the city limits.

Although Bomber Command was advancing in technology and strength, particularly in the number of Lancasters coming off the production line and in the fields of radar and electronic countermeasures, so were the Germans. Despite the continual bombing of their industries, the- night-fighter arm was increasing in potency with new twin-engine fighter designs having improved electronics, firepower and range. More than half of the 'Tame boar' aircraft had been fitted with the new FuG 220 Lichenstein SN-2 air-to-air intercept radar. Because of its ninety megacycle working frequency and shorter wavelength compared with the old sets, it could not be jammed by the 'Window' method in use at the time by the British bombers. The U-Boats out in the Atlantic Ocean sea-lanes had used a radar warning receiver in their fight against radar equipped Coastal Command and US Navy patrol aircraft, codenamed Naxos. On picking up the aircraft's radar signals the U-Boat dived to safety. The Lancaster and Halifax H2S radar was similar to the ASV (Air to Surface Vessel) sets used by Atlantic patrol aircraft. An adaptation of Naxos was developed for the Luftwaffe night-fighters to seek out the H2S carrying bombers. At this time, and for some months to come, Bomber Command was not aware of this.

The next innovation proved to be even more devastating for the bomber force than anything else, it being as simple as it was ingenious. Two upward firing MG151/20 20mm cannons were installed aft of the night-fighter's cockpit, usually a Junkers Ju88 or Messerschmidt Me110. The night-fighter now stalked the bomber from below and behind, coming in from a quarter that the rear gunner could not easily cover. When satisfied that it was in a good position, the pilot would fire up into the bomber's wing tanks and engines. Gone was the risk of detection by the rear and upper gunners. Until a Ju88 was captured in the summer of 1944, Bomber Command and its crews suspected nothing.

A raid was ordered for the night of January 15/16th, thought to be Frankfurt, but fog rolled over the fields of Lincolnshire and Yorkshire and it was cancelled. Both of Wickenby's squadrons were stood down. This bad weather lasted for the next four days and nights. To have five days off from operations in the middle of a no moon period was indeed a rare occasion. Although the Lancasters were idle, the crews were not as more training lectures occupied the days off flying.

On the morning of the 20th January the press were invited to RAF Ludford Magna nearby to see the workings of a typical bomber squadron. At the last moment, it was realised that it was the home of 101 Squadron's Lancasters. These aircraft were unique as they had powerful radio transmitters aboard to jam German night-fighter radio communications with their ground controllers. Since these top secret Lancasters were very conspicuous with their seven foot aerials, the press was transported to nearby Wickenby for press photographs. The raid that day was to be on Berlin again, a maximum effort called for by Bomber Command headquarters at High Wycombe in Buckinghamshire. After the Wickenby crews had prepared, they posed in front of their Lancasters for the press photographs. Twenty-one bombers and the sixteen crews of both squadrons for the night's raid were involved for the presentation.

The teleprinter message, though sent earlier on in the morning, called for fourteen of 626 Squadron aircraft to take part. Zero hour (ZH) was to be 1935 Hrs Four of their Lancasters were selected to bomb in the first wave after the Pathfinders, at four minutes after ZH and another four seven minutes later in the forth wave. These were to be manned by the Squadron's most experience crews. A minimum of 1690 gallons of fuel was ordered for each Lancaster, the Mk.III type, with the more powerful engines than Mk.Is, carrying extra incendiaries.

The straight-in straight-out route to Berlin proved all too costly in past raids for aircrews and aircraft alike where the night-fighter force controllers were easily predicting the target and path taken by the bomber stream. On the 20th January the bombers were to follow a northern route over Schleswig Holstein to the target out by swinging round west over Central Germany, to the

north of the Ruhr industrial area and on to Northern Holland
before crossing the North Sea coast.

```
                        SECRET

20/1.  201251.  626-14 A/C. BERLIN.

Mablethorpe-5425/0800-5337/1055-5328/1240-Target
5220/1330-5138/1220-5207/0750-5330/0545-5340/0400-
Mablethorpe.

ZH1935. Sect 1 ZH+4 Min. 4 X 626.
        Sect 2 ZH+4 to +8.  132 Halifaxes.
        Sect 3 ZH+7 to +11. 131 Halifaxes.
        Sect 4 ZH+11 to +15 4 X 626.
        Sect 5 ZH+14 to +18 all remaining Lancs of
        1 Group.

All Mk.III Lancs carry extra 150 X 4Lb incendiaries as
opposed to Mk.I with Merlin 20 engines.

Min load 1690 Gall.

9 A/C transmit the winds.

Window: Start 5402/0502. 5307/1255. 5155/1248.
Stop: 5358/0425.

Mosquito attack on Minnow with bombs and red TI. Spoof
fighter flares 20 miles east of Whitebait and drop spoof
routemarker TI red and flare red 5233/1000 homeward bound.

Attack to open with red TI in target area. Aiming point
marked with green TI and kept marked throughout attack. In
addition release point marked with bundles of red flares with
green stars. Main Force to aim at centre of all green TI. If
clouds appear aim at centre red flares green stars on 165M.
Bombsight set at true height and airspeed and zero wind.

Rondesvous 5425/0800. 19/20000 Ft. Cross EC @ 20/22000 Ft.
After target climb as high as possible 21/23000 Ft until
cross EC.
```

Document 2. Battle order for 20th January.[6]

To help the navigation, some of the turning points were at
large expanses of water like the Schaalsee, a lake thirty miles east
of Hamburg. The Muritsee was another lake and turning point
about fifty miles south-east of Rostock. The Pathfinders were to
drop route marker 0 here. On the way home, a large lake formed
on the River Mulde, halfway between Dessau and Leipzig, was
chosen as the place to drop route marker R. The bomber stream
was to drop 'Window' along the flight path at designated points,

---

[6] From Air 25/11 1 Group Operational Records. Public Records Office.
Author's note: 'Minnow' was the codename for Kiel. 'Whitebait = Berlin.

invariably it was ineffective due to the advance of German night-fighter technology. The strips of aluminium were too long to jam the airborne radar on the Ju88s and Me110s.

As a diversion, four Mosquitos were to conduct a spoof raid on Kiel with bombs and red target indicators and in addition three more Mosquitos were to fly to Hamburg to carry out a similar raid. When the attack was to take place, dummy fighter flares were to be dropped twenty miles east of Berlin. To further confuse the enemy defences, red target indicators and flares were to be dropped near Celle as a dummy route marker. Bomber Command Pathfinders were actually using green flares with yellow stars as route markers this night.

To open the attack the Pathfinder force would find the target and mark it with a red target indicator. This aiming point would then be illuminated with a green target indicators throughout the attack. In addition, the release point was also marked by red flares with green stars sky-markers in the event of cloud and bad weather.

The morning of the 20th January started with thick fog but soon cleared enough for the press photographs in the morning and a late afternoon take off after four o'clock. The bomb load was the maximum the Lancasters could take, 10,700 pounds for the Mk.Is and 11,080 pounds for the Mk.IIIs with more powerful engines. To utilise the extra power the propellers were wider on the Mk.IIIs, hence some crews called them 'Paddle steamers'. 626 Squadron's aircraft were loaded with the usual 4,000lb 'Cookie' or 'Blockbuster' blast bomb plus fifty-six of the 30lb incendiaries, ninety type 4X 4lb incendiaries and 1260 or 1170 of the ordinary four pound incendiaries. As well as the incendiary material, the 4X type had a small explosive charge to deter fire-fighters dealing with them.

Of the fourteen Lancasters of 626 Squadron that took off, two were early casualties. ME584, piloted by F/O Breckenbridge, failed to take off. F/Sgt Stewart eased back the control column of ME589 to get airborne just after twenty-five minutes to five. At 20,000 feet and fifty-five miles off the enemy coast, ME589 turned back with a sick wireless operator. After crossing the English coast at Mablethorpe for the second time it landed back at Wickenby at nearly a quarter to ten. Seventy-three other bombers of the force also aborted their sorties but nearly 700 crossed the enemy coast with the heaviest bomb load since the previous November 22nd raid.

As the bomber stream neared the enemy coast, they were detected by a radar ship the Germans had stationed in the Heligoland Bight. At the first turning point, about fifteen miles north of Heligoland Island, the Pathfinders released route marker P. According to listening stations in England, the Germans detected the attacking force before they crossed the enemy coast, the fighter controllers vectoring their fighters onto them. These proved to be the older marks of night-fighter and no intercepts or combats took place. The Lancasters and Halifaxes dropped 'Window' some time before this, forty-five miles off Tershelling Island, which might have been of some use against these older aircraft.

The bomber stream continued across the peninsula of Schleswig Holstein to turn south-east and pick up the large lakes in Northern Germany. The third turning point was at Lake Muritsee with route marker Q ten miles after it. Not all crews saw it, those that did said it was well placed, helpful and concentrated although by now there was a lot of cloud about.

Down on the ground the weather was bad for flying. Less than a hundred experienced crews were selected to scramble and meet the bombers. The northern route paid off to a degree but eventually the night-fighters were fed steadily into the stream from about 200 miles to go to the target. Lake Muritsee was the final turning point before the target, sixty miles away and bearing 165 degrees magnetic (165M). By now there was a cloud layer of over 12,000 feet over Eastern Germany and the fighter controllers were certain that their capital was the target. The Pathfinders knew that they would not see the target and had to mark it blind with the aid of H2S, sky-markers, a timed run from Muritsee and navigational skill.

Over the target area the target indicators went straight through the clouds as on many occasions before, only the red flares with green stars floating down on their tiny parachutes were left to aim at. 626 Squadron crews reported good visibility above the clouds 5000 to 8000 feet below where the searchlights were playing on the underside to silhouette the attacking force. F/Sgt Jaques in DV171 saw smoke rising up to 25,000 feet to the east of the target, his bomb aimer finding a cluster of ten flares to aim at. S/Ldr Neilson flying JB599 came in at 20,000 feet and over the target at 19:36 Hrs His rear gunner, Sgt O'Meara saw fires staring down below the cloud even at this early stage of the attack. A very experienced crew, they would have been in the first wave. A little later at 19:43 Hrs, Australian bomb aimer F/Sgt Lafferty in ME587 found the sky-markers scattered but dropped the bomb load on one anyway and hoped for the best. What was also seen was a large fire glow below the clouds already and it was only eight minutes into the attack.

F/Sgt Lone took ED424 into the target area at 22,000 feet towards the end of the raid. Dropping the bombs on some scattered flares, the crew noticed the increasing fire glow below the clouds. Their Lancaster was fitted with 'Boozer'. This was the code name for a radar warning device but it did not pick up the Ju88 night-fighter coming in fast from behind while still in the target area. The keen eyes of Sgt Begley, the rear gunner, saw it from 800 yards dead astern and 500 feet below. At that attitude he was probably lining up ED424 for an attack with his upward firing cannon. Immediately Sgt Begley ordered the pilot to corkscrew the Lancaster to port. Sgt Begley kept calm and waited till the Ju88 was 600 yards out and fired a long burst of 200 rounds from his Frazer-Nash FN20 turret. At 200 yards the Ju88 broke away in diving to starboard without firing a shot and was never seen again; another lucky escape for the second time that month. The same rear gunner, with the help of the mid upper gunner, had scared off a Me109 on the night of 2nd January. Tonight the Ju88 was not seen by Sgt Rees, the mid-upper gunner, as it was obscured by the Lancaster's rear fuselage.

The Lancasters and Halifaxes left Berlin and continued on heading 165M until the next turning point, about fifteen miles south of the centre of the city, where the stream turned south-west to find route marker R, halfway between Leipzig and Dessau. As night-fighters ran out of fuel, others took their place and the defenders' score steadily mounted. It was known that nine bombers were shot down over Berlin that night. Most crews found route marker R, even though it went straight through the cloud; the glow of it could be seen below. The next leg was over the Ruhr industrial area. Near Osnabruk, Sgt Allan's rear turret on ME587 developed a fault and would not work. Although it was not far to go to the coast on the map, this was the area of the crack 1st Nachtjadgeschwader Division with their airfields in Holland, Belgium and Northern France. However, all of 626 Squadron's aircraft, including ME587, reached the North Sea safely where the route home crossed the east end of Ameland

Island in the West Frisian Islands. All twelve Lancasters landed safely at Wickenby within an hour of midnight having flown for nearly seven hours.

This was the heaviest raid on Berlin so far in the Battle where 2348 tons of high explosive and incendiaries were dropped by the Lancasters and Halifaxes in twenty minutes. Compared with an artillery barrage, it took eight hours for guns to deliver 1400 tons of shells on the Saugn front in the Italian campaign. Such was the advantage even then airpower as a modern weapon.

The weather was appalling over Europe in the later part of January 1944, so bad that photographic reconnaissance aircraft could not overfly Berlin with any success until at the end of the month, after the next four raids. When the photographs were available, it appeared that most of the bombs fell to the east of the aiming point, from Horst Wessel (Weissensee) to Neukolln to the south. 243 people were killed and about 10,000 were made homeless. The Lichlenberg power station was knocked out cutting electricity to large areas of eastern Berlin and the supply to the railway connecting Hamburg. There was evidence of several large fires. A couple of small but important parts of the German war industry suffered, a company making Luftwaffe radar was completely wiped out by a direct hit from a 4,000lb Blockbuster and a firm making gun fire control systems was very badly damaged. When the photographic evidence came through at last the raid was judged as better than a medium success but the cost to the Command was 4.6% of the force that went, twenty-two Halifaxes and thirteen Lancasters. 172 airmen were killed and seventy-five became prisoners of war but ten managed to evade capture and return home later.

The crews finally got to bed in the early hours of the morning but unknown to them twelve out of fourteen would be detailed for another raid later on in the same day, 21nd January. Only S/Ldr Neilson and his crew were exempt with F/Sgt Henty and his crew having their sortie cancelled altogether. Irrespective of what it was like over Germany, the weather remained favourable for take offs and landings in Eastern England for the next twenty-four hours at least. The target was thought to be Berlin again but it was switched to Magdeburg, an industrial city about sixty miles to the west of the capital. This was the first major raid on this city, the target being the industries and communication networks in the southern suburbs.

On 626 Squadron, the bomb load was to be the usual 4,000lb 'Blockbuster' or 'Cookie' plus a mix of the thirty pound, four pound and type 4X incendiaries. This amounted to 10,540 pounds total for the Mk.I Lancasters with an extra 150 of the four pound incendiaries added on to that for the Mk.IIIs, a few more than the night before.

The northern route to the target was to be tried again but with a variation on the previous night's course. After leaving Mablethorpe behind on the Lincolnshire coast and crossing the North Sea, the first navigational point on the route was sixty-two miles north of Borkum Island off Friesland. Here, the bombers would turn right and head for the enemy coast and into Germany, picking up route marker P, green flare with a yellow star, along the way. There would be no natural features to guide them this time, the course taking them south of Hamburg, finding red spot route marker O, twenty miles south of that city, and flying straight in the direction of Berlin on a heading of 110 degrees true. It was hoped that the fighter controllers would vector their night-fighters there to defend it. Sixty miles from the centre of Berlin, the bomber stream would turn sharp right and head for Magdeburg, fifty miles away. A decoy raid on the capital would be carried out by 22 Five Group Lancasters and eight Mosquitos of Eight Group's Pathfinders; this idea was met with much trepidation by the crews when they were briefed for the operation.

After bombing the target, the bombers would then carry on south-west for another twenty miles and then turn right on a heading of 323 degrees true completing a circular route back to the second turning point south-west of Hamburg. A red spot route marker would be dropped halfway between Braunschweig and Wolfsburg to help navigation. After leaving Hamburg twenty-five miles to starboard, the Lancasters and Halifaxes would follow the reciprocal course flown hours before to get out of Germany, across the North Sea and home via Mablethorpe.

The Pathfinders were to mark the target by the combination of 'Newhaven' ground markers and 'Wanganui' sky-marking in case of cloud obscuring the aiming point. When found, the aiming point was marked by salvoes of red target indicators at ZH minus four minutes and to carry on for not more than ZH plus five minutes. Under combat conditions over a defended city that nine minutes was not a long time in which to find it. In this time bracket, the target having been identified, green target indicators and red with green stars sky-markers were dropped on the initial red TIs for the Main Force to aim at throughout the raid. Zero Hour was at 2300 hrs

Fourteen of 626 Squadron's Lancasters were prepared for the raid but F/Sgt Henty as captain of ED263 was told his sortie was cancelled. The remaining thirteen sped down Wickenby's main runway around eight o'clock. This was later than the previous evening but they did not have so far to go. A total of thirteen proved to be an unlucky number for three as problems started to occur soon after. Both W4967, with F/Sgt Stewart at the controls and LM380, piloted by W/O Rew, had engine trouble and in addition, the heated suit of LM380's rear gunner would not heat up. The prospect of continuing their missions on three engines was impractical and almost suicidal. They would not be able to gain operational height or keep up with the rest considering the weight of the bomb and fuel load on each aircraft. As the Lancasters were too heavy to land, part of the bomb load was dumped into the sea approximately seventy miles north-east of Mablethorpe.

The crew of LM393 (UM-W2) in January 1944.
(left to right) F/Sgt Egan (mid-upper gunner), F/Sgt Atherston (rear gunner), F/O Knight (navigator), P/O Wellham (pilot), P/O Moore (wireless operator), Sgt Lamb (bomb aimer), Sgt Groom (flight engineer). (photo: W. Lamb)

While ME 587 was climbing out over the Lincolnshire countryside, Sgt Allan found that his rear turret would not work, therefore the pilot, F/O. Wilkinson, had to abandoned the sortie which was at thirty-seven minutes after take off. After jettisoning the load out in the North Sea about the same place as the other two, F/O. Wilkinson landed ME587 at eleven minutes past ten back at Wickenby. Abandoned sorties were not taken lightly by either the crews or Squadron Commanders; crews had to have a good, proven reason to turn back. It meant that the bombing potential of the force was lowered and also the crew had to do an extra mission to complete their thirty mission operational tour. Abandoned missions where there were no bombs dropped on trepidation by the crews when they were briefed for the operation.

The crews had to have a really good proven reason to turn back. It meant that the bombing potential of the force was lowered and also the crew had to do an extra mission to complete their thirty mission operational tour. Abandoned missions where there were no bombs dropped on enemy territory did not count and who knows, the extra flight to finally end the tour might prove fatal.

The remainder of the 626 Squadron Lancasters flew across the North Sea and into Germany without incident. Most crews saw route marker P on the way, but due to the cloud, the red spot route marker Q was obscured and not seen by many. The German fighter controllers took longer than usual to determine the target. The diversionary raid on Berlin was ignored by the night-fighters but a 630 Squadron Lancaster was shot down by flak over the city. Predicting the target only served to give a warning to its defences. At this stage of the Battle the 'Tame boar' tactics were developing well and many night-fighters were directed into the bomber stream as soon as it crossed the German coast.

On every raid a small number of aircraft were detailed to find the wind speed and its direction on route and in code, radio the information back to Bomber Command. They in turn would re-broadcast it to the bomber stream. This night they got it wrong, the result being that the winds were stronger than forecast. Nearly thirty bombers even got to the target before the ZH and the Pathfinders. Some flew round looking for something to bomb, others unknowingly overshot the target altogether and flew on.

S/Ldr Spiller, pilot of JB559, was over the target at eleven o'clock. His navigator estimated the broadcast wind for the run in to Magdeburg half an hour before to be at least 65mph out, consequently they overshot the target on the first approach. Eventually they bombed on a green target indicator on time but off the heading as ordered by Command. To his crew, the attack seemed quite concentrated from 21,000 feet but also seen at eight minutes before they bombed was some red flares with green stars. These were the wrong type and in the wrong place so it was assumed that they were laid by the Germans as a decoy.

F/Lt Wright's crew had problems soon after crossing the enemy coast in the Hamburg area where the direct reading compass and the P4 magnetic compass would not agree with each other. The navigator knew they were off track due to the compass complication but carried on as best as they could. On the run up to Magneburg they found no target indicators or sky-markers, it was only after they overshot that some were seen by the tail gunner, Sgt Hardy. Some red and green target indicators were seen by the River Elbe but they were probably the same decoys that JB599's crew had seen. Eventually their bomb load was dropped on some fires at eighteen minutes past eleven from 21,000 feet.

As fighters had gun cameras to record and prove their scores, so bomber aircraft needed to show if the target had been hit. When the bomb load was dropped, a 250-pound photoflash bomb went with it where by design it detonated a few thousand feet above the impact point of the bombs. Meanwhile, a downward pointing camera had the shutter open to record the explosions on the ground. There was stiff competition between the crews to get the best photograph on the Squadron notice board after a raid.

Australian pilot P/O Wellham was flying LM393 this night, all except the bomb aimer, flight engineer and wireless operator were fellow Australians. Up to reaching Magdeburg the flight had been uneventful. Route marker P had been picked up over the North Sea on the way in but the red spot Q had not been identified. Cloud was 5/10ths and vertical visibility was considered good for bombing, better than past raids over Berlin. Like many, they were victims of the badly forecast winds. Flight Engineer Sgt Groom remembers the time he and the same crew visited Magdeburg:

"*Each crew of seven had a sweep, sixpence each – 3 shillings a crew (which amounts to 18p today); the one who got the nearest to the aiming point got the lot. That was a lot of money in those days, sixpence bought a pint of beer. This night, I will always remember it, the navigator, Noel Knight said. "We must be past it (the target) by now, are you sure you could not see it Jock?"*

Jock was the Scottish bomb aimer Sgt Lamb. So the rear gunner, Johnny Atherton, said. "Just a minute, it's about twenty miles behind us, just seen the markers go down." Twenty miles is not a long way really, when you think we were going about 180 miles per hour ground speed. Someone said.

"Will we go round again?" The reply was. "No, get rid of them Jock, bomb doors open."

The bombs all went. We came back with this photograph, it was magnificent. Some little town, I know it is terrible to talk about it now, it had got a layout similar to this one we were suppose to bomb, river, roads and things like that but obviously not as big. We came back, and the next day we went down to the

*the Squadron and ours was the number one definite photo-
graph. Many said.*

"How did you get that?"

*Well they clobbered it (Magdeburg) but ours was twenty
miles from the aiming point. But that was it, we could have
gone back, some people did, but it was getting hairy in those
days."*

The town they bombed could have been any one of a dozen
about twenty miles south of Magdeburg.

It could be said that the crew of JB599, with F/Sgt Jacques as
captain, was leading a charmed life. They were to meet for the
second time in January 1944 one of the Luftwaffe's finest fighters. Their Lancaster was over the target area on time at 22,000
feet. Five minutes after dropping their bombs the flight engineer,
Sgt Phillips, spotted a Focke Wulf 190 night-fighter dead ahead
at 500 yards. The flight engineer sits next to the pilot in the
cockpit in a Lancaster. Immediately the pilot carried out evasive
action by diving the Lancaster to avoid collision and to expose
the Fw190 to the main gun turrets. The collision speed would
have been about 500 miles per hour so there was only a split second for the mid-upper gunner, Sgt Holford, to fire off thirty
rounds and Sgt 0'Donnel to fire twenty rounds from his rear turret as the fighter passed overhead and astern. No hits were seen,
if there were any, as it all happened so fast. The enemy fighter
did not fire at all and made no attempt at a second attack. Once
again a lucky escape by the crew of JB599 as an FW190 was one
of the fastest and most agile single seat fighters in the Luftwaffe.

Having cleared the target area the main force turned slightly
right and flew on for a further twenty miles. At this fourth turning
point they headed on to 323T to join the route they came in on
again at a point twenty-five miles south-west of Hamburg. Some

626 Squadron crews still saw the fire glow at Magdeburg 200 miles away. Even from this distance and from about 20,000 feet, the rear gunner of JB595, Sgt Webb, reported seeing two explosions. On the way the Pathfinders dropped red spot route marker R but it was not seen by many. After flying back over the North Sea from the Heligoland Bight all 626 Squadron Lancasters landed safely back at Wickenby in the early hours of the morning. Not all squadrons shared the same fortune.

Fifty-seven aircraft of the 648 that set out were lost this night; 22 Lancasters and 35 Halifaxes. Due to the underestimated winds, many aircraft overshot the target arriving before the Pathfinders arrived and zero hour. Some of first to arrive, anxious to get out of the area, bombed prematurely and started fires. Those coming up behind bombed and added to these fires. Some were duped into bombing the decoy target indicators the Germans laid. The end result was that the damage was not concentrated but scattered and as far as the fifty-seven losses, a disaster. Including the Lancaster shot down over Berlin on the decoy raid, this was the Command's heaviest loss since the War started.

But it was not all one sided. Major Heinrich Prinz zu Sayn-Wittgenstein was the Luftwaffe's top scoring night-fighter ace with eighty-three kills to his credit and a holder of the Knight's Cross with Oak Leaves. This night he had already shot down four bombers before the stream reached Magdeburg. While attacking a fifth in the target area he himself was shot down and killed. Nachtjagdgeschwader 1 was the crack division of the Luftwaffe's night-fighter arm. Being based in the Low Countries, it was the first line of defence of Nazi Germany. Of the five bases they operated from at this time, Deelen, Venlo, St. Trond, Twenthe and Leeuwarden the premier unit was I/NJG 1 at Venlo. The Commanding Officer was Hauptmann Manfred

Meurer, holder of the Knight's Cross with Oak Leaves and the third highest scoring night-fighter pilot, with 65 kills. He also met his death this night, when the bomber he was attacking exploded above him, causing his aircraft to crash.

To this day, ex-Bomber Command crews respect the Luftwaffe night-fighter pilots and radar operators of fifty years ago – after all, they were only defending their country from an invader, just as the Royal Air Force pilots had done in the Battle of Britain. Crews that were trying to kill each other many years ago over the dark skies of Germany now find friendships in the many invitations to each other's Squadron and Association reunions. Gemeinschaft Der Jagdflieger is the Luftwaffe Fighter Association in which about 10% are ex-night-fighter crews. One such is Herr Herbert Thomas, who now lives in Bochum in the Ruhr area of Germany. He learnt to fly and joined the Luftwaffe long before the War to eventually become a night-fighter pilot but it would be best to let him tell the story:

"The first night-fighter squadrons were raised in June 1940, they were I./NJG and II./NJG with the Ju88, Do17 and Me110. In 1937/38 the Luftwaffe did try with biplanes, the Heinkel He51 and the Arado Ar58 and began training in night fighting. They had thirty machines in three squadrons and a fourth squadron as night-fighters but this did not work because the pilots could not land at night, also they made errors while flying and got lost. After the Polish campaign, the Luftwaffe tried to use the Me109 with out the canopy but it gave no advantage.

I./ZG76 was a Zerstorergeschwader (heavy twin engine fighter squadron) unit with Me110 aircraft at Aalborg in Denmark. Hauptmann Falck trained the pilots to attack the English Wellingtons, Blenheims and Halifaxes. The first one shot down was a Wellington by Feldwebel Wiese on 16th June.

Hauptmann Wolfgang Falck was promoted to Commander. A short time later Gerneralmajor Kammhuber took over the organisation of the night-fighters. I./NJG flew at the beginning with the Me110 then later with the Ju88. II./NJG was designated for long distance nightfighting or intruders. The first machine for this was the Do17. Not a single machine was built as a night-fighter instead they were bombers or heavy fighters that were modified. Until the end of the war there was always technical advances but never a specialised night-fighter put into production. The Me262 was designated as a night-fighter just before the end of the war in an emergency situation.

The most successful night-fighter squadron from 1940 to 1941 was II./NJG, first operating from Dusseldorf and then Gilze Rijen in Holland. They flew to England as intruders and in this time shot down 121 aircraft. This was because the aircraft were landing and very slow. At the end of 1940 the Beaufighter interfered with operations as it had its own radar. Long distance nightfighting was curtailed in October 1941 by Hitler because the invasion of Russia required every effort. English historians have said that from a military point of view this was a grave mistake. Just before the end of the war, the Luftwaffe night-fighter, with its special group 'Gisela', had another high point, but that was another story. (Operation Gisela was on the night of 4th March 1945 when 142 Ju88s flew intruder missions over England, shooting down about 35 four-engined bombers, a Hudson and a Mosquito. Over thirty Ju88s did not return from this last ditch effort.)

By now Kammhuber had three night-fighter squadrons but also at this time the Lancaster came into service. In 1942 the air war over the Reich began and more night-fighter groups were needed. The first large night attack by the RAF was the 1000 bomber raid on Cologne where at first the Luftwaffe was out-

numbered. In time, thirteen night-fighter squadrons were formed with six of them holding special responsibilities for defending German airspace. On the night of 2nd February 1944, 385 bombers dropped 1401 tons of bombs on Berlin in which twenty-eight bombers were shot down.

The German day and night-fighters. suffered the largest losses. The price they had to pay, including that against the USAAF, was 1115 fighters and their crews. On the night of the 3rd January 1944, Berlin was the target in which twenty-seven out of 311 bombers attacking were shot down. In the late evening of 15th February 1944, a large British force of 806 bombers attacked Berlin including 139 Lancasters from No. 1 Group. 2647 tons of bombs reduced Berlin to a hell of fire and smoke. The attack on Berlin on the 24th March was the high point of the March campaign. 726 reached the target and dropped 2944 tons of bombs but seventy-two were shot down. After these losses the attacks on Berlin were halted.

Between 18th November 1943 and the 31st March 1944, 9111 bombers had flown over Berlin dropping approximately 16,000 bombs or 27,951 (Imperial) tons of high explosive and incendiaries, the heaviest attacks of any bombing war in history. Above and around Berlin were 367 Lancasters and 111 Halifaxes shot down. Of those that got back to England, 745 were heavily damaged and sixty-nine Lancasters and 199 Halifaxes were written off. During this time approximately ninety German night-fighters were lost. The German capital after these attacks had 9.5 square kilometres of area flattened but the industries were not heavily damaged. Bishop Bell on the 9th February 1944 in The House of Lords gave his open statement to the (British) Government.

"The English bombing offensive has achieved exactly what Hitler wants, that is to maximise the efforts of the German people against England."

It happened that the air battle became more pointless from day to day but no one from the night-fighters gave in while beneath them their Fatherland was burning and women and children were being killed. Only one traitor defected, flying with his machine, a Ju88, complete with all the new German inventions including the Lichenstein radar, to Dyce in Scotland. This treachery cost the lives of over 10,000 in Hamburg because the RAF confiscated the machinery and using aluminium strips cut to the same wavelength of the radar frequency, jammed it so the German controllers only saw 'Snow' on the screens. This was a tremendous advantage to the British.

The first strike against Berlin in the Battle was in the late evening of 18th November 1943 followed by four more nights of raids. By the fifth raid 2212 British bombers had dropped 8656 tons of bombs on the Reich Capital. In the bitter fight against the flak and night-fighters Bomber Command in those five nights lost 123 bombers. There followed another eleven attacks on Berlin in which 2700 died and 250,000 were made homeless. In December Berlin was again visited by the RAF, the defences shooting down forty bombers. On one raid, 23rd December, 358 machines dropped 1288 tons of bombs for the loss of fifteen bombers. Bishop George Bell of Chichester said, as reported in a Swedish newspaper, that bombers had dropped bombs purely on domestic housing. He was making an attempt to try and stop the bombing.

"We fighter pilots and night-fighter pilots from the age of fourteen before and after 1933 sat in gliders and believed that we could get close to Heaven and God. When we flew up in the air we felt as free and good men. From 1935/6 we were in the

146

luftwaffe where we served and believed in a good Germany. Out of 20,000 fighter pilots, 18,000 are buried or missing in all parts of Europe and Russia. Even today we feel the idiocy of war in our hearts but the killing goes on as if nothing has ever happened. We pilots shortly after the end of the war met our erstwhile enemies and asked for understanding and to start friendships. I have learnt never again to have death on my side, instead a brother, no matter where he comes from."

It would seem from his last paragraph that Herr Herbert Thomas is a religious man, not all Germans were goose-stepping Nazis. Captain Landsdorf of the pocket battleship *Graf Spee* was not, he was a sailor, neither was Field Marshall Rommel, he was a soldier. Herr Herbert Thomas was an airman defending his country. Of course the opinions, facts and figures are his own but the tonnage of bombs dropped that he mentions could be in metric tons. I hope there is not too much lost in the translation.

For the next three days the Squadron stood down from operations, however there was still training to do, aircraft battle damage repairs and routine servicing. On the 25th January, 1 Group Squadrons were detailed to take part in an attack on Berlin again. Throughout the day, twelve aircraft had been prepared, fuelled and bombed up. Later the aircrew were briefed and after the usual meal of bacon and eggs were driven out to their respective aircraft. While actually sitting in the Lancasters waiting for the order to go the operation was cancelled at a quarter to five, probably due to the weather ever England being too bad for landing some hours later. Some with relief, some with disappointment, the crews got out of the Lancasters and waited for transport back to Operations and the various messes. Some crews, like F/Lt Belford's on LM380, left their parachutes in the aircraft, as seeing it as pointless to lug them back only to bring them out again at the prospect of being on another raid later on in the week. The navigators already had their green navigator's bag containing maps and almanacs to carry also the cumbersome box containing the astro sextant all on a full crew bus.

It was still early evening, plenty of time for some crews to go to Lincoln or the pubs in the nearby villages. F/Lt Belford's crew decided to see James Cagney in the film 'Yankee Doodle Dandy' showing at Wickenby's camp cinema. Out on the airfield the Lancasters waited for their next foray over Nazi Germany. Being at the end of January it was very cold and it rained all night.

The next day brought cloud and rain with poor visibility down Wickenby's runways. There was no operational flying, the aircrews going to training lectures. Dawn heralded a clear and bright day on Thursday the 27th January. Later, the Operations Block teleprinters informed the Wickenby squadrons that an attack on Berlin was on for that night. Much of the work had been done on the Lancasters for the previous cancelled raid but the aircraft still had to have a pre-flight check by the ground and aircrews alike. F/Sgt Lee, the navigator of LM3B0, thought his parachute to be damp as it had been in the Lancaster for two nights. He decided to change it by cycling round the the perimeter track to the Parachute Section. The rest of the crew kept the ones they were issued with two days before in the aircraft.

Take off times were to be about Five-thirty in the early evening according to aircraft with a time over target between 20:28Hrs and 20:48Hrs That gave over 500 Lancasters just twenty minutes to drop a little over 1700 tons of high explosive and incendiaries. The route to Berlin and back featured more diversions and feint attacks than ever before to counteract the ever-increasing expertise of the Luftwaffe Night-fighter Arm. The biggest diversion was to be a force of eighty Stirlings and Wellingtons mine laying off the Frisian Islands just before the main force was due to approach the enemy coast further to the west. Meanwhile, twenty-one H2S equipped Halifaxes were to bomb the Island of Heligoland to the north. The route for the Main and Pathfinder force was straight in over Northern Holland and head for a target that could have been Magdeburg again, Braunschweig or faraway Leipzig. At About twenty-five miles south of Hanover the stream would turn left to execute a confusing dog-leg course to Berlin. Mosquitos would drop dummy fighter flares, dummy route markers and 'Window' in two places while the bombers were en route and more fighter flares north-east of Berlin when the bombers were over the target. On leaving Berlin the bombers would fly south-west and west over Central Germany, Belgium, Northern France and across the English Channel to home.

In the early evening, thirteen Lancasters of 626 Squadron were ready for take off but once again the figure thirteen was to daunt the Squadron's effort as on the previous raid. W4990 with F/Sgt Welford as captain, failed to take off. ME589 cleared Wickenby's runway just after half past five. Three quarters of an hour later saw them on their way back with no intercom between the seven crew and an unserviceable Monica radar warning system. A load of incendiaries were dumped in the North Sea to lighten the aircraft before landing at twenty minutes to ten but they brought back the 4,000lb 'Cookie' and 210 incendiaries to use in the next raid.

Australian F/Sgt Jock Torrance was the pilot of JB646 this night and got his Lancaster Mk.III off the ground just before a quarter to six. Out over the North Sea it was found that Sgt Smith, the mid-upper gunner, could not communicate with any other member of the crew. Other helmets were tried and with the ten-foot extension lead that was always carried, they were plugged into another station box but still without success. It was decided to fly on and to attack the nearer secondary target; the flak batteries on the island of Texel. This they did from 20,000 feet at nearly half past seven. This place was a good secondary target as the Germans had placed guns there to catch the bombers flying to and from their targets in Germany. JB646 landed back at Wickenby just before half past nine but since the bombs were dropped on the enemy the sortie was counted towards the crew's thirty sortie operational tour.

The diversion raid on Heligoland and the minelaying sorties around the Frisian Islands drew many night-fighters out to sea while the Mainforce turned south-east into Holland and Germany. By the time the Germans realised what had happened many night-fighters were in the wrong place and running out of fuel. Bomber Command's tactics were working well. The Mosquitos were dropping dummy route markers and fighter flares to the north of the bomber stream and when the bombers turned left for the dogleg route to Berlin Mosquitos again carried on south-east dropping large amounts of 'Window'. Because of the high westerly tail wind of about 100 M.P.H., all these events were happening quicker than the fighter controllers could keep up, consequently very few bombers were intercepted by night-fighters on the way to the target.

F/O Breckenridge, pilot of ME584, saw a Lancaster crash in flames when he was flying twelve miles south of Wilhelmshaven at 1931Hrs On route, the crew also saw green and red markers complete with incendiary fires. Perhaps a load spilled out from a crashed bomber or a decoy laid by the Germans. Wing Commander Haynes, 626 Squadron Commanding Officer, was not required to fly as often as other aircrew but this night he was leading his Squadron in JB599. The last leg before the target involved flying due east. While over Brandenburg, the aircraft was caught by heavy flak where a piece of shrapnel came flying through the right side of the cockpit damaging F/Lt Phillips's engineer's panel, at this time they were twenty minutes from the target.

The Berlin target was covered in cloud therefore the not so accurate 'Wanganui' sky-marking method had to be employed. The Pathfinders made a standard H2S attack picking up on radar the towns of Genthin, Brandenburg and Potsdam in a straight line flying east. Only to be expected, the marking was scattered in some parts and concentrated in others owing to the wind's effects on the floating sky-markers. F/Sgt Lamb, the bomb aimer of LM393, bombed a concentration of fourteen green and red flares. P/O Poushinsky, the bomb aimer of ME584, also found a concentration of sky-markers to aim at. Overall, most crews reported that the marking was scattered.

Not many night-fighters made it to Berlin to defend the city as were expected thanks to the diversion tactics along the bombers' route. Although the crew of W4967 did see some single engine fighters they were attacked by them. To help divert the fighters from the target area, Mosquitos dropped fighter flares to the north-east of the city. The bomber force on leaving the city turned clockwise and headed south-west and then west over Central Germany for the long 450-mile route to the French coast. Now the strong west winds were against them. The economical cruising speed of a Lancaster was about 150-160 M.P.H. and with a headwind of about 100 M.P.H. groundspeed was slower than a speeding German staff car. This made the Lancasters more vulnerable and with the location of the stream now known, night-fighter attacks increased and their successes steadily rose.

The southern route home passed two important night-fighter bases at Erfurt and Mainz-Finthen before passing the industrial cities of Frankfurt and Koblenz. At Erfurt the unit was IV/NJG5 while Mianz-Finthen operated the Messerschmitt Bf110G-4 belonging to I/NJG6 which had previously transferred from France. These aircraft were equipped with the latest Lichtenstein SN-2 radar- and two upward firing 20m.m. canon in *Schrage Musik* (jazz music) installation just aft of the cockpit.

Flt/Lt W.N. Belford RAAF (pilot) and Sgt T.S. 'Tommy' Trinder (W/op) of Lancaster LM380, both killed during a Berlin raid on 27th January 1944. (photo: E. Lee)

F/Lt Belford in LM380 left Berlin heading east and then turned round clockwise on a dogleg course to the west across Central Germany but about ten miles south of track. A little before eleven o'clock, unknown to him or his crew, German ground radar had found his Lancaster. Somewhere in Central

Germany in a Master Control Centre, Women Communication Auxiliaries, Luftwaffenhelferinnen, were plotting an intercept with a night-fighter. Between Koblenz and the River Rhine, LM380 was soon to be seen as a blip on a night-fighter's radar.

F/Sgt Arthur Lee, only survivor of LM380's crew when shot down on 27.1.44 and founder member of the Wickenby Register. (photo: E. Lee)

The night-fighter was a Messerschmitt Bf11OG-4 of I/NJG6 believed to be piloted by Ober-leutnant Birkinstoctc. Being fitted with upward firing canon, it stalked the Lancaster- from below and a little to one side and when in the ideal position, raked the bomber's wing tanks and engines with devastating effect. From 23,000 feet the blazing Lancaster began its last dive with a mid-air explosion and an engine separating from the wing on the way down. Only one crew member survived, the navigator, twenty-two year old F/Sgt Arthur Lee who parachuted down to land in some trees on the edge of a wood near the village of Katzeneinbogen, seventeen miles east of Koblenz.

The village was the home of Rudi Balzer, a soldier of the German Army who was on leave at the time, like Arthur Lee he was twenty-two years old. He saw the stricken bomber spiralling to earth and in the light of the falling wreckage, a lone parachute. Gathering some *Volksturm* (German Home Guard) and a few Hitler Youth he set out quickly in the direction of the crashed Lancaster, where he found the shocked and dazed navigator.

In Germany at this time, Royal Air Force bomber aircrew were known as '*terrorfliegers*' and, if shot down, the most dangerous time was from landing till being taken prisoner by the Luftwaffe authorities, whose responsibility it was to take custody of airmen as POWs. It was not unknown for airmen to be strung up on lampposts and trees by civilians, the SS and Gestapo alike. Katzeneinbogen had its fair share of Nazis, particularly since people made their way into the rural areas having been bombed out in nearby Frankfurt and Koblenz, but Rudi Balzer got to Arthur Lee first and escorted him to the village. Showing great courage, he refused to leave Arthur Lee until the Luftwaffe arrived the following afternoon and at great risk to his own life he refused to hand him over to any other authority or obey orders he knew conflicted with the Rules of The Geneva Convention regarding Prisoners of War. The young soldier took the frightened

Arthur Lee to the Burgomaster's office, where he organised food and first aid for his burnt hands and face. He used the parachute as a mattress and covered him with his own greatcoat. The two young men were in great danger, one of being lynched and the other of being court-martialled for disobeying orders no matter how unlawful. Rudi Balzer, although Arthur Lee's 'enemy' at the time, showed great kindness and compassion that was not to be forgotten, as will be seen later.

The graves of the crew of LM380, Rheinberg War Cemetery

F/Lt W Belford (captain/pilot), Sgt T. Trinder (wireless operator), Sgt J. Lee (bomb aimer), Sgt H. Hill (flight engineer), Sgt H. Mewburn (mid-upper gunner), F/Sgt R. Gould (rear gunner). They were originally buried in the village churchyard of Klingelbach, about 20 miles south-east of Koblenz, a couple of miles north of where their Lancaster crashed. Like many other airmen who perished in the night sky of Germany, they were moved to Rheinberg after the war to finally rest in company with their comrades in arms.

No one else in the Lancaster survived, F/Sgt Arthur Lee becoming a POW until liberated in 1945.

How did Arthur Lee parachute to safety when the rest of the crew were found dead alongside the wreckage? He was sure he had been the last to leave the burning Lancaster. Their parachutes did not open, he believes, because they were damp after being left in the aircraft for two nights and had then frozen at 20,000 feet or more. F/Sgt Lee had changed his chute for a fresh one before take off and believes it saved his life. His six friends were first buried at the Klingelbach Churchyard but were later transferred and finally laid to rest at the Rheinburg War Cemetery to the north-west of the Ruhr industrial area.

~ ~ ~ ~ ~

With a near 100mph headwind, P/O Currie and his crew were making heavy going of it. JB559 was not a good a flyer as their previous Lancaster as it would not trim correctly to fly in a straight line and the autopilot seemed to have a mind of Its own. It was found that by increasing each engine speed by 100 R.P.M., the flight engineer could get a bit more speed out of it as they flew between Bonn and Koblenz and across Belgium via Naniur and Charleroi. The English Channel was a welcome sight and more so the English coast, crossing it at Dungeness. Despite their slow speed JB559 was back at Wickenby first, landing gust before half past one in the morning.

For P/O Moore, wireless operator of LM393, this was his big night as this sortie was to be the last of his operational tour. While at 21,000 feet and flying in the Aachen area, LM393 and his tour nearly came to an abrupt end there and then. The aircraft was shot at by flak but luckily only the main wheel doors were damaged by the flying shrapnel in a near miss. Three hours later P/O Wellham landed LM393 safely at Wickenby.

LM380 was 626 Squadron's only casualty that night, the rest landed back in England in the early hours of 28th January. Berlin was always a long haul no matter what the route, a strong headwind on the way back added to the problems. After crossing the English Channel and heading north, some aircraft landed away from home having run out of petrol. F/O. Breckenridge landed ME584 at Wittering near Peterborough while W4967 did not even make it across the River Thames and had to land at West Malling, a Fighter Command airfield south of London.

The 'Wanganui' method of target marking was not 100% accurate, especially on a night with high winds. The damage to Berlin was over a larger area than planned. More bombs fell in the south of the city than elsewhere, including over sixty small towns and villages outside the capital. Some important industries manufacturing war materials were severely damaged including fifty factories. 20,000 inhabitants were reported to have been made homeless and 567 were killed. Later, when all the evidence came to light, no photographs were brought back by the bombers of the damage, the raid was considered to be a medium success. Thirty-three Lancasters did not return with 172 airmen killed. Fifty-five aircrew sat out the rest of the war in Stalag Luft POW camps including F/Sgt Arthur Lee.

After the War and some years later in 1979, Arthur Lee, with the help of some old Squadron friends, formed the Wickenby Register, the 12 and 626 Squadron Association. Following a lot of investigation and research to his whereabouts in Germany, Arthur Lee met Rudi Balzer once again in Katzeneinbogan on 13th October 1984, over forty years later. A few days after his return, Arthur Lee put his story before the Central Committee of the Wickenby Register. For his outstanding courage and Christian fellowship', Rudi Balzer was appointed an Honorary Membership for saving the life of the young navigator on the night of 27th January 1944. Sadly, Arthur Lee died on 21st October 1986. As

co-founder and President of the Wickenby Register he left behind over five hundred reunited aircrew and ground staff. In
1998 the membership was over 1000.

The 28th January dawned cloudy with rain in the morning but
by sundown in the late afternoon it cleared up to reveal a clear
night with good visibility. In the morning the ground crews had
been hard at it arming, bombing up and refuelling the Lancasters. Of course to them and most of Wickenby the target was a
secret but by the quantities of fuel required and the size of the
bomb load, they and the aircrew could make an educated guess.
There had been all the indications that the target was a long way
away, in fact the loads were the same as the previous night. For
P/O Hodges, the mid-upper gunner and F/O Newman the bomb
aimer, both of JB599 and all the crew of LL772, it was their last
sortie of their operational tours. It will be remembered that it was
Bill Newman that devised the Squadron badge. F/Sgt Brettell of
LL772 had double the reason to celebrate; it was the last operation of his second tour.

The 91 airmen, thirteen crews, of 626 Squadron, filed anx-
iously into the Wickenby briefing room at four o'clock. As the
curtain was pulled back to reveal the red tape across the big map
of enemy occupied Europe, it was seen that a Berlin finish was
the order for those completing their tours. The captains and
navigators had known for some time from their briefing earlier.
This gave them extra time to work out the course to the target
and back with the latest available information on the winds and
weather. High flying Mosquitos would have ranged far over
Germany to bring back all this information during the day. It was
always a trying time for the crews between briefing and take off,
being all keyed up knowing where they were going but having to

stand around the dispersal waiting for the word to go. 'Butterflies' in the stomach was not uncommon for new and old hands alike.

Take off was delayed for an hour which left crews in some doubt to whether they were going at all as sometimes a delay was followed by a scrubbed operation. Some gunners polished turret perspex, others read books, smoked or drank tea in ground crew huts alongside the aircraft. Anxious moments. Then word came that the operation had been delayed a further four hours and transport was coming to take the crews back to the messes. Some went to the camp cinema to watch 'Casablanca'; others sat it out in their accommodation to write a last letter or to contemplate the next few hours. A little after eleven o'clock the crews were driven again to the waiting Lancasters.

Bomber aircrews were a superstitious lot. Some preferred a particular seat on the crew bus or carried a girlfriend or wife's stockings about them. Many carried good luck tokens or wore 'lucky' items of clothing. For crews to relieve themselves on the tail wheel of their aircraft before take-off 'for luck' was also a common practice. By midnight the still Lincolnshire air was shattered by straining starter motors and Merlin engines bursting into life as one by one the Lancaster's captains and flight engineers brought the temperatures and pressures of the engines to take off and flight readiness. When ready, the ground crew removed the starter trolleys and wheel chocks, then marshalled the aircraft out of their dispersals to the taxiway track. Once again 626 Squadron was operational.

Not all answered the green Aldis lamp of the runway control van for take off as pilot F/O. Breckenridge of ME584 and W4990 captained by F/Sgt Welford failed to take off due to technical problems with the aircraft. LL722 was P/O Currie's Lancaster for the night, Having Packard Merlin engines and large Hamilton propellers it proved a more powerful aircraft than previous examples he had flown. With greater rate of climb and thrust on take off with eighteen pounds boost from the superchargers, this Mk.III Lancaster easily cleared the runway at 00:18Hrs to head for Mablethorpe and the North Sea. Crossing the English coast at 17,000 feet it continued on to gain operational height of 20,000 feet long before reaching Denmark 350 miles away. The wind was behind the bombers this night making speed over the sea of about 250mph.

677 bombers were flying across the North Sea in which 432 were Lancasters. Stirlings and Pathfinder 8 Group Halifaxes took part in a minelaying diversion in Kiel Bay off the North German coast. Mosquitos bombed the night-fighter airfields of Deelen, Leeuwarden, Venlo and Gilze Rijen in Holland. Another new idea was tried this night. Six Mosquitos flew from Oakington in Cambridgeshire to bomb Berlin four hours before the main raid. Each carried four 500-pound bombs and took less than four hours to complete the flight there and back. Mosquitos of Eight Group's Light Night Striking Force flew many spoof raids throughout the Battle to draw the defending night-fighters away from the attacking force, always bombing a different city to the night's main target. This night it was different as the same target had never been attacked twice on the same night before.

The route this night was to head for the fifty-five degrees north latitude line about sixty miles to the west of the Danish coast and fly due east across Denmark to the east coast of Fyn Island, then go straight in a south-easterly direction of the Berlin target. After leaving Berlin, turn left in a wide circle and fly back on a direct route to Fyn Island again until the fifty-five latitude was reached, then back home westwards the same way as the inward route.

Just after two o'clock in the morning the stream was off the Danish coast. The Pathfinder Force in the van dropped red marker flares and broadcast an accurate wind speed of 87mph from 310 degrees. Half an hour into the south-easterly leg to Berlin the wind was found to have changed on the approach to the target. To help navigation the lead Pathfinders laid down more route markers as planned. The windspeed had risen so making the groundspeed of 280 MPH too fast, throttling back by some aircraft prevented them arriving at the target too soon.

At 0310Hrs the target markers went down again on Germany's capital. It is always a source of amazement that, as on this night, 677 individual aircraft can arrive at one place at a pre-determined time after flying almost across a continent. It says a lot for the skill of the navigators for when flying independently all these aircraft take off from different airfields, fly along a set route and bomb a target all within an actual time of fifteen to twenty minutes duration. Navigational systems were crude compared to those fitted to say a Tornado of today's Royal Air Force. No radio beacons, no radio direction finding, that was jammed and not all bombers had H2S radar.

On arrival at the target it was found that in some places there was thin broken cloud, some crews seeing Berlin streets for the first time in weeks. S/Ldr Neilson's crew had borrowed JB716 from 12 Squadron equipped with H2S radar but having no training on the system they had it switched off. F/O Simms, the bomb aimer, dropped their bomb load from 21,000 feet on some red and green flares noting that the ground and sky-marking was well concentrated. By this time, 0330Hrs, fires were quite extensive with a lot of smoke. Three very large explosions were seen by most crews between 0315 and 0325Hrs W4967's bomb aimer sighted on a cluster of sky-markers at 0325Hrs, shortly afterwards the starboard outer engine caught fire which was eventually extinguished. With the propeller feathered they flew on three engines but lagging behind the stream. JB559 was also experiencing trouble where the pilot, S/Ldr Spiller, could not get it flying above 18,500 feet.

P/O Currie and six of his crew with (most likely) EE133 UM-C2.
(left to right) P/O Myring (bomb aimer), P/O Currie (pilot), F/Sgt Brettell (rear gunner), Sgt Protheroe (mid-upper gunner), Sgt Walker (flight engineer), Sgt Fairbairn (wireless operator). (photo: G. Walker)

For the last time bomb aimer F/O. Bill Newman looked down at a target and the markers. One can almost imagine the anxiety of the crew with wondering if the bombs dropped by the others flying 3000 feet above them would hit their Lancaster. Widespread fires and several large explosions were seen by most but at 0314Hrs there was one enormous explosion lasting many seconds and nine minutes later the Berlin West Power Station blew up in a blinding flash.

This night the Luftwaffe fighter controllers had predicted the target in time. Ju88s and Fw200 Condors of III/KG3 dropped fighter flares above the bombers and turned parts of the Berlin sky into day, many crews and their aircraft met their fate over the target. Fatigue and tiredness began to tell at this point, for many of the crews this was the second night of attacking Berlin on the trot. Single engine night-fighters were in the stream in competition with twin-engined types for targets. Seventeen Halifaxes and ten Lancasters were shot down in the target area. Despite all this the Pathfinders put down very accurate markers and most of the Main Force coming up behind bombed on them just as accurately as good photographic evidence was to prove later. The Battle of Berlin was over half way through and it was beginning to tell on crews and aircraft alike.

Often as not, early return of bombers, a long cold route and a lot of opposition in the target area by flak and fighters usually gave a poor bombing result. Not so this night. Devastation was mainly on the southern and western side of the city but seventy-seven places outside were also hit. It was estimated that 180,000 people were made homeless but by now, the end of January, the damage was so great that records were not often kept. There were a number of hits on important buildings, five embassies, six hospitals, the State Patent Office, four theatres and the new Chancellery were all extensively damaged.

After leaving the burning city behind the stream turned left all the way round and headed back the way they had come, flying into the 95mph headwind that had aided them for such a long time. Once out of Germany most of the flight home was over the sea and Scandinavia, which was not so heavily defended as the direct route home westwards. But it was still a long way to the Baltic Sea. LL772 headed north-west with the rest of the

Squadron in darkened accompaniment as 626 was to loose none this night. No route markers to give away the route home fell as it sped along at about 150 MPH over the Northern Plain of Germany. Much cloud was about and being out of the range of the GEE navigational aid the navigator, Australian F/O Cassidy, had to resort to an astro fix. Before crossing the coast near Rostock, fires could still be seen raging in Berlin from over 120 miles away. Flying over the coast between Rostock and Lubeck they caught the attention of a flak ship anchored in Kiel Bay but out-manoeuvred its gunners to carry on and fly due west on the fifty-five degrees north latitude line across Denmark and the North Sea. Giving the Island of Sylt a wide berth the enemy coast was left behind for the last time on their tour and with 360 miles to go LL772 raced ahead over the sea for the coast of Lincolnshire at Mablethorpe.

At six o'clock and 250 miles to go the GEE aid picked up a signal for a fix, LL772 having flown beyond Germany's jamming range. An hour later and for the last time the friendly coast and its welcome searchlight beacon at Mablethorpe were flown over. Next the distant Lincoln Cathedral was seen on the hill above the city surrounding it. A beacon of another kind that welcomed crews home before landing at one of the many bomber stations in the county. Today the Cathedral remembers the ones that did not come home in the Bomber Command Chapel of Remembrance. There were tired hands but an alert mind at the controls as Lancaster LL772 lined up with Wickenby's runway. The landing check list was gone through by pilot and flight engineer as it had been many times before: *Auto pilot OUT, superchargers M RATIO, air intake COLD, check brake pressure at 250-300 PSI, flaps DOWN, undercarriage DOWN, propeller controls at least.*

2850 RPM and fuel booster pumps ON *in tanks in use at the time.*

This was no time for a sloppy landing as many people were watching. A crew ending their operational tour was an occasion and the Group Air Officer Commanding was on the Station. LL772 was one of the early ones to land at twenty past seven in the morning. W4967 limped home all the way from Berlin on three engines to land at Wickenby just after nine o'clock when most other aircraft had been back an hour.

9. They Also Served…

It was customary for tour expired aircrew to go on a couple of weeks leave and on return to be notified of their next posting and 'clear' the Station. Before they went there was one more important duty to perform and that was to take the ground crew on a night out as a token of appreciation of a job well done while the Lancaster was in their care. What of these men and women who worked all hours and conditions to keep the Lancasters serviceable and available when required. Not much has been written, in fact too little.

There was always something to do in maintaining the aircraft if only to wash them, grime caused drag and decreased airspeed. That vital knot or two could mean the difference between life and death escaping from a night fighter's cannon. An aircraft of the Lancaster's size was looked after by a team of ground crew led by a Sergeant in the Airframes or Engines trade. Under him were well trained and qualified tradesmen and women to maintain the four Merlin engines, the airframe and all the armaments including guns and bomb loads. No less skilled were the specialists in the electrical, instruments, radio and radar fields. Usually the engines, airframes and armaments trades would work on a variety of aircraft but the other four tradesmen, in addition to their basic training, sometimes needed specialist knowledge and courses appertaining to the aircraft they were to work on.

Training, if one was a 'regular' and 'signed on' for twelve years or more, was second to none. One of Sir Hugh Trenchard's priorities at the beginning of the Royal Air Force was training, equal emphasis being given to the technical and administrative as the flying aspect. He set up the Technical Apprenticeship scheme at RAF Halton for the training of ground crews and other branches of engineering. By the beginning of World War Two the cadre of well qualified, adaptable NCO technicians who could be relied upon to act on their own initiative when required was in place. Many ex-RAF Halton 'brats' were awarded Commissions, becoming Engineering Officers and aircrew, some attaining Air Rank. To cope with the many thousands of conscripted men and volunteers in wartime, women as well as men, technical training schools are already established up and down the country.

Unless at the age of sixteen to attend the RAF Halton Apprenticeship Establishment to become a Fitter for three years. Young men or women would spend four to five days at a reception centre like RAF Uxbridge or RAF Cardington on joining up. It would be there that after some practical and written tests, his or her trade would be determined. Then a posting to a basic training camp to learn Service discipline, combat skills and of course 'square bashing'. This took eight weeks for men but only three weeks for women as they were regarded as non-combatants. This was followed up by another posting to a specialist training establishment to train as a Mechanic if in a technical trade. In 1943 aircraft ground crew were Group I and Group II with all the support trades such as drivers, parachute packers, catering, radio and radar operators right down to the officers batmen and musicians in Group V. No matter who, all had their part to play and each no less important that the one beside them. On the pay scale the ground crews got paid the most per day moving down to the Group V people the least.

Tom Hughes is in retirement, having spent a lifetime around aeroplanes. He lives in Ringwood near the New Forest, where he uses some of his time writing a journal of his career for his grand-

grandchildren. "Hopefully, when I have done my final take off," he says, "it will answer questions such as 'What did Grandpa really do in the RAF?'"

"I was born and educated in Ireland and joined the RAF as an Aircraft Apprentice in January 1937. I was dubbed 'Paddy', which I accepted and carried right through the War. I then reverted to my rightful handle of Tom, much to the joy of my family.

My Halton entry, 35ᵗʰ, were trained as Fitter 2s (Airframes & Engines) but on passing out No.1 Wing were declared Fitter 2E and No. 2 Wing, to which I belonged, Fitter 2A. I was more au fait with engines!

My first squadron was number 98 with which I spent the first year of the War in U.K., France and Iceland. Our aircraft were Fairy Battles. I was posted to number 12 Squadron at Binbrook in November 1940, who were in the process of converting from Battles to the Wellington Mk.2. As a Corporal I took over a repair party in the Maintenance Flight. In July 1942 I was promoted to Sergeant and moved to 'B" Flight in charge of the Airframes tradesmen. In September 1942 I moved with 12 Squadron to Wickenby, where after several months a third flight was formed, 'C' Flight. This was later to become the nucleus of 626 Squadron when it was formed in November 1943. I was posted to 626 and remained with it until its disbandment in late 1945".

Tom stayed with the Royal Air Force after the War coming out in 1969, the last six years as a Vulcan Bomber Crew Chief at Finingley and Waddington. Continuing his career on aircraft, he joined Airworks Ltd. on their contract in Saudi Arabia. On return to England two-and-a-half years later he was promoted to Branch

Chief Engineer working on another one of their contracts. This was serviceing the RAF's 7 Squadron Canberras at St Mawgan in Cornwall until they moved to Marham in January 1982.

The corporals of the Wickenby bowser pool.

On a bomber squadron, like 626 at Wickenby, for the ground crews the work was hard, long hours and especially in winter, under appalling outside conditions. Promotion was slow, pay was poor for the work one did and comforts little. For every flight of maybe twelve Lancasters, up to three on a large squadron, there would be a Flight Sergeant delegating his authority to a Sergeant Fitter in charge of each aircraft. He would most likely be of the Engines or the Airframes trade. Each bomber's ground crew would consist of an NCO Fitter with an Engine Mechanic for each engine while the airframe would be looked after by an Airframe Fitter and three or four Airframe Mechanics. Early in the morning after breakfast the daily work routine would start with the D.I., Daily Inspection, on all the aircraft on the flying program for that day. Sometimes the bomber would have just landed after a raid and seen in by early risers or a night shift. Rectification and repairs would be done in the open as other servicing. Refuelling and rearming would be carried out as required by Operations after a ground test prior to going on a raid. There was always pressure after a raid to get the aircraft fully serviceable, sometimes having to remove and re-use an item from a grounded aircraft to do it if the Supply Squadron did not have it. As the Lancasters were spread out all over the airfield a bicycle was essential. Each dispersal had its own ground crew hut made out of any material to hand, corrugated iron, packing crates, canvas in fact anything for a shelter from the weather and a place to make a brew of tea on a cold day.

Like the aircrew, the ground staff had a language of their own. A non-NCO was an 'Erk'. The three 'Heavies' were 'Fitters', Engine tradesmen, 'Plumbers' who were the Armourers and dating back to when the RAF had biplane's braced by wires, 'Riggers', the Airframe tradesmen. Many Armourers volunteered for aircrew to become Air Gunners, likewise quite a few 'Fitters' became Flight Engineers. What was known as the ancillary trades were specialists in Electrics, Radar, Radio and Instrument systems. Because of the delicate nature of the altimeters, the airspeed indicators and gyroscopes that they serviced and handled, the Instrument people were called 'Instrument bashers'. Sometimes ancillary tradesmen would be assigned to more than one bomber. On the flight line all servicing, refuelling and re-arming would be done in the open come all weathers. Only on a long inspection or for major battle damage repair would a Lancaster go into one of Wickenby's large black hangers, its own ground crew sometimes going with it to do the work. On being posted to a squadron, for just about all ground crew it was for the duration, which for 626 Squadron it was to be at disbandment in October 1945. With training over, after a short time enthusiasm would build up and it became a matter of professional pride to get one's 'Kite' serviceable before the rest after an operation the night before.

Being an Armourer on a bomber squadron meant a life of handling heavy and dangerous explosives, not a few in the Command were killed in accidents. Sid Field was a Leading Aircraftman (LAC) in the trade and was on 626 Squadron right at the beginning in November 1943 to the end of the War. He is now retired and lives in Birmingham:

"I was an Armourer at Wickenby from June 1943 till the end of the War, being with 12 Squadron when I arrived. My first job was with another L.A.C. Loading flashes into a chute in each of the aircraft. I was transferred to 626 Squadron when it was first formed in November 1943, serving until it was disbanded at the finish of the War and was one of the few who was transferred to help direct the new personnel in the technicalities in servicing and bombing up on Lancasters. We had one Armoury serving both Squadrons but whereas we serviced 626 we bombed up 12 as well.

At first it was a thrill working on Lancasters. We were allocated two aircraft to service each day, the job comprising of looking after the turret's hydraulics, component parts and ammunition, which was loaded in large containers each side of the aircraft with belts of cartridges running down ducts to the guns in each turret. The guns we rarely touched as each aircrew looked after their own. The average life of a Lancaster was only a few missions so I did not get to know each aircrew very long. Wickenby opened in late 1942 and at the end of the War we had lost about 1080 aircrew, which is a lot of aircraft when each had seven crew members.

Towards lunchtime we often learned if operations were on or not for that night. We were formed up into regular bombing crews and more often than not, had about four aircraft to do. When 626 came to us the Corporal of our team asked me if I would see the bombs loaded in the bomb bay. As I was more conversant with it I did this right to the end of operations.

The bomb bay consisted of fifteen stations. In the middle was always, without exception, the 4,000lb 'cookie', shaped like a huge dustbin with a canister acting as a tailfin. Quite regularly we loaded three delayed action 1000-pounders on the three rear stations. The rest of the bomb load were cans of incendiaries. Each hexagon-shaped can carried ninety bombs in three compartments held in by an iron bar, which was released electrically from the Bomb Aimer's panel. Normally, each aircraft carried at the most eleven cans, with one can carrying explosive incendiaries (4X Type). Most times the bomb load varied because of the distance to the target where we had to balance the bomb load with the petrol load; a light load for Berlin and Nuremberg, heavier for Essen, Cologne and the Ruhr".

Wickenby was a wartime built airfield and the accommodation for all was not as good as many brick built pre-war stations like Scampton or Lindholme. Administration buildings and servicing bays were of drab concrete while the airmen lived in Nissan huts. When it rained some said the mud was like Flanders. It was up to the occupants to make the huts homely, and many did as far as regulations allowed. Each Nissen but had a pop-bellied stove in the middle, but never enough coke to keep the place warm in winter. At night, greatcoats were donned and a foraging party would go out and raid boiler houses and other stockpiles for fuel.

The WAAF had their own but similar accommodation on a separate site near the village of Holton, a couple of miles to the west of the airfield.

At the time of the Battle of Berlin there were about 18,000 women in the Women's Auxiliary Air Force who worked alongside their men counterparts, in many cases doing the same job but only for two-thirds of the pay. It was to be four decades later that this diabolical anomaly was rectified for the women of the now Women's Royal Air Force.

About fifteen per cent of the Wickenby workforce were girls of the WAAF. Most of the driving on 626 Squadron was done by the 'Waffs', as they were known, from towing bomb trollies to the Lancasters to taking and bringing back aircrew from their aircraft. Administration and supply were two trades that women did in civilian life as well as in the RAF but there were many jobs they did on an RAF station that was normally quite alien to them. They worked in servicing bays carrying out all sorts of tasks from cleaning spark plugs to maintaining radio and radar systems. Many worked alongside the men actually on the Lancaster flight line and shared the same conditions and weather all the year round. They were also involved in looking after the aircraft safety equipment and parachutes, including packing them. When a Lancaster crew had been flying on an operation for about eight hours, being shot at by flak and night-fighters, it was always pleasing to hear a female voice in the earphones belonging to a WAAF air traffic controller after crossing the English coast. The women and girls of the WAAF volunteered from civilian life, they were not conscripted like some of the men, although the alternative was to join the Land Army in the fields or work in an armaments factory. For their work in Bomber Command and elsewhere, the magnitude of their contribution is immeasurable.

As with the other two services, uniform was worn all the time on and off duty unless at home on leave. There was a 'Best blue' uniform for parades, ceremonial duties and going off the station for an evening out or for the journey home on leave. The jacket had brass buttons that needed to be polished every time before wearing. For work there was the 'Working blue' of wool serge, shabby by the standards of today, that was hard to keep pressed and tidy. On a nice summer's day it was hot and uncomfortable where in winter, although warm, it soaked up rainwater like a sponge, after which the creases would drop out and smell a musty odour.

For off duty entertainment the Corporals and ranks below had the NAFFI canteen while the SNCOs had the Senior Non-Commissioned Officers and Warrant Officers' Mess. There was a cinema at Wickenby for all ranks, occasionally there would be a dance. In the surrounding villages there was the pubs and regular dances in the village halls. Wickenby was, and still is of course, miles away from any big town or the nearest city, Lincoln. The big problem was transport; very few officers owned a car, of the ground crew, none at all. There was always the bus but very few and far between in a country district. The only solution was the bicycle which was either brought from home or purchased second-hand but even that idea had its complications. Torch batteries were very scarce in wartime England and many an airman 'Ran the gauntlet' with the local village policeman when riding back to Wickenby at night with no lights.

Although the working day could be long, especially if the Lancasters were on operations, off duty time could be spent in many ways, even with wartime restrictions. There was humour and for a person with initiative, ways of supplementing the low pay. Sid Field explains:

"It takes some believing but it is true. One night when I arrived back at my billet, there was a new arrival who was already in bed. When I awoke the next day I bid him good morning. I could not believe my eyes when he reached under his bed and pulled out a false leg and proceeded to fit it on. He was a very likable fellow, name of George Pitt from Gateshead. He walked with a slight limp and was issued with a ladies bicycle to ride, we all had bicycles to get about. His job, as an assistant armourer, was to drive a tractor bringing the bombs to the dispersal points. There were many amusing incidents relating to George's leg, I could write a book about it.

Believe it or not but two other fellows in the hut along with myself, purchased a ferret, keeping it in a cage in the air raid shelter. Averaging about two to three rabbits daily, we sold them to the N.A.A.F.I canteen for nine pence each which kept us in fags as I smoked in those days".

Very few lasting friendships between the ground crews and aircrews were struck up, aircrew life expectancy on average being too short. When a Lancaster did not come back there were some long faces on the flight line but soon another aircraft and crew would arrive and all was back to normal again. It was not callous; it had to be like that. Of course some crews did complete their thirty operation tour, after which it was tradition that the jubilant aircrew would take the ground crew for a night on the town before being posted on, usually to a training unit.

Bomber Command was the only British fighting force hitting at Germany in between the evacuation of Dunkirk and the Normandy landings and they were doing in night after night. The unsung heroes of Bomber Command were definitely the men and women of the ground crews and their supporting staff. They came from all walks of life, from the Commonwealth countries as well as all over the British Isles. All the WAAF, as stated before, were volunteers but so were many of the men, not all were conscripted. The ground crews that served on the flight line did so in inadequate protective clothing and the pay was not good for the hours they put in. The War did not stop at weekends, Christmas or bank holidays.

Mr. E.G. England was a Cpl. Fitter in 1943/44 at Wickenby and is now (1998) nearing eighty. Before employment in Bomber Command he was on 266 Fighter Squadron in the Battle of Britain and saw action in the landings in North Africa later on. He still remembers what life was like on a front line bomber squadron:

> "I was with 626 during the Battle of Berlin and was on 'C' Flight 12 Squadron that became 'A' Flight 626, moving to the other side of the airfield. Being ground staff on a bomber squadron was not very exciting. The work was mainly routine, getting aircraft ready for flying, I've had a few unofficial trips in them, then service and repair to the aircraft's Form 700 (aircraft fitness for flight document) requirements. One bit of excitement I had was an unofficial trip over Holland to drop food. The Lancaster was a good aircraft to work on and of course you can get attached to them and your favourite crew. Time off usually meant a trip to Lincoln or the local village pub for a few pints. I also played football for the Station. I had my wife with me for a few weeks staying at a cottage near the railway station that helped".

Still with aircraft, Mr. England left the Royal Air Force after the War and became a Planning Engineer working for British Aerospace for thirty years at their factory at Brough in Yorkshire.

Upon the ground crews technical skills, dedication and pride in the job the lives of the aircrew relied and therefore they could not afford the luxury of making a mistake as in some other professions. Once the bomber had taken off it was too late to right a wrong or remember something that was forgotten. Bomber Command had a tremendous task, which was not always appreciated by historians and politicians after the War – a task that could not have been accomplished without the professionalism of the Command's ground crews.

626 Squadron 'A' Flight Groundcrew
(left to right) top row: Stoneman, Batchelor, Tunley, ???, Agar, Christmas, Peg, Smith, Miley, Duxbury, Mathews, Wilkins. Second row: Moxley, Hastings, Jones, Wood, Mullen, Clarke, McCabe, Newall, Milbury, Skeling, Excell.
Third row: Sgt Cranidge, Sgt Hughes, F/S Booker, F/Lt Downs, W/O Bull, Sgt Sarfas, Sgt Asprey, Sgt Tregunna. *Front row*: Jakes, Barson, Cpl Forney, Cpl England, Cpl Cottey, ???, LAC Orrall, Cpl Carter.

On the 29th January after returning from the raid to Berlin the Command's crews were given a stand down for the next twenty-four hours. Although the day started fair it became cloudy with haze near the ground over the Lincolnshire countryside.

The only flying carried out over enemy occupied Europe was by twenty-two Mosquitos on a nuisance raid to Duisburg and to a flying bomb site in Northern France. The next day 446 Lancasters, 82 Halifaxes and 12 Mosquitos were brought to readiness for yet another raid on Berlin.

Take off at Wickenby was after five o'clock in the early evening with a return about midnight. This time ME584 managed to take off without incident unlike the previous night, F/O. Breckenridge again as its captain. For this crew the trip was to be one of tragedy and valour.

A maximum effort was called by Command for this night but the older marks of Halifax were left behind. The northern route to the target was chosen again but a little more to the south crossing Schleswig Holstein and out over Kieler Bucht. When south of Lolland Island the Force was to turn south-east and head straight for the Berlin target the same as the previous raid. After bombing they would turn and fly straight across Germany and Holland avoiding the Ruhr industrial area to the south. Conditions were ideal for operations in England but thick cloud covered most of Europe and with the cloud came icing conditions to encumber the defending night-fighters. The moon was waxing and this was to be the last raid before the two-week moonlight period. As this was the third raid on Berlin in four nights the crews were looking forward to the next two weeks or so off operations.

When the bomber stream came up on the coastal Freya long range radar screens the Germans thought it was another minelaying diversion. Also they did not think that Berlin was the target and that the northern route would be used again. Consequently, the Night-fighter Arm was slower to respond than usual, eventually assembling their twin engine aircraft south of Bremen and near the mouth of the River Elbe, still some miles away from the bomber stream. The bombers got to within seventy miles of Berlin before the night-fighters got in amongst them in force. Two thirds of the bombers shot down this night met their fate approaching, at or leaving the target. There was a small diversion raid to Braunschweig by five Mosquitos but they were not taken notice of.

At the target there was 10/10ths cloud, the Pathfinders were using 'Wanganui' sky-marking as well as target indicators on the ground. Zero hour was between 2013 and 2027Hrs The marking was well concentrated and even after the first five minutes of the attack good fires were beginning to get a hold. F/Sgt Higgs piloting JB595 reported large fires and smoke spiralling up through the cloud to 14,000 feet or more. S/Ldr Spiller who was pilot of LL775, his bomb aimer finding a green target indicator to aim at, saw a very large explosion to the west of the target area at 2017Hrs JB646 arrived late and bombed the estimated position of the red and green sky-markers at 2038Hrs from 21,000 feet. The pilot, F/Sgt Torrance and his bomb aimer saw a good and well concentrated fire-glow below the clouds with smoke now rising to 18,000 feet. Of course his gunners would deliberately avert their eyes from the scene below so not to ruin their night vision. Fighter flares were being dropped and therefore there were night-fighters about.

For ME584 the long haul to Berlin started just after five o'clock, the watery winter sun having gone down some time previous. Although the Lancaster flew through some of the most heavily defended airspace in Occupied Europe and Germany it arrived over the target unmolested by night-fighters or Flak. Luck was not to hold out for very long. On the actual bomb run when the aircraft was being held straight and level, it was found by an unidentified night-fighter. At the time fighter flares were being dropped and there was the glow from the underside of the clouds for the Lancaster to be silhouetted against.

The fighter's first attack raked the bomber from nose to tail killing the wireless operator Sgt Hall. Both gunners, rear gunner Sgt Schwartz and mid-upper P/O Baker, were hit and left wounded and unconscious. The Lancaster was hit extensively damaging hydraulics and oxygen systems, the bomb doors, which were still open for the bomb run and would not close. To the rear the elevators and rudders were damaged and in the cockpit the pilot's instruments were either inoperative or smashed. Some electrical cables caught fire and burnt out which included the intercom circuits but worse of all, one of the fuel tanks was punctured causing high-octane petrol to pour out into the slipstream. One of two things could have happened at this point. Either the petrol would ignite and that would be the end of ME584 or the petrol would react chemically with the material the tank was made of and 'Self-seal'. Luckily, fate chose the latter.

After taking evasive action, the crew continued on with the bomb run from 20,000 feet but since both gunners were out of action, no warning came when the fighter came in for the second attack with a five second burst of machine gun and cannon fire. Thrown about in their cramped compartments during the evasive action could not have been worse for the wounded gunners but once again the fighter hauled round for a third attack from 400 yards out. This time, apart from inflicting more damage on the aircraft and its systems, W/O Meek the navigator was severely wounded in the chest by one bullet and another struck his left shoulder blade in his back. The pilot, F/O Breckenridge, faired better when a bullet grazed his leg.

Meanwhile, bomb aimer F/O Poushinsky still managed to bomb a concentration of red and green sky-markers in the middle of it all at 20:27hrs. W/O Meek, despite his wounds causing loss of blood and a lot of pain and with most of his navigational aids and other supporting systems shot to pieces or burnt out, continued to work out the course home. By now the mid-upper gunner was recovering and in a better shape than his comrade at the back, then the fighter came in for a forth and mercifully a last attack. This time the mid-upper turret rear and side panels were shot out, P/O Baker avoiding the splinters. With much skill the pilot took evasive action when he saw tracer with no warning from the rest of the crew and in complete intercom silence. Once more the Lancaster was hit and so was W/O Meek. P/O Baker managed to get Sgt Schwartz out of his rear turret and take over- where the rear gunner crawled to the rest bed and collapsed again. P/p. Baker, now in the rear turret, had no oxygen, the heated suit was inoperative and the turret had to be moved manually as there was no hydraulic pressure to operate it.

Throughout the combat W/O Meek stayed at his navigating table plotting and checking the course home with what aids and systems that were left to him. He was in great pain and weak with loss of blood. Later it was found that one of the bullets had only just missed his heart. He did not complain or ask to be relieved from his duties, he felt he had a job to do and that was to guide the others home. On crossing the enemy coast it was found that the Lancaster was only three miles north of correct track. Flying over the North Sea the aircraft suffered another electrical fire that was quickly put out. On reaching England they prepared for an emergency landing at RAF Docking but a lot of the systems were shot up and the undercarriage would not come down. After making sure the rest of the crew had taken up crash positions,

F/O Breckenridge skilfully brought ME584 in for a belly landing along Docking's runway, causing no further injury to his crew. All other 626 Squadron Lancasters were to return safely to Wickenby except one.

W/O Meek and Sgt Schwartz were both taken to the RAF Hospital at Ely, while P/O Baker received treatment at Docking's medical section. After a rest, the remaining crew returned to Wickenby. For staying at his duty station and navigating ME584 home while having been wounded twice and with most of the navigating systems and aids burnt out or shot to pieces, W/O Meek was awarded the Conspicuous Gallantry Medal on 9th February 1944. He was the only man from 626 Squadron to be awarded it this rarely-awarded medal.

The CGM was first instituted in the Crimean War in 1855, for acts of valour by Senior Non-Commissioned Officers (SNCOs) of the Royal Navy and Marines. Until then, the Army had the Distinguished Conduct Medal for SNCOs, but the Navy had no such equivalent. The Victoria Cross was not introduced until 1856. The same problem arose when servicemen, not in the Royal Navy, took to the air in battle. Available to RAF Officers was the Distinguished Service Order for extreme acts of gallantry under enemy fire but no equivalent for their SNCOs. This was put right by a recommendation by the Air Council on 13th August 1942. On 10th November 1942 the CGM was extended to the RAF and Army flying units by Royal Warrant, approved by King George V. In the following year on 7th January 1943, an Air Ministry Order was issued to Commands seeking airmen eligible for the Medal. The first was awarded in February 1943 and the last awarded to an Australian airman in the jungles of Vietnam in December 1968. Only 110 airmen have received the CGM (Flying), second only in status to the Victoria Cross.

W/O Meek recovered from his wounds and returned to finish his operational tour with 626 Squadron, later gaining a Commission. W/O Richard 'Jack' Meek was not a young man by aircrew standards, being thirty-three years old. He hailed from Vancouver in Canada, joining the Royal Canadian Air Force in 1941, arriving in England with many of his fellow countrymen after navigation training. August 1st 1944 saw him as a Pilot Officer and being recommended for a Distinguished Flying Cross, having completed 28 operations over enemy occupied Europe.

There were no photographs brought back from this raid by the bombers, the clouds over Berlin being too thick but with the reported explosions, the glow of the raging fires below the clouds and later reconnaissance, it was deduced that this was the third successful raid in a row and all in less than a week. So many dwellings, industrial premises and other important buildings were being severely damaged and destroyed each night that accurate records could not be kept up by the Berlin authorities. The toll of important and public buildings hit on this and the other two nights read as follows: The West Berlin Power Station, six gasworks where three of them were totally inoperative, the underground train depot at Krezburg destroying nearly 100 pieces of rolling stock and damaging over 200 more, a Luftwaffe barracks and the Leibstandarte barracks. (Hitler's personal bodyguard was drawn from these troops.) The list goes on to include two district town halls, the Charlottenburg Opera House, the 3erlin University, three main bridges, five embassies, six Hospitals and a prison in Moabat. On this day, 30th January, eleven years before in 1933, Hitler came to power. Bomber Command had marked the anniversary well.

Thirty-three aircraft did not return this night, all Lancasters except a RCAF Halifax, eight of the Lancasters were from the

Pathfinder Force. 193 airmen were killed and fifty-three were captured as prisoners of war. One of the Lancasters that was posted missing in action was 626 Squadron's ME587. With F/O Wilkinson as pilot, it took off From Wickenby at 17:18hrs and was never heard of again. ME587 was never found so it must be supposed that it crashed in the North Sea, the Baltic or the Kieler Bucht between Schleswig Holstein and Denmark. All seven members of the crew had been together since training on 1662 Heavy Conversion Unit and arrived on 626 Squadron on the first day of the Battle of 3erlin, 18th November 1943. Because the crew have no known grave, they are remembered on the panels of the Royal Air Force Memorial at Runnymede.

10. Two Weeks Off!

The bright moon period brought a welcome stand down for the next fourteen days and nights. By the end of January, the aircrews were physically and mentally tired out but with the satisfaction that the last three raids on Berlin had gone better than the previous ones. The ground crews had done well too, keeping the Lancasters serviceable night after night. With hard work came the rewards. Although there were a few cross-country training flights and night landing practice for few crews, rest and recreation was the order for most people at Wickenby for the next couple of days. On the 2nd February Wickenby played football against teams from nearby Ludford Magna and Faldingworth, also bomber stations. Not all were relaxing however, as the crews of W4990 and W4967 were on training flights that day. After the work was over there was a dance in the WAAF Canteen in the evening.

At Wickenby, as on other stations, the WAAF lived separately from the airmen. Their accommodation was a collection of Nissen huts and a canteen out in the countryside just to north of the village of Holton and half a mile east of the airfield. The girls were very popular, working alongside their male counterparts in all trades except of course aircrew. On the squadrons they shared the same weather and hangars when working on aircraft with high octane fuel and live bombs on board as the airmen. They also shared the same relief with the ground crews when the aircrews came back and the sorrows when they did not. For an evening's entertainment off the Station there was not much in the way of a variety in places to go, noisy local pubs, the NAAFI canteen or a cinema many miles away in Lincoln. Dances were popular and held frequently in the Station canteens and surrounding village halls.

Jean Hawkins was a Corporal MT Driver at RAF Wickenby who met her husband while serving there. After fifty-four years she still remembers:

"I was posted to Wickenby in 1942 when the station was first opened and I recall that the construction work had not been fully completed so we all had to deal with a lot of mud. Having previously stationed at Binbrook, a peacetime station with all its 'Spit and polish', the change was a cultural shock but it was great fun with great deal of camaraderie.

The WAAF were accommodated on a site about half a mile from the main camp where we were issued with bicycles for transport back and forth to the MT yard as well as for recreational purposes. We lived in Nissan huts, with ten to twelve girls per hut, but there were few facilities except for an iron stove in the centre of the hut and an ablutions block on the site for washing etc. Meals were served in the Airmens' Mess on the main station site and I remember well a frequent high tea menu of cheese and potato pie, which we attempted to improve by liberal dowsing of Daddy's brown sauce.

Once a week the girls had a 'domestic night' when we were confined to camp and required to polish the brown lino on the hut floors, do our laundry and other domestic chores. It was fortunate for the girls in my hut that one of the other drivers had contact with a Chinese laundry in Leeds where she sent all our detachable shirt collars to be later returned, laundered to perfection, very stiff and shiny.

A great deal of our leisure time was spent in the NAAFI or going to one of the local pubs with friends, usually the nearby

186

*White Hart or the Adam and Eve at Wragby with sometimes a
visit to the cinema at Lincoln by the camp liberty bus when
funds permitted. There were also camp dances from time to time
and very infrequent variety shows put on by airmen and women,
maybe two such shows in my stay. Generally we had to be back
on site by 22:00hrs each day (except when on duty) but were
given late passes on two days per week when we were allowed to
stay out until 23:59hrs. We were nearly always short of money
and I well remember one occasion when it was only possible for
me to go to the cinema with a friend using a foreign coin, which
I had been given as a shilling in change. The coin was used
with great foreboding and equally great relief when it was accepted, unknowingly, by the cashier.*

*The Transport Section was indeed an extremely busy place,
especially at times when flying operations were being prepared.
It was commonplace for young girl drivers to be required to drive
vans, staff cars, twenty-four seat buses, lorries up to three tons
and the like. Such a variety of vehicles and even wider variety of
tasks including taking crews to their planes at the dispersal
points around the airfield and collecting them on their return.
My husband was a bomb aimer with 626 Squadron at the time
and it was whilst driving a crew bus that I met him. My abiding
memory of this duty is of the unfailing cheerfulness of the young
men as they went out to their planes amid lots of laughter and
repartee, many carrying mascots, some with bits of informal
dress and in some cases little rituals to be carried out before take
off. When collecting them on return laughter had been replaced
by extreme tiredness and quiet perhaps hiding concern for
friends who were late or would not return. These collections were
often performed in darkness, with hooded lights on our vehicles
and I personally found it very frightening to be driving around
the same perimeter tracks as the returning bombers as, at times,*

they appeared to be perilously close and one hoped that the dimmed rear lights could be seen from the planes.

Another task I remember was transporting bombs from the bomb dump at Norton Lindsay. Generally girl drivers transported bombs up to 250 pounds and the airmen the larger bombs up to 4,000lbs. The journey passed through Lincoln, northwards up a steep hill where it was a great relief to reach the top. Despite all the drama and excitement, of a kind, life was generally made up of a lot of mundane events and many memories are buried in the past".

Jean eventually married her bomb aimer who, unlike many of his fellows, survived the war. They both now live in Exeter, but once a year they make the journey north to the annual Wickenby Register reunion to meet old Squadron friends like Paddy Grove. She too was a driver, an LACW. Although having more to do with 12 Squadron, she still remembers what Wickenby was like, having served there from 1943 to 1946.

"I suspect that the life of a WAAF driver was much the same on either of the squadrons at Wickenby, I think most of us were of the opinion that we had the best job of all. There were plenty of rules and regulations of course (largely ignored) but we had a fair amount of freedom. We drove our crews out to their aircraft and then hopefully drove them back again for their de-briefing. We cheered with them when they finished their tours and wept over those who did not come back. They were all around the same age as us; too young to die.

There were a few options for off-duty time, a favourite haunt being the White Hart at Lissington, our local pub. Then there was the camp cinema or the NAAFI, which was probably considered rather tame. On days off (afternoons really) we went on the liberty coach to Lincoln, where we had tea in a café and visited a 'posh' cinema for a change. (The films were good at the camp cinema but the seats left much to be desired!) We very rarely went into a pub in Lincoln, there wasn't really much time before catching the bus back to camp.

The White Hart at Lissington, as it was during WW2.

On Saturday evenings we often cycled to Wragby to the weekly dance. We were nearly all into dancing in those days... not the sort of thing that passes for dancing these days but real cheek-to-cheek stuff. Ah, nostalgia!

We lived in Nissen huts; my bed was near the stove, which obligingly glowed red hot if properly stoked up. I am amazed that my bed did not go up in flames at times, but since I was, and still am, a chilly mortal, I really appreciated the warmth. We had a coke allowance and I seem to remember crawling under wire somewhere to pinch a few pieces of real coal to get the stove started ... but perhaps we should draw a veil over that strictly forbidden activity!

The bath huts were a short walk from the living quarters. It was jolly cold in the winter, no heat in there of course, just wooden duckboards on bare concrete floors. Looking back, I am amazed I did not remain filthy for the duration. The mere memory of it makes me shudder. The water was hot though ... bliss ... unless of course one fell asleep and awoke in a lukewarm bath.

It was not a very exciting life, but we thought it was at the time, and I would not have missed it for the world."

The White Hart at Lissington – 50 years on.

Another trade that came in close contact with the aircrews were the people that looked after them in their messes from she domestic and personal point of view. Officers were assigned servants to tend their needs from tidying rooms and cleaning uniforms to bringing them a cup of tea first thing in the morning.

Sadly when the aircrew officer did not return from a raid it was their job to gather his kit together, with probably the Squadron Adjutant, for forward shipment to his text of kin. In the Royal Air Force they are called batmen and batwomen but although not belonging to a technical trade they were no less important. One such lady was Dorothy Stilwell, who was an LACW Officers Mess Batwoman at Wickenby. She worked at the Officers Mess at No. 6 Site just south of she airfield near the hamlet of Fuinetby.

"I came to Wickenby in 1942/3 I believe it was. Being there for two-and-half years I saw 626 start and was there when it finished. I met a WAAF called Daisy Blythman and we worked together. I was around twenty and Daisy was twenty-four. We remained friends all through and although she got married we still kept in touch till she died about sixteen years ago.

We did get some laughs (and shed a few tears). One incident was with a S/Ldr Gould of 12 Squadron. Daisy and I asked him to take us up on a trip. After a lot of aggravation, he did and we went all over Lincoln. I shall never forget it, although he told us never to tell a soul and we didn't. Daisy sat on the engineer's seat and I stood behind the pilot hanging on like mad. The cathedral looked a sight from the sky, we always treasured that memory. Although we were attached to 626 and worked on 6 Site, I guess somehow we came to speak to S/Ldr Gould and his crew. I believe later he was killed, such a waste of life.

We liked our job and the aircrews were wonderful and always treated us with respect. One little incident always sticks in my mind. Often when we woke the crews up and they were very sleepy, we would say, "You will die in that bed!"

On this occasion the reply was, I believe he was a Canadian, "I can't think of a better place!"

They called us 'Gert and Daisy'[7] – well I am a Londoner and Daisy came from Mansfield in Nottinghamshire.

We used to cycle from '6 Site' every night, home to the WAAF Site and our Nissan hut. One night Daisy and I walked into the hut and shouted "Attention!" but the girls in the hut yelled "Shut up you two…" Blow me, the other door opened at the end and there was a WAAF Officer! She didn't know how to stay sober faced and we could have fell flat! When the WAAF Officer went out we all laughed and I daresay she did too…"

Dorothy now lives alone by the sea in Essex but still writes to old wartime friends and enjoys visits by her family and grandchildren.

On the 3rd February Wickenby played another station, RAF Kelstern, at rugby and won by 29 points to nil. The 4th to 13th February was a stand down period from major operations for the whole of Bomber Command except for a few units. Small flights of Mosquitos roamed Germany far and wide, dropping bombs on industrial cities and generally keeping the inhabitants awake. Meanwhile Stirlings and Halifaxes carried out minelaying duties from the Baltic to the Bay of Biscay. No.3 Group Stirlings, now exempt from operations over Germany on most raids, were gainfully employed dropping secret agents and arms supplies to Resistance groups in the occupied countries. Only four aircraft were lost in this period. The Germans were also busy in Berlin, clearing away the rubble and digging out the hundreds of bodies. In this month of February 1944, the Armaments Chief of the Luftwaffe, Generaloberst Erhard Milch, was heard to encourage his staff to see the destruction in Berlin for themselves. It was his

---

[7] Two comediennes called 'Gert and Daisy' were a popular music-hall act during and after the war.

department that supplied the night-fighters to the Luftwaffe. Ten more raids like those on Berlin in late January, he estimated, would finish off the city.

Back at Wickenby there was more training for the raids to come in the continuation of the Battle. Lectures were given by crew members to enlighten others in their crew duties. On 6th February a station self help scheme was started where all worked on a road widening project from the Officer's Mess to No.3 Domestic Site. For the next week it was back to flying training, starting the next day for the crews of EE133, W4967 and W4990 followed by fighter affiliation exercises, more lectures and finishing up with a Command 'Bullseye' exercise on the 11th. The previous afternoon, the 10th, the whole station had a 'stand to' alert where the personnel 'defended' the airfield. In reality, much of the defence would be left to the newly formed Royal Air Force Regiment.

On 11th August 1942 after the Battle of Britain, the fall of Crete and Greece, the defence of Malta and with the Desert Air Force in North Africa, a high-level meeting was convened by the Air Officers Commanding of all Commands and Air Members for Personnel and Training. They came to the conclusion that although ground crews did their best at defending their airfields, they were not mentally or physically equipped to fight battle hardened paratroopers, as in Crete, who were well equipped and determined to capture their airfield. Although there were many acts of courage by the ground crews, their trades were technical with only a minimal amount of small arms experience in a Basic Training Camp on joining the RAF and afterwards for couple of days a year when posted to a squadron. After discussing the defensive capabilities of the average airman in defending his airfield under attack, he was found to be lacking, although through no real fault of his own. To defend the airfields The RAF Regiment was formed soon afterwards. They have been the RAF's infantry and anti-aircraft gunners ever since being distinguished by their 'RAF Regiment' badge on the shoulders of their- uniform. They still do the same job today but with automatic rifles, guided missiles and light tanks.

11. Back to 'The Big City'

The weather on the 12th February was not good for flying being cloudy, hazy and visibility down to half a mile, which was just as well. The Officers Mess celebrated the award of the Distinguished Flying Cross to Pilot Officers Curry, Hutchinson, Drew and Oliver. The next day at 0945, Operations ordered nine Lancasters to be readied for a raid on Berlin that night. The stand down and training was over. By four o'clock in the afternoon the operation was cancelled. The next day began with low cloud and fog coming later, needless to say there were no operations called for that day. The following day, 15th February, the Squadron was back on the line with a raid on Berlin ordered for that night and this time 'Ops were on'.

In the late afternoon in Yorkshire, Lincolnshire and East Anglia nearly 900 Lancasters, Halifaxes and Mosquitos were starting their engines and preparing for take off. This was to be the largest raid on the German Capital yet, in fact the largest non-1000 bomber raid on Germany since 23rd May 1943. The Command now had more than 500 Lancasters in front line squadrons at its disposal. Also the aircraft this night were carrying over 2600 tons of bombs between them, another record.

The route to Berlin was once again over Denmark, The Baltic and an approach from the north to Berlin. Time on target was between 21:13 and 21:35 Hrs. The route home after the attack was west over Central Germany and Holland with a small dogleg north to avoid the guns of the Ruhr industrial area. In support of the Main Force, 23 Mosquitos were to bomb five night-fighter bases in Holland using the accurate Oboe electronic blind bombing aid. As diversions, forty-three Stirlings and four Path-finder Lancasters were to lay mines in Kiel Bay. Proceeding the Main Force was a flight of Mosquitos to drop target indicators, bombs and fighter flares on Berlin followed some time later by a force of twenty-four Pathfinder Lancasters simulating the start of an attack on Frankfurt-on-Oder, some fifty miles to the east. Flying home, the bomber stream would separate into two halves, two streams flying about forty miles apart.

The weather that Tuesday was cloudy to start with but becoming fair in the afternoon. To meet the time on target the Wickenby force took off in the late afternoon, 626 Squadron fielding eleven Lancasters.

The Pathfinders and the Main Force from all Groups involved met over the North Sea off the Danish coast north of Heligoland Island and continued over Denmark to the German Baltic coast. By this time of course they were attracting the attention of the Luftwaffe Nachtjagd, the night-fighter force. The night-fighter airfields in Belgium, Holland and Northern Germany were brought to readiness for the pending night battle, although the minelaying operation in Kiel Bay was ignored. The pilots were patient to wait for the more important prey that they knew was just over the horizon. Action took place from the Baltic coast right up to the outskirts of Berlin, the flak perimeter, where the night-fighters were forbidden to fly further. Just getting to Berlin the stream suffered at least twenty casualties shot down, mostly stragglers at the rear.

Berlin was covered in thick cloud, tops to 15,000 feet in places, bomb aimers seeing nothing of the city except the sky-markers raining down on top of it. The mid-upper turret of W4990 had not worked since after half an hour of leaving the English coast, likewise the starboard engine had been giving trouble from that same point. F/Sgt Welford as pilot came in on the third wave where in his opinion the green target indicators were scattered but his bomb aimer dropped the bombs on four close together at 21:22Hrs from 22,000 feet. A few minutes later W/O Henty came in piloting ED623 at 23,000 feet. His bomb aimer identified the target by the green-red sky-markers up ahead but when the Lancaster arrived over the target there was only two of them to aim at. It was satisfying though to see a bright red glow below the clouds. ME589 was one of the last of 626 Squadron's Lancasters over the target area with F/L. Wright as pilot. Although the bomb aimer found a shortage of sky-markers by this time he managed to aim the bomb load in the centre of a cluster of four.

806 Lancasters and Halifaxes dropped over 2600 tons of bombs on the city, mainly in the western and southern areas. There was more explosive dropped this night than on Hamburg that caused the firestorm in the summer of 1943. Included in the loads dropped were 470 4,000-lb 'cookies' and 15 huge 8,000-pounders, the whole raid lasting only thirty-nine minutes. Over 3,000 fires were started, nearly 600 of them classed as large causing extensive damage and destruction to all kinds of domestic and industrial property. One was the vast Siemensstadt electronics and electrical complex to the north-west of the city. Flak was quite extensive but it was estimated that only three bombers met their fate over Berlin. The twenty-four Lancasters that flew to Frankfurt-on-Oder as a diversion failed to draw any night-fighters away from the main attack but they evaded the flak defences of that city and all returned home safely.

The attackers headed south for about thirty miles, joined once again by the night-fighters, then turned west for the Dutch coast where for a welcome change the bombers had a tailwind from the east to speed them home. The Luftwaffe wisely held some of the fighters on the ground until the stream left Berlin. Before the bombers reached the North Sea nearly fifteen were shot down. One of these was 626 Squadron's JB595, crashing near Erfurt, sixty miles south-west of Leipzig and way south of track. The captain and pilot, F/Sgt Jacques and five of his crew survived to become prisoners of war. Records are conflicting about the fate of the flight engineer Sgt Phillips. True that he is buried in the Berlin War Cemetery but whether he died of his wounds as a prisoner of war or when JB595 was shot down it is not clear.

JB595 was the only casualty on 626 Squadron this night. Being crippled or short of fuel, two aircraft from other squadrons were abandoned over the North Sea and tragically, three aircraft crashed in England in sight of their airfields killing thirteen out of the twenty-one aircrew. All the 626 Squadron Lancasters that crossed the English coast landed safely around midnight leaving the eleventh aircraft of the Squadron lost in the Battle of Berlin burning in Germany.

The final toll was 43 bombers lost plus five abandoned or crashed in England, 265 airmen killed, 54 taken prisoner of war, five managing to escape and evade the clutches of the German authorities. And on the other side, apart from the damage and destruction already mentioned, 320 were killed in Berlin, including some foreign workers and a POW. Some 260 or so people were known to be buried under the rubble the next morning. By now, the middle of February 1944, unless they had really essential duties, many Berliners had evacuated to other parts of Germany, hence the low casualty figures compared with those of six months previously. Many industrial premises were wrecked, but like the people, much of the work had been relocated out of the city.

By virtue of the number of bombers that had reached the city and the tonnage of the explosives dropped, it was the heaviest raid on Berlin in the war so far. Although some bomb loads were wasted, having been dropped outside the city up to thirty miles away, the raid was still regarded as a medium success.

After the 15/16th February raid, Sir Arthur Harris attempted to follow it up with another the next night but his plans were thwarted by the weather. Over Europe it was not so important, the bombers had improved H2S radar and navigational systems but on return, bad weather with fog and snow had proved in the past to be disastrous.

On 16th February at ten o'clock in the morning a message came through on the Operations Room teleprinter for a raid on Berlin that night. Ten Lancasters were made ready but it was cancelled just after three o'clock in the afternoon. The next day the same thing happened. The day after that, exasperated crews trudged back to their accommodation at half-past-four in the afternoon where this time the raid was cancelled due to snow, some of it falling at Wickenby.

For some time now the Americans and British had been practicing what Churchill called in a speech in Parliament as the 'Round the clock' bombing of Germany, as agreed at the Casablanca Conference in February 1943. The American 8th Air Force did not have a suitable escort fighter to fly with the Fortresses and Liberators to targets in Eastern Germany in daylight. The entry of the Mustang into combat over Europe was still some weeks away. The main adversary of the bombers, RAF by night USAAF by day, was the Luftwaffe fighter. The American bombers, although heavily armed compared with the RAF's Lancasters and Halifaxes. were suffering from appalling losses in some of their daylight raids. On one such raid every B17 Fortress belonging to a squadron of the 90th Bomb Group was shot down. An attempt at an answer came as a joint effort between the 8th Air Force and RAF Bomber Command to attack the German aircraft industry, especially fighter production, in the remaining days of February 1944 in what the Americans called 'Big Week'. Bomber Command shared the targets with the 8th Air Force such as Augsburg where Messerschmidts were made and the Schweinfurt ball-bearing factories where the Americans had been before and many had not come back. On Saturday 19th February bomber Command ordered a 'Maximum Effort' for a raid that night on the aircraft assembly plants of Leipzig, about ninety-five miles to the south-west of Berlin.

The route to Leipzig was designed to cause maximum confusion to the German fighter controllers with no less than four turning points before reaching the target. At one point it would look as if the Force would be heading straight for Berlin again. After leaving Mablethorpe behind the stream would rendezvous about seventy miles north of the Frisian Islands and head across the northern tip of Holland and into Germany as if going for Hanover. Twenty-five miles north of Osnabruck they would turn to port and head east for Berlin but from about fifty miles to go to that city they were to swing right and attack Leipzig from the north. Fifteen Mosquitos would fly with them but go straight on for a diversion raid to Berlin. Earlier, as the bomber stream was entering enemy airspace, 45 Stirlings and four Pathfinder Halifaxes would try to draw some of the night-fighters away with a minelaying operation in Kiel Bay. Mosquitos would attack night-fighter airfields in Holland beforehand, which was now commonplace before a raid.

Twelve Lancasters on 626 Squadron were made ready for take off between eleven o'clock and midnight, zero hour or time on target was around four o'clock in the morning of 20th February. For the 823 Lancasters, Halifaxes and Mosquitos the planned route was good but for one fact, the speed and direction of the forecast winds that had been given to the navigators at briefing had been overestimated.

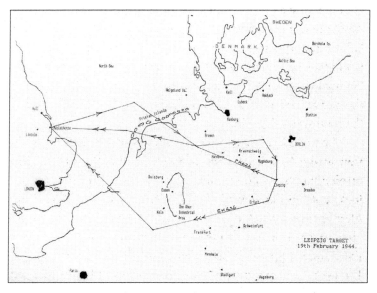

Map 3. Target Leipzig, 19.2.44.

The calculation to determine the track that they were to fly incorporated a steady head wind from the east. In actual fact the wind was light from the north, which meant a tailwind going into the target. It was that simple fact that would cause the disaster to follow and make it easy for the Luftwaffe 'Tame Boar' operation that night. Soon after the take off, some of the more experienced navigators detected the correct wind and realised that the Force had taken off too early. Quickly a new track to the target had to be worked out, 'Doglegging' their way across Europe so as not to get to the target before the Pathfinders. Unfortunately many of the less experienced crews did arrive early which lead to the bomber stream being stretched out, consequently giving the German fighter controllers more time to direct the night-fighters into the attacking Lancasters and Halifaxes. Of the bombers that did arrive early many started to circle the target awaiting the Pathfinders, consequently, with disastrous results as many were shot down. When at last the markers were dropped, nearly 800 bombers tried to fly in and off load their bombs at once, with the inevitable collisions.

One Lancaster that did not make it very far was 626 Squadron's W4990. One hour forty-five minutes after take off the aircraft suffered a complete oxygen failure at 21,000 feet. From eighty-seven miles east of Spurn Head the crew had to turn back, the pilot, F/Sgt Welford landing W4990 just after- three o'clock in the morning with all the bombs still in the bomb bay.

Pilot F/Sgt Matheson and his crew had not been on the Squadron long, all having been posted in from 1667 Conversion Unit on 2nd February. It is not certain how their Lancaster, ME589, met its fate but on the outward leg of their flight over the North Sea it crashed near the Dutch Frisian Islands. It was known that the bomber stream had been detected before reaching the Dutch coast and that night-fighters had been sent to intercept. Nothing was heard from the crew after- take off at 23:33 Hrs until a few months later. On 8th May the body of Sgt Bodycot was washed up on the shore of Schiermonnikog Island, one of the West Frisian Islands and was buried in the island's cemetery. He was the mid-upper gunner. A little to the east and over a month later the body of the bomb aimer, Sgt Mitton, was washed up on a beach at Ameland Island and was buried at the General Cemetery on the island. The other five were never found but they are remembered on a panel of the Runnymede RAF Memorial.

The rest of the stream carried on 'Doglegging' across the North Sea, Holland and Germany like JB559 with W/O Rew at the controls. This aircraft's crew were lucky, with most of the stream criss-crossing the track to eat up the time it was estimated that at least four bombers collided. Along the way Dornier Do17s were dropping fighter flares but it was known that at least one was shot down by a bomber's gunner. JB559's navigator calculated correctly the aircraft's new track to arrive on time, as on approaching the target at about 0350 Hrs the Pathfinders were marking it with red/green flares and red target indicators. Leipzig was covered in cloud, the red target indicators going straight through it. As JB559 was leaving the city at 23,000 feet the crew saw the glow of fires below the clouds. JB559 was shortly followed by ED424 in the third wave at 22,000 feet. This Lancaster, piloted by F/Sgt Lone, had been hit in the port wing by heavy flak in the Bremen-Hanover area at 02:47 Hrs but kept on flying. His crew noticed a German decoy target with lots of green and red target indicators after bombing the real one at 04:08 Hrs.

On leaving Leipzig a new tactic was tried to further confuse the fighter controllers and protect the bombers on the way home. South of Leipzig the stream split up, half going back north-west over Northern Germany, the other half swinging south between The Ruhr and Frankfurt and out over Belgium and Southern Holland. Five Lancasters of 626 Squadron were to take the northern route and seven the southern.

About twenty-five miles south of Leipzig the stream, including the remaining ten Lancasters of 626 Squadron, turned and headed for home along their respective tracks, being attacked by twin and single engined night-fighters all the way to the enemy coast. Both gunners of LM393 could see good fires still raging at Leipzig from eighty miles away on the return journey. Being short of fuel, pilot Sgt Margetts had to land LM393 at RAF Bardney, the wheels touching the runway just before seven o'clock in the morning.

While 626 Squadron lost F/Sgt Matheson and all his crew the rest of the Command lost 77 more Lancasters and Halifaxes, 9.48% of the 823 bombers that were sent. The Americans bombed Leipzig the next day so a proper assessment of Bomber Command's effort could not be obtained by photographic re-connaissance. Over 960 Leipzig citizens were killed with nearly 51,400 made homeless by both raids. With the large number of dwellings destroyed it was assumed that the both raids were a success but at a terrible cost to Bomber Command.

With the largest loss rate of the War so far, three immediate shifts in policy came about. The first was that the Halifax Mks 2 and 5 would no longer be included in the Order of Battle for raids to Germany. Being inferior in performance to the Mk.3, their casualty rate was too high and the moral of their crews too low because of it. Secondly, because of the mistake of the fore-cast winds, in future and if the situation warranted it, the time on target could be moved while the bombers were on their way. When airborne, experienced navigators would check the wind and compare it to that given at briefing before take off. If differ-ent, Command would be advised by radio and time on target would be updated accordingly and broadcast to the crews in the air.

The third change was the most important of all. After fifteen raids on Berlin from the start of the Battle, 18th November 1943,

Sir Arthur Harris gave up the idea of 'Wrecking Berlin from end to end'. That does not mean that the Battle was lost, far from it. Many industries producing war material had been wrecked and large areas of the city laid to waste. Thousands of Germans were tied up in Berlin's defence and it was better that they stayed there than be available to meet our soldiers on the beaches of Normandy a few months later or to fight our Russian allies to the east. Many other factors caused Bomber Command to switch targets mainly as a necessity. There were many other industries that needed to be curtailed such as aircraft production, the synthetic oil plants and the U-Boat was still a menace. The time was nearing for the Command to start preparing the way for the Normandy invasion. In the coming months bombing rail, road and canal communications or anything that could move troops, vehicles and supplies would soon become top priority along with beach defences, gun emplacements and radar sites. Two new threats were just emerging at this time that were directly aimed at the civilian population of South-Eastern England, the V1 Flying Bomb and the V2 Rocket. Both needed to be stopped ideally at their launch sites in France although the VI could be shot down by anti-aircraft fire or a fast fighter. Of the V2 there was no defence, it had to stopped on the launch site or the storage and assembly area. Until overrun by allied troops only bombing by Bomber Command and the American 8th Air Force could achieve this.

12. Switching Targets

Bomber Command could not be active over every target every night. On the long nights of the winter months the Command's bombers had hit the industrial areas of the North and North-east of Germany like Stettin, Braunschweig, Magdeburg and Berlin fifteen times. The northern routes to the targets were patrolled by an ever-increasing efficient night-fighter force, the targets themselves being defended by radar assisted flak guns and searchlights. The losses were not beyond what Bomber Command could sustain or what was predicted in November 1943 but very near it. In the 1943/44 Winter campaign, firstly the Stirling was withdrawn from the Order of Battle over Germany and now after Leipzig, the earlier types of Halifaxes, with the Mk.III and their crews still soldiering on. The Battle was sapping the strength of the front line squadrons in aircraft and more important, crews. Aircraft were easier to replace than well trained experienced crews, which took time. The moral was still there for the Halifax crews but only just, the withdrawal Mk.IIs and Vs was just in time. The Lancaster squadrons on the other hand were faring better, the crews had great faith in their aircraft to do the job and bring them back safely. This could be put down to the superior performance of this magnificent bomber compared to the Halifax and Stirling. But even the Lancaster crews were getting tired of the long haul over cold and heavily defended Northern Germany night after night. If they were pushed to far there was the risk that they would not be fit for supporting the Allied armies when they waded ashore in Normandy in the coming June. So far, 626 Squadron had launched 242 sorties against Berlin and other targets since 18th November- 1943, when the Battle of Berlin had started. Seven Lancasters had been lost over Europe, two had crashed in England, one killing all the crew trying to land at Marham and at least two were at the bottom of the North Sea. Of the fifty-six airmen lost over Europe and the North Sea only seven were alive as prisoners of war in Germany.

After the Leipzig raid with its so many losses, it was decided that the industrial cities of Southern Germany would get some long overdue attention. The route across the English Channel, Northern France and up into Southern Germany spent less time over enemy occupied Europe and many miles south of the main night-fighter airfields. And this was the way nearly 600 bombers attacked Stuttgart on the night of 20th/21st February 1944.

On 626 Squadron, eleven Lancasters were made ready for a take off around midnight. During the day it had been cloudy with scattered wintry showers but by late evening the weather had improved with visibility good enough for operations throughout the Command. After take off these eleven joined 587 more bombers heading south for the English Channel instead of the usual Mablethorpe/North Sea route. Three were not to make it very far. The first casualty was five minutes after take off where F/Sgt Bennet's LL772 developed a fault in the rear- turret gun sight. His Lancaster could not land again unless it got rid of some weight, so out to the North Sea it flew where everything in the bomb bay was dumped except the 'Cookie', sixty-five miles east of Spurn Head from 5500 feet. LL772 landed back at Wickenby at nearly four o'clock in the morning. F/Sgt Welford, piloting W4990, got some way further, as far as Reading, where due to the crew's oxygen supply system failure at 17,000 feet they could not breathe properly. F/Sgt Welford quickly got the aircraft down to below 10,000 feet to prevent hypoxia killing his crew. Turning north-east across Eastern England the Lancaster headed out to the North Sea and dumped the bombs 100 miles north-east of Grimsby, then headed back home to land a few minutes before LL772.

The Force sped out over the English Channel leaving Dungerness behind. At the same time 132 bombers from the Operational Training Units and twenty-four from the front line squadrons reached their assigned objective, a point in the North Sea sixty-five miles north of Texel Island, and then turned back for home. Although this was a major training exercise, it was also a feint to draw off the Luftwaffe night-fighters from the Main Force to the south and as it will be seen, it seemed to have worked. Also as a diversion, seven Mosquitos were detailed to drop bombs on Munich. Once again, as common practice now, night-fighter airfields in Holland came under attack also by Mosquitos.

Two hours into the flight and sixty-five miles north-east of Paris, F/Sgt Lone's aircraft, LM393, became the third and final 626 Squadron Lancaster to drop out of the stream and return home. Over the Channel the rear gunner complained that his special heated suit was not working. On crossing the French coast he was found to have lost consciousness and all attempts to revive him failed. His oxygen supply was suspect and it was decided to turn back, re-crossing the English coast at Beachy Head. By losing height over the English Channel they managed to save him. To lighten the aircraft for landing an attempt was made to dump some of the fuel but it was found that the fuel jettison valve was stuck. There was no other alternative but to drop the bombs in the North Sea, which they did, except for the 'Cookie', at 0425 Hrs and 85 miles north-east of Grimsby. Forty minutes later LM393 landed back at Wickenby.

The bomber stream flew on over Northern France, Southern Germany and then turned a little east of north to attack the target. HK539, with Sgt Bladon as pilot, encountered a 'Wild Boar' Fw190 near Epinal in the north-eastern corner of France but survived the action. His Lancaster was carrying the electronic countermeasure 'Mandrel' which was meant to jam the German defence radar by transmitting on the same frequency. Although the weather en route was noted to be mainly clear and therefore ideal for night-fighter operations, especially for the 'Wild Boar' fighters, they were conspicuous by their absence for most of the time, although some were met in the Lake Constance area on the Swiss-German boarder. JB409, flown by F/Sgt Marriotte, was severely damaged by a Ju88 here but the Lancaster and its crew carried on into the attack. On approaching Stuttgart the thin cloud started to thicken, ending up to 8 to 10/10ths in places. There was a decoy target thirty-two miles west of Stuttgart as seen by HK539's crew at thirty minutes to time on target but it was ignored by this crew the rest of the attacking force.

The markers were scattered over the target and not concentrated. The green target indicators went straight through the cloud where only a few were seen on the ground but these were combined with red/green sky-markers above. Time on target was around 0400 Hrs. ED623, with W/O Henty as pilot, was in the third wave. His bomb aimer dropped the bomb load on three green target indicators at 0406 Hrs from 23,000 feet on a heading of 020 degrees magnetic. By this time into the attack they observed many fires below, especially south of the railway marshalling yards which was probably one of the aiming points. As the bombers were coming from the south these fires were most likely caused by what was technically known as 'Creep back'. There was a tendency for some crews to get rid of their bombs as soon as possible and get out of the target area as quickly as they could. About this time many crews reported later at debrief to have seen a tremendous explosion, the crew of Hk539 also seeing three large fires elsewhere as well as many small ones. W/O Gallagher, captain of W4967, reported seeing two green target indicators overshooting the main but loosely-concentrated markers by at least a mile. Looking down on the run up to the target, his bomb aimer saw many burning buildings through the gaps in the clouds.

The Stuttgart flak defences did not put up a very stiff barrage, as would a northern target and it was also noted that the night-fighter activity over the city was not as much as the crews were use to on previous raids. As the bomber stream turned for home, the fires could still be seen from 100 miles away, the rear gunner of HK539 seeing the glow from fifty miles further on from that. Although fighters were seen occasionally on the way to the enemy coast, none were to attack a 626 Squadron Lancaster this night, all eight landing safely around seven o'clock in the morning. But it was casualties of a different kind that the Squadron suffered this night where two of the aircrew had had enough of combat and could not take it any more. Unfairly, as we now know through the advancement of medical science, they were stripped of rank and posted away from Wickenby branded as having 'Lack of Moral Fibre'.

After the recent losses over Leipzig and the earlier Berlin raids, Bomber Command had a better night with only seven Lancasters and two Halifaxes failing to return. Sadly, another four Lancasters and a Halifax crashed in England nearing their bases. It was thought that the not so heavily defended southern route, the diversions by the Operational Training Units and the seven Mosquitos dropping large amounts of 'Window' on the way to and bombing Munich over 100 miles to the south-east, contributed to the low casualty figure. Most of Stuttgart was covered in cloud causing the bombing to become scattered. There were large concentrations of fires in two areas as seen by 626 Squadron crews but these were at least five miles apart in a line north-east to south-west. However, much damage was caused to the centre of Stuttgart and the north-east and north-west suburbs. To the north-east in the district of Feuerbach, the Bosch factory manufactured all kinds of electro-mechanical components for ships, aircraft and armoured and non-armoured vehicles. This very important complex in Germany's war effort was extensively damaged. In the civic section of Stuttgart the Parliament building of the region, the State Art Gallery, the State Theatre and the State Archives were all badly damaged. 125 citizens were killed in the raid and when digging in the rubble, 510 people were found to be injured.

On landing, the Wickenby Squadrons learnt that the rest of the day was a stand down from operations although three Lancasters from 626 Squadron's 'A' Flight and four from 'B' Flight were down for training exercises. The next day, twelve Lancasters were bombed up, fuelled and pre-flight inspected for a raid on Schweinfurt as ordered at 0955Hrs. By 1220hrs the target had changed to Frankfurt. A new tactic was to be tried this night where the Force was to be split, the first attack being at 2245Hrs and the remaining half of the Bomber Force attacking two hours later when the defenders thought it was all over for the night. As a diversion, a spoof attack was to be carried out on Stuttgart. At 1745Hrs a message came from Command and 1 Group Headquarters that the raid was off due to bad weather. Elsewhere 111 Halifaxes and Stirlings were recalled from a minelaying sortie to the North German coast.

The next day, 23rd February, was also a stand down for the Wickenby and 1 Group Squadrons from operations. Three new crews carried out training flights, Sgt Bowditch, F/Sgt Bernyk and Sgt Newton who were captains of HK539, JB559 and LL148 respectively for these flights. This night heralded a 'First' for Bomber Command. A new type of Mosquito with an enlarged bomb-bay and modified bomb-bay doors dropped the 4000-pound 'cookie' for the first time on an enemy target. The city of Dusseldorf being chosen for this debut.

One of the many problems that beset design engineers of machinery is the friction and wear of moving parts that come into contact with each other and how to deal with it. This problem has been in existence since the invention of the wheel and the shaft that it rotates on. Archaeology tells us that ancient wheelwrights made a crude bearing out of leather, which was soaked and lubricated with animal fat. For many centuries afterwards the shaft and wheel was lubricated with copious amounts of oil or grease to keep the two surfaces separate and running smoothly, which was quite acceptable for the horse drawn transport at the time. Luckily when the steam engine came along, which of course made of steel, mineral oil was available that had better lubricating properties. As engineering science progressed into this century the internal combustion engine and the electric motor took over many tasks. Machinery rotated faster as the means to propel it became more efficient and powerful. The old problem of friction and wear still remained but even more so. The development of more efficient lubricants only solved part of the problem. The solution came in the form of a bearing that reduced the bearing contact surfaces. The arrival of hardened alloy steel ball and roller bearings did this dramatically. Compared to ordinary plain bearings they are almost frictionless, need far less lubrication, little attention 'and when required can be changed easily. By WWII they were used in all kinds of engines, motors and machinery in ships, aircraft, vehicles and weapons.

The manufacturing process of ball and roller bearings employs a highly specialised branch of engineering working to extremely fine tolerances. The main centre for this industry in Germany in WWII was Schweinfurt although there were individual factories elsewhere but not many. One other was at Erkner to the south-east of Berlin but on the 23/24th December 1943, it will be recalled, four loads of miss aimed bomb loads all but demolished the plant causing much concern for Albert Speer, Germany's Armaments Minister.

On the night of 24/25 February 1944 a raid on Schweinfurt was ordered. Sir Arthur Harris had been specifically told to attack this target in support of 266 American USAAF B17s that bombed the factories the day before. It was the first time that Bomber Command had targeted Schweinfurt, which is sixty-five miles east of Frankfurt in Southern Germany. The tactic of sending two waves of bombers to hit the town two hours apart was also a 'first', the idea thought up for the cancelled Frankfurt raid two nights previously. 392 aircraft including fifteen from 626 Squadron, would attack first, then when it was hoped that the night-fighters would be on the ground refuelling and the defences thinking it was all over, another 342 bombers would arrive, two hours after the first wave. In support, nearly 180 aircraft from the Command training units were to fly in a stream over the North Sea towards the enemy coast. As another diversion, over 100 Stirlings and Halifaxes would be laying mines in Kiel Bay and the Kattegat. Once again Mosquito fighter-bombers would attack night-fighter airfields in Holland.

This was indeed a night of 'firsts' where Wickenby for the first time put thirty Lancasters in the air, fifteen from each squadron, for a raid with no cancelled take offs. It was also the first time that 626 Squadron's new Commanding Officer, W/Cdr Ross, was to fly operationally with his Squadron. He flew as second pilot for W/O Gallagher, the captain of LL772.

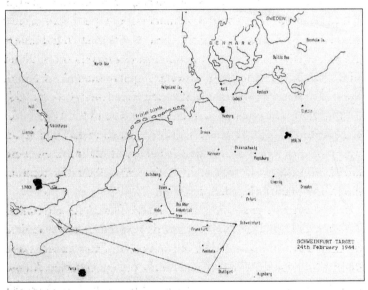

Map 4. Target Schweinfurt, 24,2,44.

Zero hour for the first wave to attack this target was 2305Hrs and to meet it take off time for 626 Squadron's Lancasters was just after six o'clock in the early evening. Once again the route took to the south, much the same as the last raid, crossing the enemy coast between Dieppe and the mouth of the Somme. From then on it was a straight line to a turning point between Strasbourg and Stuttgart where a sharp turn to port would bring the stream on a heading to the target. After bombing, the Force would carry

214

on for about another twenty miles and turn west, flying between Bonn and Koblenz to exit France at the same point as they came in; across the Channel to Beachy Head then Reading and Wickenby.

Not all of 626 Squadron's Lancasters reached the target or indeed saw the shores of England again. The night-fighter airfield at Metz in North-East France was headquarters of Nachtjagdgeschwader 4 of Luftflotte 3 (France), equipped with a few Me110s. 110 miles to the south-west was another night-fighter airfield at St Dizier. Here another Staffeln (squadron of about nine aircraft) belonging to Nachtjagdgeschwader 4, II/NJG4, operated the Me110 plus some Do217s. These two airfields straddled the flight path of the Bomber Force to the target. F/O Hutchinson DFC was piloting LL797 on this raid. The aircraft was shot down over North-East France and all the crew were killed. The flight would have been the last of their 30-operation tour if they had made it home.

All the crew except one had transferred from 12 Squadron on 7th November 1943, taking part in 626 Squadron's first raid to Modane three nights later. F/O Young, the bomb aimer, came from 460 Squadron stationed at Bimbrook, near Grimsby. All the crew started their operational tours in the summer of 1943. Sgt Bowditch was a young pilot who came to 626 Squadron from 31 Base on 19th February, five days before. He flew with his new crew on a training flight the day before the Schweinfurt raid. Policy dictated that a new captain was to carry out an operation with an experienced crew to 'get to know the ropes' before going with his own crew on a raid. That night, Sgt Bowditch was flying 'second dickey' with LL797 and died along with its crew when it was shot down. It does not require much imagination to discern the feelings of the six members of Sgt Bowditch's crew, who he had left behind at Wickenby, when he did not return.

The last resting place of F/O Hutchinson and his crew, with Sgt Bowditch, in the village church cemetery at Marsal, a tiny hamlet just east of Nancy in north-east France. Even in this remote area, The Commonwealth War Graves Commission tends the graves regularly. Nestling in a farming community, Marsal appears to be a very old village, surrounded by a circle of protective earthworks. It is obviously of some historic note as some of the very old and important buildings are being carefully restored. Below, the church as it is today, seen from across the fields.

All seven members of LL797's crew and Sgt Bowditch are buried in the village church cemetery at Marsal, a small hamlet twenty miles north-east of Nancy. It is quite feasible to assume that LL797 was shot down by a night-fighter belonging to either the Metz or the St Dizier airfields as the purpose of Nachtjag-dgeschwader 4 in Northern France and Belgium was to protect the southern route into German airspace.

The first leg of the route was covered without further incident for 626 Squadron Lancasters, the south of Europe being more lightly defended than the northern part. W/O Rew, flying JB559 at 20,000 feet, saw the Pathfinders opening the attack when his Lancaster still had twenty miles to go to the aiming point. There was only a slight haze or fog on the ground and no cloud for a change. Firstly a string of flares went down followed by green target indicators and finally red target indicators by the 'Back-ers-up' Pathfinders. Less than ten minutes later JB559 was over the target itself and dropped its bomb load at 2317Hrs. By that time the area below was well alight with many large fires getting a hold causing smoke to spiral up to 6000 feet or more.

At this time pilot Sgt Bladdon and his crew of HK539 saw a very large explosion on the ground. After the initial success of marking the target, some target indicators were seen to drop to the west of the aiming point and become generally scattered. Sgt Margetts and his crew of LM393 could see that the 'backers-up' and the first of the Main Force bombers were causing 'creep back' by the location of the bomb explosions and resulting fires. His bomb aimer dropped their bomb load in the centre of some red target indicators at 2319Hrs from 20,500 feet. The town's defences put up fairly intensive flak between 18-24,000 feet and searchlights were reported to be quite active in the northern side of the target. No attacks were made by night-fighters in fact none were seen by 626 Squadron crews over Schweinfurt.

The remaining fourteen Lancasters of 626 Squadron flew back over Southern Germany and Northern France, returning safely to Wickenby, landing after two o'clock in the early hours of 25th February encountering little flak over the French coast before crossing the English Channel.

Despite the reports of large fires, explosions and smoke the raid suffered from the target being undershot by the Pathfinder 'Backer-ups' shortly after the initial markers went down. This was compounded by the Main Force crews following behind, with they in turn undershooting, which caused the damage level to be disappointing. As for the ball bearing industry, it was found later that much of it had been moved to other parts of Germany to safeguard the supplies of this vital product. In the combined effort of the USAAF and Bomber Command over 360 citizens died. The idea of two separate raids, two hours apart to the same target was considered a good tactic that paid off. Twenty-two bombers were shot down out of 392 in the first wave, the second wave was not expected by the defences and only eleven out of 342 did not return home.

As the crews were debriefed, had breakfast and eventually went to bed, plans were being made at Command for the next raid, which was to be that night, 25/26th February. The target chosen was Augsburg, once again in support of the USAAF and their 'Big Week'.

On the 17th April 1942, S/Ldr Nettleton led twelve Lancasters of 44 (Rhodesia) Squadron to the old Bavarian city of Augsburg. This was no sightseeing tour, it was to destroy the MAN U-Boat engine factory in daylight. At that time the Battle of the Atlantic was at its height and allied merchant shipping was being sunk by

German U-Boats at an alarming rate. The factory was hit, but seven aircraft did not return and S/Ldr Nettleton was awarded the Victoria Cross for his leadership in the raid. This was only the third raid for the then new Lancaster. Sadly, in July 1943, now W/Cdr Nettleton was shot down and killed over the English Channel while returning from an attack on Turin.

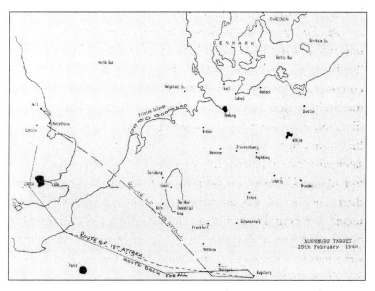

Map 5. Target Augsburg, 25.2.44.

But on the night of 25th February 1944, nearly two years after the first attack on Augsburg, 1 Group's orders were not to disrupt U-Boat engine production. To follow an attack by 194 American B17 bombers in the afternoon, Bomber Command Lancasters and Halifaxes were to bomb the Messerschmidt aircraft factory and other aircraft component assembly plants on the outskirts of the city.

Two waves were again to be sent into the attack, two and half hours apart, each on separate routes out but both following the same route home. Time on target for the first was to be 2245Hrs, the second being in the early hours of the next morning at 0115Hrs. Even more Mosquitos than last time, twenty-two, of 8 Group's Light Night Striking Force were to be engaged in attacking night-fighter airfields in Holland. As a diversion, over 130 bombers were to be sent minelaying in Kiel bay again.

The southern route out and back was to be tried once more on the first wave as it was paying dividends as far as crew losses were concerned. Compared to attacking a northern industrial city the casualty rate was about half. The second wave had a more direct flightpath. After passing Sherringham on the north Norfolk coast the stream would head out to the North Sea and make for the enemy coast a few miles south of Rotterdam and keep going to a turning point near the Belgium city of Liege. Turning a few degrees to starboard they would then make for a point sixty-five miles south of Stuttgart, then fly due east until due south of Augsburg. On turning sharply to port the target would dead ahead with about thirty-five miles to go. 626 Squadron fielded fifteen Lancasters for this raid, those of the first wave taking off after 1800Hrs for the four-and-half hour trip to Augsburg with 2,000 gallons of high-octane petrol apiece. Unfortunately, like the Schweinfurt raid before, there were some aborts on the way out. The first two Lancasters turned back over the Channel within two minutes of each other.

Pilot F/Sgt Bennet could only get 135 MPH out of W4967 at 20,000 feet and that height was difficult to maintain. Somehow the engines were not giving their best. His navigator calculated that at this rate they would get to the target thirty minutes after the rest, that is if they were not shot down, quite often stragglers were. About forty-five miles from the enemy coast and twenty miles south-east of Beachy Head it was decided at 2000Hrs to turn back. The Lancaster had used up quite a lot of fuel so allowing it to land back at Wickenby at a safe landing weight. This was 55,000 pounds, 10,000 pounds less than the maximum take off weight for a fully loaded Lancaster.

About the same time and only thirty or so miles away from W4967, the rear turret of P/O Stewart's JA922 developed a fault and would not work. JA922 at this time was twenty miles north of Dieppe and the enemy coast but 2009Hrs saw it heading back and out to the North Sea. Sixty miles east of Spurn Head the bomb load was dumped except the 'Cookie', this they brought back, landing at 2336Hrs.

The first wave of the bomber stream crossed over the English Channel into Northern France following the now familiar route south of the French-Belgium boarder before dipping in a large arc to the south to come up under Augsburg heading north. Just before nine o'clock two more of 626 Squadron's Lancasters dropped out of the raid having passed Rheims to the south-west. LL829, with F/Lt Ravenhill at the controls, had an oxygen supply fault, a serious problem at 23,000 feet! He turned the aircraft back for home at 2058Hrs. To lighten the Lancaster's weight the 'Cookie' was dropped in the Channel between Dieppe and Treport while heading for the English coast at Littlehampton. Later, LL829 landed at Wickenby at 2330Hrs.

Meanwhile, about ten miles to the south of LL829, and at the same time, the rear gunner of JB409 was found unconscious, also the navigator and the wireless operator were feeling sick and breathing with difficulty. Lack of oxygen due to a possible leak was suspected. At 21,000 feet, F/Sgt Marriott as captain was taking no chances with his crew's well-being and the aircraft's safety. He quickly turned the Lancaster round and headed for Dieppe and home via Beachy Head at a lower altitude. JB409 was at a sufficient safe weight for landing when reaching Wickenby and touchdown just a few minutes after LL829.

While LL829 and JB409 were heading north across the English Channel for home, the rest of the Bomber Force in the first wave were approaching the target from the south having made a large loop towards the Swiss border. ED623 with Sgt Smith as the pilot, arrived early and started to orbit the target while waiting for the markers to go down. 626 Squadron's 'A' Flight Commander, S/Ldr Neilson, was flying JB599 and came in on the bomb run dead on time, dropping the load in the centre of a cluster of target indicators. Still in the area afterwards, his crew saw that there were concentrated fires in the built up areas with a large explosion at eleven o'clock.

As the red and green target indicators went down ED623's bomb aimer now had something to aim at and the bomb run was started. As the Lancaster made the approach the target indicators went out. There was a lot of snow on the ground and before reaching the target the red route markers had been put out by it. Not daunted, the bomb aimer estimated the centre of the extinguished cluster when lining up the bombsight aiming gratical and pressed the bomb release button.

Nothing happened... the bomb load 'hung up'. Emergency bomb jettison procedure was carried out using the Bomb Containers Jettison Switch and the Bomb Jettison Control Handle on the instrument panel. Still the bomb load refused to drop. After repeated attempts the flight engineer and the bomb aimer started looking for the reason why. Lingering in the target area was dangerous, there was always the risk of being caught by flak or nightfighter and collision with another bomber. ED623 headed for home, bomb load intact, with the rest of the stream. Still large fires raged below with more explosions including a huge yellow one at 2305Hrs as seen by the crew of HK539. Smoke haze on the ground and smoke spiralling up to 10/12,000 feet could be seen as the attack progressed.

Eventually the bombers left the burning city by flying west, heading for just below Strasbourg. The flight engineer and bomb aimer of ED623 worked at getting rid of their unwanted bomb load for over half an hour after leaving the target. At 2335Hrs while flying over the 4000 foot peaks of the Schwarzwald Mountains forty miles south-west of Stuttgart, the six tons of incendiaries and 'cookie' were finally released, the fault being found. Their departure from the Lancaster's bomb bay no doubt giving the inhabitants of some mountain village a very rude awakening. The route back was a little to the south of the track to the target over Northern France but still crossing the enemy coast at the same point, just north of Dieppe, then on to Beachy Head, Reading and home to Wickenby.

The 626 Squadron Lancasters landed later than the previous night, mostly after half-past-two in the morning but at least they all landed with no casualties, all safe. ED623 was later than most, the drag of the bomb doors being open when starting back from the target for over half an hour could not have helped. Sgt Smith landed the Lancaster at 0310Hrs.

As the first wave was leaving the target the second was making their way across the North Sea but they had their share of aborts as well. DV177, with F/O Kewley as pilot, took off late at 2154Hrs but tried to catch up. The Lancaster might have achieved that with a wise use of the throttle but the P4 compass let the crew down. Thirty-five miles from the Dutch coast the navigator calculated they were at least thirty miles north of track and heading in the wrong direction due to the faulty compass. By this time it was too late to try and catch up so the aircraft was turned for home, dumping the bomb load on the way at 11 o'clock from 15,000 feet. Flying back via Cromer they landed back at Wickenby at a few minutes before one in the morning.

The attack on Augsburg by the two waves was very successful, the weather being clear and the flak contributing little to the city's defence. The night was also very cold and because of this the water froze in many of the firefighters' hoses rendering them useless. Bombs and incendiaries did rain down on the aircraft factories as planed in the northern and eastern outskirts of the city but the centre itself was completely gutted by explosions and fire. The marking of the Pathfinders and the bombing by the Main Force that followed was extremely accurate. Nearly 3000 dwellings were destroyed, 5000 damaged and nearly 90,000 people were made homeless by in excess of 2000 tons of bombs and incendiaries. The City Hall was completely destroyed along with sixteen churches, eleven hospitals and many establishments of Art all seriously damaged. With foresight, all the patients in the hospitals were safely evacuated beforehand with not one life lost. About 700 citizens were killed and over 2000 injured. The German media made much propaganda out of the raid saying that it was 'Terror bombing' in the extreme.

On the Bomber Command side. The two separate waves in the raid, the diversions, the clear weather over the target, the southern route again and the not so efficiently defended target all contributed to the reduction of crews and aircraft lost. This was the last raid in which route markers were used. It was found that once dropped the German night-fighters would fly towards them knowing that the bomber stream would be in the vicinity. Twenty-one aircraft did not return, four crashing due to mid-air collisions and not enemy action.

On 26th February there was a stand down for all of 1 Group, which was just as well as it rained and drizzled all day. The next day it was even worse with sleet and snow. Every one that could handle a shovel was out clearing Wickenby's main runway of snow until it was cleared in the evening. Wickenby woke up the next day with more heavy snow from the north wind. Operations were ordered for a raid on Munich, time on target to-be at 0305Hrs the following morning. Needless to say it was cancelled by seven o'clock in the evening due to bad weather on route, the cloud over Europe being up to 25,000 feet thick. On Tuesday 29th February, although he had flown already operationally with 626 Squadron, W/Cdr Ross took over the unit as its new Commanding Officer. Outgoing W/Cdr. Haynes was posted to RAF Standtoft as acting Group Captain. Not for the first time this week all personnel not on essential duties took to the shovels again to clear snow off the runways. That was the end of February 1944, in which 626 Squadron flew 442.4 hours operationally in 44 sorties, dropping 212 tons of bombs and incendiaries on the enemy. It was also the end of the period in support of the USAAF's 'Big Week'.

The next full moon period was due soon but there was a few nights left yet where it was relatively safe to fly over Germany. On the night of 1st March 1944, Stuttgart was chosen once again for the target. There was still a lot of cloud over Europe but not so bad as two days previous, flying conditions over England were better too. Thirteen Lancasters of 626 Squadron were made ready for take off between eleven o'clock and midnight to meet a time on target at 0300Hrs in the following morning. From start to finish the bombing period was sixteen minutes.

Operating at Wickenby this night were six special Lancasters belonging to 101 Squadron from Ludford Magna. These were highly secret aircraft, which flew in support and with the Main Force and Pathfinders. They carried bombs the same as any other Lancaster but in addition, there was 800 pounds of radio counter measures equipment code named 'Airborne Cigar', ABC for short and an extra crewmember to work it. They were German-speaking radio operators, not necessarily, Englishmen as some of them were airmen that had fled from the now occupied countries at the beginning of the war to continue the fight in the Royal Air Force.

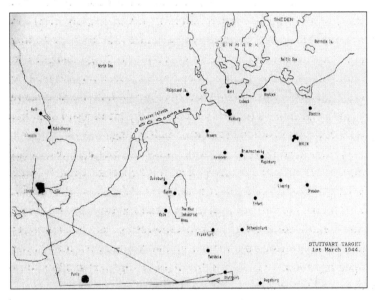

Map 6. Target Stuttgart, 1.3.44.

While flying, they listened out for the German fighter controllers' instructions to their night-fighter pilots in the VHF radio band. On noting the frequency they were using, the Special Duties Operator in the 101 Squadron Lancaster then tuned one of three powerful radio transmitters on board to that frequency and broadcast a warbling jamming signal. With two more transmitters to hand, they caused considerable annoyance to the German controllers and pilots alike. These special Lancasters were conspicuous by their three 7ft transmitting aerials on top of and down the length of the fuselage.

The route was the familiar southern one, down to Reading and out over The Channel via Beachy Head and crossing into France about twenty-five miles up the coast from Le Havre. From then on, down to a turning point about eighty miles south-west of Paris, east to just south of Strasbourg and then straight for Stuttgart. After bombing the target, fly clockwise round the bottom of Stuttgart and head back to the same turning point near Strasbourg. Here the stream would go straight over Northern France to exit the enemy coast just south of Boulogne, leaving Paris to the south on the way. The hundred mile crossing of the English Channel would see Beachy Head again and then up Central England to Wickenby via Reading.

When it came to take off time, nearing midnight, two of 626 Squadron's aircraft were cancelled but the rest got away on time. There was no second wave as on previous raids of late, all 557 Lancasters, Halifaxes and Mosquitos starting out together. There was the now usual attacks on the airfields in Holland and eleven Mosquitos provided a diversion raid to Munich. No mine laying operations were carried out this night or flights across the North Sea by the Operational Training Units.

One of the crews new to 626 Squadron aborted one-and-half hours after take off. DV177's navigator found it difficult to determine the Lancaster's position and cope with the navigation in general. Since there was cloud ahead denying the crew any chance of pinpointing their position with a ground feature, the pilot, F/O Kewley, turned the Lancaster towards the North Sea.

Here the 'cookie' was dumped before heading for Wickenby and landing at five o'clock in the morning.

Another aircraft in trouble was JA922, P/0 Stewart as captain. About the time of their crossing of the enemy coast, the crew found that the 'Monica' device was unserviceable. This was an active radar that detected an aircraft in the Lancaster's vicinity, possibly a night-fighter. Likewise the rear turret would not work correctly, altogether not a good situation to be in over enemy occupied Europe. Many would have turned back at this point but, with much credit to this crew it was decided to carry on in the hope that they did not encounter a night-fighter along the way. They did not know it but luck was with them this night. There was thick cloud all the way to and from the target making it difficult for any night-fighter that managed to take off in the murk to get into the bomber stream.

Out of the 557 aircraft that were detailed for the raid 502 actually reached Stuttgart to attack it. The city, apart from being difficult to find down a long narrow valley, was covered in cloud. The Pathfinders' green target indicators went through it, while the red/green flares floated above it on their tiny parachutes for a little while longer before being consumed by the cloud. Consequently, the marking looked scattered to the bomb aimers above. W/O Jackson, piloting JB599, had to circle the target twice before his bomb aimer found some flares at 0317Hrs to aim at. By this time, over fifteen minutes into the attack, the fires below had got a hold and large explosions were seen by many. F/Lt Wright, flying HK539, found the sky-markers sparse when his Lancaster arrived on the scene but his bomb aimer managed to aim the bomb load at three Wanganui flares at 0310Hrs. The crew reported seeing fire's rapidly spreading under the clouds with explosions.

As JB409 approached the already burning city with still some miles and minutes to go and flying in the third wave, the crew saw a decoy of about five target indicators on the ground. But these were just not the right shade of colour in comparison with what the Royal Air Force used. Brocks Fireworks Ltd made the fillings for Bomber Command's pyrotechnics and the Germans never, throughout the war, simulated them perfectly. Over Stuttgart, JB409's bomb aimer bombed a cluster of three red/green flares at 0310Hrs. The marking was scattered and the attack was creeping back, the opinion of Sgt Temple, pilot of LM393. Sgt Abbot, his bomb aimer, aimed the bomb load at the centre of a group of five markers at 0313Hrs from 22,000 feet. Two large fires were seen by the crew with buildings aflame under the clouds.

Unable to seek the bombers out en route to the target, the night-fighters that did manage to make it into the air concentrated their efforts over Stuttgart. P/O Stewart captain of JA922, saw some of them while over the city but luckily they did not see him. This was just as well as it will be remembered that JA922 had an unserviceable rear turret and 'Monica' radar warning system. The only 626 Squadron aircraft that came up against a night-fighter was LM393 on the way to the target. This was in the Orleans area south of Paris but no damage was inflicted on the Lancaster. Many crews reported huge fires spread over a large area of Stuttgart, which could still be seen from 150-200 miles away by the rear and mid-upper gunners on the way home. Between seven and eight o'clock in the morning of 2nd March, all 626 Squadron Lancasters on the raid landed safely back at Wickenby.

Not having a major attack for many months and then being bombed for the second time in ten days, the raid came as a surprise for the citizens of Stuttgart. In addition to that inflicted on the 20th February, the Bosch complex, the main railway station and the Daimler-Benz vehicle factory were once again seriously damaged. In the morning after the attack, more new damage was found in the western, northern and centre of the city including a lot of housing. 125 people were killed and over 500 injured were taken to the city's hospitals.

Because of the thick cloud to and from the target, only three Lancasters and one Halifax were reported missing in action after the raid, one of the lowest casualty rates. of the Battle.

At 1015Hrs on the morning that the Lancasters landed the message on the teleprinter from 1 Group stated that there was to be no operations that night, although the day was fine and with good visibility. The next day the Station continued to rest with no operations for that day either. The wind however had veered north-west and it was a lot colder. One aircraft from 626 Squadron went on a Command 'Bullseye' exercise at 1115Hrs with others from the Operational Training Units. On the 4th March orders came through from 1 Group for Wickenby's Lancasters to have maximum fuel on board for a nearly 2000 mile round trip to Munich. Time on target for the raid was to be 0025Hrs after midnight with a late afternoon take off. Visibility was good in the morning but deteriorated throughout the day. At 1910Hrs the operation was cancelled when visibility was down to less than 2000 yards with falling snow. This was frustrating for the aircrews who were all keyed up to go and for the ground crews who had put in a lot of effort, as always, to get the aircraft bombed up and ready. The next day the operation was tried again with sixteen Lancasters of 626 Squadron participating. By 1000Hrs the weather was too bad over most of the country and the raid was once again scrubbed. Konigsburg, fifty-five miles north-east of

Berlin, was selected for the next night's raid. Ten aircraft and their very best crews were chosen for the long flight over the North Sea and the Baltic. Navigation had to be precise as there was not much in the way of ground references until crossing the North German coast and heading inland. Time on target was just before midnight but the whole of the operation was cancelled at 1645Hrs.

On the 7th March the Squadron got down to some training as there were no operations. Four Lancasters went on a bombing exercise to the ranges, another four for fighter affiliation exercises, six on an air-to-air and air-to-ground firing detail and one on a night cross country navigation flight. For the next couple of days the welcome break continued although there was a visit by a F/Lt Hopson from 156 Pathfinder Squadron at Upwood on liaison duties. Another crack at Konigsburg was tried on 10th March with 18 Lancasters of 626 Squadron available and ready. By 1045hrs the target was changed to Kiel at the western end of the Baltic, a large German Naval port, but just before one o'clock in the afternoon that raid was cancelled. No operations were declared for the next day or the one after.

Most of the Squadron's Lancasters were serviceable, as they had not flown for nearly a week. Because of this, many ground crew were allowed with the aircrew to attend a lecture and slide show given by a S/Ldr Morris from Bomber Command Headquarters. The next day was for sports where Wickenby played the Army's King's Own Border Regiment at rugby and football, Wickenby loosing the rugby, the score being 3-40 points. No operations were called for the next two days, the only real activity being an airfield defence demonstration by the Royal Air Force Regiment on the 13th March.

With no operational flying for some time and little flying training taking place, it gave a chance for the ground servicing crews to get as many aircraft to operational readiness on the flight-line as possible. Normally there was always aircraft in the big black hangers for battle damage repair and routine deep servicing. Apart from four operations to France by 3, 4, 6 and 8 Groups to bomb aircraft factories and railway centres in preparation for the invasion, only minor operations were carried out over Germany by the Command's Mosquitos in this period.

Across the other side of the North Sea, in enemy occupied Europe, Bomber Command's adversaries were going through a similar period. Many units of the Luftwaffe Nachtjagd were also enjoying and utilising the inactivity to build up their operational strength. One such unit had been busy for some time where they had not long converted from the Messerschmidt Bf110G-4 to the Junkers Ju88C-6. This Staffeln was III/NJG2 based at Gilze Rijen in Holland. The Staffeln had had a chequered career over the past months since returning home from Mediterranean duties in the late summer of 1943 to Stuttgart to receive Bf110G-4s. Then on to Schiphol (Amsterdam), Neuruppin (north-west of Berlin), back to Holland at Venlo and finally to Gilze Rijen near Breda. Converting again from the Messerschmidt to the Junkers Ju88C-6 did not just involve waving goodbye to the old and flying in the new. Along with the new aircraft would be different specialist ground and test equipment for the aircraft's systems and armaments. There would be a period of time, although not long, when the air and ground crews would work up and train with the new aircraft to get the unit up to fighting fitness. III/NJG 2 at this stage of the Battle of Berlin had not long been flying the Ju88C-6.

As a night-fighter, this aircraft was the most dedicated killer that Bomber Command crews had to encounter. Its fire power and electronics suite gave it the ability to shoot down more night bombers in World War II than all other Luftwaffe night-fighter types put together. In the nose of the Ju88C-6, the version that equipped III/NJG 2, a typical offensive armament would be three MG FF/M Oerlikon 20mm cannon and three MG17 7.62mm machine guns. With their combined rate of fire, a two second burst meant that 54 explosive shells and 118 machine gun bullets would hit a Lancaster, Stirling or Halifax all at once and often did, with devastating effect. The night-fighter pilots found that the most efficient way to bring down a bomber however, was not with the forward facing armament. It was found that if two Mauser MG 151/20 20mm cannons were placed behind the cockpit and angled upwards and slightly forward at about seventy degrees to the fuselage, the attack could be made from 100 to 120 feet below the unsuspecting bomber. The Ju88C-6 would creep up slowly and out of sight of the bomber's rear and mid-upper gunners to deliver the fatal coup de grace to the wing fuel tanks and engines using dim tracer ammunition. The crew would not know what hit them and from what quarter.

The Ju88G-6s air-to-air radar was the latest Telefunken FuG 220 Lichtenstein SN-2. Unlike the earlier sets that were tuned to 54 megacycles, it was designed to be impervious to jamming by the 'Window' aluminium strips in use by Bomber Command at the time as the SN-2 worked on the switchable frequencies of 91, 81 and 72 megacycles. The Ju88C-6's radar/radio operator could also home onto the emissions from the bomber's 'Monica' tail warning radar with its FuG 227 Flensburg receiver. It was also equipped with the FuG 350 Naxos receiver that homed on to the bomber's H2S navigation and bombing radar pulses. Until an intact Ju88 was captured in the summer of 1944, Bomber Command was not aware of this.

The Ju88 was designed in the mid thirties as a bomber, the first prototype flying on 21st December 1936 at Dessau. By the end of WWII no less than sixty-seven variants were in service all having been designed from the same basic airframe, from the Ju88A-1 Bomber to the Ju88Z Destroyer (Heavy fighter). There was probably no other aircraft anywhere in WWII on either side that was so versatile and adaptable. In modern terms a true multi-role-combat-aircraft. It wasn't the fastest night-fighter and it did not climb as fast and as far as others that came after it but it was, as claimed by many that were associated with it in Germany, the Star of the Luftwaffe.

When the 15th March dawned the rest and training period was over. The days off operations had been well spent, the crews were refreshed and more aircraft had been repaired and serviced than ever before. When the teleprinter message came through from 1 Group for a raid on Stuttgart for the third time in a row, Wickenby was able to put up thirty-six Lancasters, twenty of them from 626 Squadron. The southern route was to be taken again over Northern France crossing the coast a few miles south of Le Havre. Although the route was similar to last time, the last turning point was about sixty miles below Stuttgart, attacking it from the south. After the attack and fifteen miles to the north of the target, the Force would make for the familiar turning point south of Strasbourg, avoiding the defences of the industrial city of Karlsruhe. Heading for the French coast just north of Dieppe, a dogleg turning point was introduced between Paris and Rheims. After crossing the English Channel a friendly landfall would be made at Selsey Bill in Sussex. Time on target was to be between 2315Hrs and 2330Hrs, which necessitated a take off time of around seven o'clock in the early evening. Once again there were no cancellations and all thirty-six Lancasters took off in forty-two minutes and headed south leaving London to port and out over English Channel via Reading and Selsey Bill.

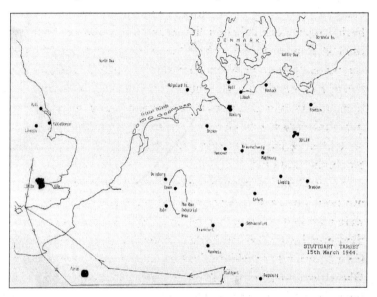

Map 7. Target Stuttgart 15.3.44.

DV244 took off at 1909Hrs. Thirty minutes later over Lincolnshire at 12,000 feet and still gaining height, number two port wing fuel tank developed a leak and the rear turret had an electrical failure. F/Sgt Bernyk, the captain, made the decision to abort the sortie and headed the Lancaster east to the North Sea. Here a majority of the incendiaries were dumped and later at nearly eleven o'clock DV244 landed back at Wickenby with the 'cookie' and twenty-four thirty-pound incendiaries.

Sgt Margetts eased the control column of Lancaster LL798 back and was airborne at 1917Hrs where he headed the aircraft south with the rest of the Force. With over 860 other Lancasters, Halifaxes and Mosquitos in this raid it was not surprising, with navigation lights on over England, that LL798 found itself in the company of another Lancaster travelling towards the English Channel. The pair continued south and then south-east heading over the water for the French coast. The unknown Lancaster had been in front of LL798 since passing Reading so it came as a complete surprise when thirty-seven miles north-north-west of Le Havre at 2041Hrs the rear gunner of it raked LL798 with two four second bursts from his four machine guns. Sgt Margetts veered the stricken LL798 away instantly while the rest of the crew reported in the damage. The starboard outer and port inner engines were on fire and as this was priority the flight engineer pressed the fire extinguisher buttons. Each engine bay had its own extinguisher on a Lancaster for such an emergency.

Taking stock of the other damage, the direct reading compass was out of action, the rear turret perspex was holed and the bomb bay had received hits but luckily no one was hurt. The decision to abort was made as two engines could not be relied on to last and there was a useless direct reading compass which was used to steer and navigate by. Only the pilot's P4 magnetic compass was now left and since this was positioned in front of his left knee it was most inconvenient for the navigator. But their troubles were not yet over as when it came to jettison the bomb load for landing a canister of twelve thirty-pound incendiaries hung up. Quickly the jettison switch was tried but they still remained in the bay so the bomb doors were closed and the Lancaster sped north and home. Just over one-and-half hours later LL798 landed safely at Wickenby.

The Force continued on in the night along the now well trodden route across Northern France. While flying at 22,000 feet

feet and just south-west of the French town of Epinal HK539 was attacked by a Focke Wulf Fw190 from the port quarter. The fighter was seen from 600 yards out by the Australian rear gunner F/Sgt Jones, where he immediately ordered his pilot, F/Sgt Bladon, to corkscrew to port. Meanwhile he opened fire scoring hits with a long burst starting at 500 yards range. A large blue flash was seen by the rear gunner as his bullets found their mark, perhaps hitting something electrical. The fighter got to within 200/250 yards of HK539 before peeling off and having never fired a shot. Lucky at their escape, F/Sgt Bladon put HK539 back on course, F/Sgt Jones claiming one Luftwaffe night-fighter damaged.

The bomber stream flew on, turning north-east for the run in to the target. The night-fighter force did not find them until they were nearly there. When they eventually did, they bore in with a vengeance and many bombers were shot down just before Stuttgart was reached and later over the target. 626 Squadron's JB409, flown by F/Sgt Marriott was nearly one of them.

When thirty miles still to go and JB409 flying at 22,000 feet, the crew anticipated being over Stuttgart in about twelve minutes. All of a sudden three searchlights formed a cone of intense light 2000 feet above the Lancaster and followed it along its track. At this time, as common practice with this crew, the mid-upper gunner, Sgt Loughrey, was scanning the sky to port while the rear gunner did the same to starboard. At 2313Hrs the Lancaster was attacked by what was identified as a Junkers Ju88 night-fighter from below the starboard quarter, opening fire with its cannon and machine guns from about 600 yards out. JB409 was badly hit but the rear gunner, Sgt Brewer, retaliated by firing a long burst before the Ju88 broke away. Immediately the night-fighter hauled round and came in again, this time from dead astern and slightly above firing from 250 yards, a range that he could not miss. This time it was Sgt Loughrey that was in a better position to return fire, which he did while the pilot took evasive action causing the night-fighter to loose them.

All the crew reported in the damage in their area to the captain, which was extensive, as best as they could as the crew inter-communication system was inoperative likewise the IFF and the R/T set. The immediate problem was a fire amidships in the fuselage, which was put out by the mid-upper gunner. Surveying the other damage, the mid-upper and rear turrets had no hydraulic power to move them, the base of the mid-upper was wrecked and both gunners were cut off from their oxygen supply. Externally, the tailplane elevators and trim tabs had been hit and there were holes all down the fuselage including the astrodome and cockpit. It was only a matter of luck that the explosive cannon shells did not strike something more vital; a fuel tank, engine or wing root. It can only be assumed that being given the best night-fighter in the Luftwaffe at the time the pilot was lacking experience. Meanwhile the Lancaster was approaching Stuttgart and even though the aircraft was shot up the captain and crew still carried on to find the markers and bomb the target.

JB409 was lucky to get out of the cone of the searchlight as some were radar controlled. The Lancaster had a built in defence against being seen and caught by searchlights and that was the underside paint, which needed special attention to look after it. Ex - Sergeant Airframe Fitter Tom Hughes, who served on 626 and 12 Squadrons, explains:

> "When the aircraft arrived on the unit they were already camouflaged, the underside surface having been finished in matt black called 'Black Night'. It actually looked like black velvet. Of course the more this surface was cleaned the less 'Velvet-like' it

> *became. The policy was to leave well alone, except for the re-*
> *moval of oily streaks. It was certainly my policy on the three*
> *Lancs for which I was responsible. I suppose it was a compro-*
> *mise between being 'coned' by searchlights and 'get-away'*
> *speed."*

The weather over the target was clear in some places and 8/10ths cloud in others but adverse winds were causing the markers and target indicators to be scattered and creeping back to the south-west. Flak was heavy but exploded far too low to harm many of the attacking Force. This was noted by F/Lt Ravenhill, captain of LL829, when over the target at nearly half-past eleven. The initial markers were fizzling out before being renewed by the 'Backers up' in the Pathfinder Force. LL829 began a run up to some target indicators only to find them extinguished at the time of bomb release, the pilot then having to fly around trying to find something to bomb. Eventually the bomb load was dropped on a concentration of target indicators at 2328Hrs.

About the same time, S/Ldr Spiller with F/Sgt Dawson as second pilot and on his operational experience flight, brought LL772 in on the first wave. They had already passed a decoy area with dummy red target indicators and incendiaries and like the rest ignored it. Although the aiming point was badly marked, the centre of a cluster of target indicators was bombed at 2321Hrs. By this time there was widespread fires over the target and a huge explosion seen by many at 2320Hrs. W/Cdr. Ross believed in leading from the front and as Commanding Officer of 626 Squadron was flying JB599 this night. As a much experienced officer and pilot he thought that the Pathfinder marking was at least seven minutes late in being laid down.

What with the encounter with the Ju88 and the damage to the airframe causing drag, JB409 was one of the last to arrive at the target. By this time many fires had got hold and not many markers were still alight but the bomb aimer, Sgt Todd, found three flares to aim for at 2335Hrs. After the bomb run, the flight engineer, Sgt Willday, went back to check on Sgt Brewer in the rear turret. Although he was wounded in the left foot and ankle, had no oxygen supply and having to work his turret manually he insisted on staying at his crew station. On the way back to the cockpit Sgt Willday found Sgt Loughrey unconscious in his turret with blood on his right boot revealing wounds to his foot. This was caused by metal splinters from the attack earlier. Sgt Willday, with assistance by wireless operator Sgt Palmer, succeeded in getting the mid-upper gunner to the rest bunk and strapped in for the remainder of the flight home.

After leaving Stuttgart the Pathfinder and Main Force turned for home, still being harassed by the odd night-fighter along the way. For 626 Squadron aircraft the homeward journey proved uneventful, even for the damaged JB409. To keep a lookout the bomb aimer alternated his place in the nose with that of the mid-upper turret, the wireless operator taking up a position in what was left of the astrodome. Swapping crew places was no problem as all Bomber Command wireless operators and bomb aimers were trained gunners. Meanwhile Sgt Loughrey remained unconscious on the rest bunk causing not a little concern by the rest of the crew.

Seventeen of the eighteen 626 Squadron Lancasters that attacked Stuttgart returned safely to Wickenby at around three o'clock in the morning. Having limped across Northern France and the English Channel, F/Sgt Marriott put JB409 down on the first piece of England he could find that was big enough to land a Lancaster. This was Ford, an airfield on the West Sussex coast. After landing, Sgt Brewer was taken to hospital where he was

detained with frostbite to his face as well as the wounds to his left
foot and ankle. Sgt Loughrey was still out cold when he reached
hospital and remained that way till the middle of the afternoon
twelve hours later. More damage was found when the remaining
crew walked round the aircraft. Number two petrol tank in the
starboard wing was found to be holed and both starboard propellers hit by the night-fighter's bullets. Bullets it must have been, as
if the propellers and tank had been hit by the JU88's 20mm explosive cannon shells the crew and the Lancaster would not have
survived the attack.

Twenty-seven other Lancasters were not so lucky. As with ten
Halifaxes they did not return to England, two of them being so
badly shot up that the crews chose to land them in neutral Swit-
zerland knowing that the aircraft were in no fit state to get back
them back home. They were interned by the Swiss authorities
but at least they were still alive.

While the crews slept in the morning of the 16th March,
preparations were being made at Bomber Command Headquarters for a raid that night on Munich. Aircraft on 626 Squadron
were fuelled, bombed up and ready by the early evening, crews
were briefed and all set for take off. But Munich, as on the 4th
and 5th of the month, was leading a charmed life as at 1845Hrs
the raid on that city was cancelled.

It was not just a case of packing up and going home on these
occasions. The groundcrews had toiled throughout the day loading 14,000 rounds of ammunition into each Lancaster and hoist-
ing nearly five tons of bombs and incendiaries into every bomb
bay. For safety reasons it was forbidden to leave live ordnance in
a parked aircraft if it was not being flown. The groundcrews now
had to take all the fuses out of the bombs and shift them all plus

the incendiary canisters and ammunition back to their respective dumps and storage places.

The next morning brought fog and also the news that there was to be no operations that day. But it was not all good for the aircrew, when they tumbled out of bed they found that they had to attend a session of P.T. with the Station's physical training staff. All stations in 1 Group were on a stand down from operations but 626 Squadron put up an aircraft on fighter affiliation exercise when the fog cleared later in the day. In the afternoon the officers played a football match against the boys from the local Market Rasen Grammar School. On a more serious note there was a conference attended by the flight commanders and aircraft captains to discuss the previous raid on Stuttgart.

13. The Destruction of Frankfurt

At this time in the Battle, Bomber Command was loosing on average 154 Lancasters on operations over Europe a month. To replace them the aircraft industry was working flat out and producing 212 in the same period of time. As long as the factories were supplied with aluminium, steel and other materials to build them the lost Lancasters could be replaced within forty-eight hours, often less. The problem was crews; experienced crews, that is. Bomber Command aircrew were being trained in America, Canada, South Africa, Rhodesia and even as far away as Australia. Gaining operational experience took time and Bomber Command did not have that to spare. Flight commanders and squadron commanding officers to lead the new crews were being killed the same as anybody else.

Experienced crews were needed for the Pathfinder Force all the time. The attrition rate was such that by the middle of March 1944, Bomber Command had just about turned over or replaced its operational aircrew in the four winter months 1943/44. It says a lot for the generation of young men of those times that there was never a shortage of volunteers for bomber aircrew or the Pathfinder Force. Although with some relatively inexperienced aircrew on some squadrons, with increased aircraft production, the Command was at this stage of the Battle able to field 800 plus bombers on a raid where over 600 of them would be Lancasters. In the previous November less than 400 bombers of all types were being sent to Berlin on some nights.

On the night of 18th March 1944 Bomber Command put up 846 aircraft for a raid on Frankfurt in Southern Germany. 620 of them were Lancasters in which eighteen of them belonged to 626 Squadron. Take off time was in the early evening, again around seven o'clock. Fuel for the trip was to be just 1477 gallons of 100 octane petrol for each of 626 Squadron's Lancasters. Once more 626 Squadron was to be lead by its Commanding Officer, W/Cdr Ross. The flight to the target was out over Orford Ness and crossing the enemy coast between Dunkerque and Oostende. Making their way across Belgium, the bomber stream would reach a turning point about twenty-five miles below Liege where they would start a long clockwise sweep below Bonn and Siegen to approach Frankfurt from the north. Ninety-eight aircraft were sent on a minelaying diversion which drew off half of the night-fighter force to the north. The other half of the night-fighter force were detained until the last moment before the bombers reached the target. This was a relatively new tactic by the Luftwaffe as just before the target was reached and at the target the bomber stream was more concentrated.

Two Lancasters of 626 Squadron dropped out due to electrical and mechanical failures. 'A' Flight Commander S/Ldr Neilson, a New Zealander, had to turn JB599 back over Orford Ness. The electrical system would not change up the engine supercharger ratios on all four engines when 15,500 feet of altitude was reached. The air pressure at 20,000 feet was only 45% of that at ground level and that operational height air had to be rammed into the carburettors to maintain engine performance. JA922, P/O Stewart as captain, got a little further. Ten miles to the north-east of Dunkerque the supercharger of the port inner engine malfunctioned and the Lancaster was turned back. As instructed by flying control both aircraft lightened their loads over the North Sea to land safely at Wickenby later on that night.

244

Cloud was thin across Europe but thickened up on the approach to Frankfurt. Despite, this the marking by the Pathfinder Force was said to be good and accurate by some crews, time on target being 2200Hrs. When LL829 came up to Frankfurt, piloted by F/Lt Ravenhill, he thought the marking to be a bit scattered and late, he saw no sky-markers at all. In some places the cloud was thinner allowing his bomb aimer to see the streets of the city through the haze. It was policy that new crews bombed in the last waves and on leaving the target area it was seen by LL829's rear gunner that bombs were dropping away from the aiming point to the east.

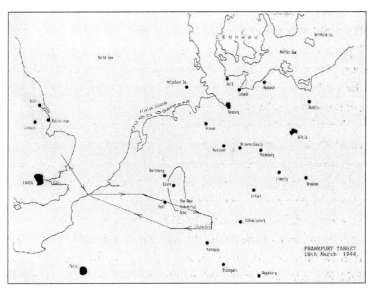

Map 8. Target Frankfurt, 18.3.44.

F/Sgt Dawson and his crew were on their first operation together flying in JB559. On the way the aircraft had to take evasive action against a night-fighter south-west of Liege over Belgium and once again on the approach to Frankfurt. The target was marked by the combination of red target indicators and Wanganui sky-markers, the so-called 'Berlin Method'. JB599's bomb aimer identified the target through the haze and smoke dropping the bomb load in the centre of three red target indicators at 2208Hrs. Two minutes later came HK539 with F/Sgt Bladon as captain who ignored the obvious German decoy site to the south with its dummy red target indicators. Fires were seen to be widespread by now and two large explosions occurred about this time. Many night-fighters were seen in the target area but it was thought that the cloud hampered their operations; certainly they attacked no 626 Squadron aircraft. After leaving the target the stream was to keep on the same heading as the approach and about fifteen miles south of the target turn east to the next turning point south of Liege. From then on it was the same way home as the inward route.

The return flight was uneventful for many, but not all... LL829's W/Op was due to listen to the Command's broadcast on wind information at 2300hrs and at 2320hrs, which was to help with the bomber stream's navigation. When F/Lt Ravenhill, the pilot, checked on the Navigator, he got no reply. It was found that the navigator's oxygen had been cut off and he was unconscious. After being revived by other members of the crew with an alternative supply, he carried on to navigate LL829 home. F/Sgt Bernyk as pilot of DV244 on leaving Frankfurt reported seeing another German decoy site with dummy red target indicators twenty miles north of the city.

The small hours after midnight saw all of 626 Squadron's Lancasters returning safely after about six hours of flying. Ten Lancasters from other squadrons did not, along with twelve Halifaxes this accounting for a loss of 2.6% of the Force that set out.

In Frankfurt nearly 5,500 dwellings and almost 100 industrial premises were either destroyed or heavily damaged. 55,000 of the city's citizens were made homeless.

No sooner than the aircraft had landed, the ground crews started their after-flight inspections, repairs if needed and rectification of snags (system malfunctions in air force jargon) encountered in flight. Some members of the ground crew were always detailed off to stay up and see the Lancasters in, if there was not a proper organised nightshift, dealing with any work if and when required. While the aircrew slept it was never known until the mid morning if an operation was on for the coming night. If an order came through from 1 Group the fuel and bomb loads would be given along with the number of aircraft needed, so it was prudent to recover them as soon as possible. Sure enough, later that morning 1 Group gave details of requirements for a raid on Braunschweig that night, ordering eighteen Lancasters on 626 Squadron to be made ready. The ground crews set to arming, refuelling and servicing the aircraft. By late afternoon the pre-raid ground testing had been done and the crews 'Bacon and egged', as the expression went, in the various messes. Frustratingly, the raid was cancelled,, the message coming through actually while the main briefing was taking place.

On cancellation, the task of removing the bomb loads from the eighteen Lancasters began, the armourers undoing all the work they had done that day. This started by making the large 4000-pound 'cookies' safe by removing the fuses. Then came the task of winching them and all the incendiary canisters down and back on to bomb trolleys below for transport to the bomb dumps. This was nearly as hard as getting them up into the bomb bays in the first place. The hand winches were heavy and awkward to carry up into the Lancaster's fuselage whereby the cables and hooks were attached to the bombs and canisters through a hole in the floor. When the individual load was released from its release unit there were many arm aching turns on the winch handle to get it down on to the bomb trolley below. The armourer's job was one of the hardest on the Squadron and not one for the unfit. In contrast, on today's Tornados, the under wing and under fuselage 'Stores' are raised and lowered to and from the pylon release units in a matter of minutes by a motorised hydraulic weapons loader.

Eventually all eighteen Lancasters were unloaded and made safe for the night. The next day at 1000Hrs an operation was announced for a raid on Munich that night. In the teleprinted orders was the codename 'Goodwood', which meant a maximum effort was required with all available aircraft. With eighteen Lancasters, as on the previous day, the process of servicing and arming up started all over again and finished the same way, as the raid was cancelled at 1645Hrs due to unfavourable weather at the target. Unbelievably the same thing happened the very next day, 21st March, when a raid was ordered for Berlin.

The 22nd March 1944 started fine at Wickenby becoming cloudy later on with a light north wind, Visibility was good. The message came through from 1 Group to mount a raid on Frankfurt again and this time the operation stayed on.

Since the aircraft had not flown for a few days the ground crew were able to put fifteen 626 Squadron Lancasters on the flight line for the raid, the take off for it being about seven o'clock in the early evening. There would have been four more but the loading of the bombs could not be completed in time. Time on target was at 2150Hrs after crossing the North Sea, the West Frisian Islands and then east into Germany, the last turning point being between Osnabruck and Hanover where the Force headed almost due south for Frankfurt. What with the new route and that there was eighteen Stirlings and 128 Halifaxes on mine-laying diversions to Kiel Bay and the Danish coast, it confused the German fighter controllers for- a period of time to what city was going to be the target.

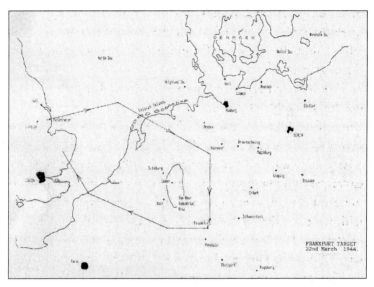

Map 9. Target Frankfurt, 22.3.44.

At one stage it was thought that the Force was going for Hanover and a large number of night-fighters must have been sent to that area to defend the city. Indeed F/Lt Ravenhill reported seeing many of them between Hanover and Osnabruck as pilot of LL829. There were two important Night-fighter airfields near the route of the bomber stream. Oldenburg was fifty miles north of Frankfurt and home of III./JG300, being the original single engine 'Wild Boar' unit it operated the Messerschmidt Me109G. Twenty miles south of Oldenburg was Vechta which was host to II./NJG 3 flying a few Dornier Do217s but mainly the deadly Junkers Ju88C-6. Not far to the west of Frankfurt was the airfield of Mainz-Finthen with I./NJG 6 and a Nachtjagd ace of whom we shall hear about later.

Because of the diversions and that Hanover was for some time taken for the target, only a few night-fighters found the bomber stream at this stage of the attack. It could be assumed that it was a night-fighter from one of the above airfields that found and shot down 626 Squadron's JB599 near the town of Luebecke, twenty-five miles east of Osnabruck. The crew had only been on 626 Squadron a little over a month being lead by pilot F/O Kewley. JB599 crashed very near the last turning point before going for the target and all the crew were killed. Their final resting place is in the nearby Hanover War Cemetery.

Although the route to the target was 4-7/10ths cloud only thin cloud covered the target in some places while in other parts as much as 8000 feet. About ten miles north of Frankfurt a dummy target area was seen with false red target indicators as on the last raid. This night the Pathfinder Force was using red and green target indicators and red and yellow Wanganui sky-markers, by all reports being laid down accurately.

LL829, with F/Lt Ravenhill piloting, dodged the night-fighters to the north and came in at 23,000 feet bombing four minutes after zero hour. Two concentrations of red target indicators were seen, one slightly north and another to the south of the aiming point, the bomb aimer choosing the first encountered. Fires that were seen below caused smoke to rise to 6000 feet or more. Three minutes later F/Sgt Bladon brought in HK539 where his bomb aimer, F/Sgt Nathanson, aimed the aircraft's bomb load at eight red target indicators. P/O Gallagher's crew had been issued with 12 Squadron's ND710, equipped with H2S radar and the electronic device 'Fishpond'. 'Fishpond' was the code name for a modification to the H2S radar. If the ground could be seen by H2S then it was thought that other aircraft flying within the scanning envelope below would also be picked up as a return on the screen.

This was found by experiment to be true and another screen was placed in the wireless operator's compartment for that purpose. Other bombers could be seen on the screen but they would show as keeping in station and about the same speed as the aircraft fitted with 'Fishpond'. Any 'Blip' that moved faster across the screen was taken as a hostile night-Fighter. Of course H2S only looked down as it was a bombing and navigation radar but it was from below where most attacks came from anyway. Although finding a cluster of red and green target indicators to aim at the navigator identified the target aiming point with the H2S. This was quite a novelty for the crew as 626 Squadron aircraft were not fitted with it.

The stream flew south before heading west for home but not before noticing another decoy target site ten miles south of Frankfurt. This and the one to the north were now quite well known, both having been seen on the previous raid four nights before. The route back was near enough the same as the previous Frankfurt raid, north-west across Western Germany, Belgium and leaving the enemy coast between Dunkerque and Oostende again, then making a landfall on the English coast at Orford Ness. On the homeward journey JA922 was flying at 21,000 feet with 10/10ths cloud whose tops were 4000 feet below. The pilot, F/Sgt Dawson, the flight engineer, Sgt Hemus and the bomb aimer, Sgt Slater up in the front turret suddenly saw four lines of tracer coming towards them from 600-700 yards ahead. F/Sgt Dawson immediately pushed the control column forward and dived the Lancaster under the oncoming tracer bullets. There was no moon and no aircraft was seen by any of the crew ahead or above. JA922's gunners did not get a chance to fire back. It was believed by the crew that the attack could have come from another bomber with a four-gun rear turret like their own or a Halifax because of the unique tracer pattern. A lucky escape never the less. The remaining fourteen Lancasters of 626 Squadron came back without further incidence, landing between midnight and two o'clock in the morning of the 23rd March.

With these two raids on Frankfurt by Bomber Command and another 36 hours later by B-17s of the USAAF, the city was just about destroyed. This latest raid was worse than the one four days previous. Half of the city was without the essential services of gas, water and electricity and remained so for a long time. The main damage to industry was in the western and south-western parts but bombs exploded all over the city wrecking churches, historic buildings, hospitals and homes putting 120,000 inhabitants out onto the streets. As far as contributing to Germany's war effort from then on, like Hamburg before it, Frankfurt was no more. Over 900 people were killed and 350 were injured.

Including 626 Squadron's JB599, 26 Lancasters were posted missing the next day along with seven Halifaxes. Luftwaffe night-fighter pilot Hauptman Martin 'Tino' Becker, flying a Messerschmidt Me110 G-4 claimed no less than six of these, although not strictly true as his funker (radio/radar operator) Karl-Ludwig Johanssen shot down three of them with his rearward facing machine gun. Their aircraft belonged to I/NJG 6 flying out of Mainz-Finthen airfield to the west of Frankfurt. Martin Becker went on to become one of the top scoring night-fighter aces of the Luftwaffe, receiving the much sought-after Knight's Cross to The Iron Cross in April 1944 from Adolf Hitler himself. He survived the war and in 1997 was still living in Germany.

14. Berlin Just One More Time

The 23rd March brought cloud and only moderate visibility at first, which reduced to about 300 yards down Wickenby's runways later on in the day. At 1000Hrs a message from 1 Group stated that there was to be no operations that day. This day saw RAF Wickenby with a new Commanding Officer, Group Captain Haines assuming command of the Station.

Sir Arthur Harris was running out of time. Earlier he wrote that 'We can wreck Berlin from end to end if the United States Army Air Force will come in on it'. Fifteen heavy raids later found the German capital heavily damaged in many areas but unlike Hamburg and Frankfurt it was still intact. The USAAF had seen fit not to venture all the way to Berlin in daylight without a proper fighter escort. One can hardly blame them as the B17 and B24 crews were sometimes being slaughtered going to and from targets nearer to home than Berlin. Time was running out for three reasons. It was spring in North-West Europe and the nights were getting shorter, which cut down the amount of safe dark flying hours over Germany available. The moon was waxing giving an advantage to the defending night-fighters, particularly the single engine types with no radar. For some time now, minor raids had taken place in France in preparation for the invasion, mainly against road and rail communications and German Army units that would impede the landings in Normandy. Also V1 flying-bomb launch sites were still a regular target. On the night of 23rd March 1944, 143 Halifaxes, Stirlings and Mosquitos attacked the railway yards at Laon, seventy-five miles north-east of Paris. Up till now, Sir Arthur Harris had a big say in what targets were to be attacked and when. This certain amount of freedom was to be enjoyed up till 1st April. After then Bomber Command would come under General Eisenhower, the Supreme Allied Commander, and be used in direct support of the invasion and the preparations leading up to it. Small forces of Mosquitos would still roam far and wide across Germany carrying out nuisance raids to Berlin and other cities but the main bulk of the Command, the four engine heavies, would be directed towards France.

There was still a little time left to execute one final blow to the capital of the Third Reich, one last chance and Sir Arthur Harris took it on the 24th March 1944. This was to be the final and sixteenth major attack on Berlin with over 800 Lancasters and Halifaxes at his disposal, nearly twice as many as the first raid of the Battle of Berlin on 18th November 1943 when 440 Lancasters took part.

When the order to go was received the teleprinter message went out from Bomber Command Headquarters to all Groups and RAF Stations involved. Only the barest details were given at this stage. On this, the Form A, would be the target, bomb load, fuel load and the number of aircraft required. The fuel load for the Wickenby squadrons was 1849 gallons of petrol for each Lancaster. If a 'Maximum Effort' was required where everything humanly possible was to be done to get every aircraft on a squadron serviced and on the flight line for the raid the message would be coded 'Goodwood'. The details on the Form A would allow the ground crews to get on with job of getting the aircraft prepared. As soon as the target was known, for security reasons, the Station was 'Sealed'. Unless on very official RAF business, nobody went in or out the perimeter or main gates and the PBX telephone exchange would cut the Station off from the outside world except for official messages and orders. Meanwhile at Bomber Command Headquarters the route would be decided with diversions and spoof raids worked out to try and draw the defending night-fighters away from the bomber stream. Sometimes they worked, many times they were ignored by the enemy.

SECRET

24/3.   WHITEBAIT - SKATE.

MABLETHORPE - 5440N/0430E - 5513N/0940E - 5418N/1221E

TARGET - 5206N/1303E - 5157/1054E - 5242N/0801E

RENDEZVOUS 17/20000 FT AT 5440N/0430E.

ZH 2230.

FUEL: 1849 GALL.

WINDOW: START   5500N/0720E. 5320N/1336E. 5201N/1218E.

         STOP   5252N/0346E.

NT. TACTICS FOR BOTH AREAS.

(A).   CLIMB ON ROUTE SO AS TO RENDEZVOUS AT 1ST TURNING POINT OUT TO SEA 17/20000 FT.

(B).   CROSS ENEMY COAST IN 20/24000 FT.

(C).   MAINTAIN THAT HEIGHT OVER ENEMY TERRITORY AND THEN CLIMB SO AS TO BOMB BETWEEN 21/25000 FT.

(D).   AFTER BOMBING FLY AT 20/24000 FT FOR THE RETURN JOURNEY AS FAR AS THE ENEMY COAST OUT.

(E).   BASES ARE TO SPREAD THEIR AIRCRAFT EVENLY OVER THESE HEIGHT BANDS AND ALL CAPTAINS ARE TO BE BRIEFED TO ADHERE TO THEIR ORDERED HEIGHT UNLESS SUCH ADHERENCE WOULD INTERFERE WITH THEIR ABILITY TO CARRY OUT A SUCCESSFUL ATTACK.

NG.

(A).   METHOD FOR TONIGHT 24 MARCH 1944 ON WHITEBAIT OR SKATE

WILL BE NEWHAVEN GROUNDMARKING. WANGANUI SKYMARKING WILL BE USED AS EMERGENCY IF CLOUD COVERS TI.

(B).   PATHFINDERS WILL OPEN ATTACK AT Z-5 WITH STICKS OF ILLUMINATING FLARES AND GREEN TI DROPPED IN THE TARGET AREA.,THE AIMING POINT WILL BE MARKED WITH LARGE SALVOS OF MIXED RED AND GREEN TI AND KEPT MARKED WITH RED TI.

(C).   IF ADDITION OF CLOUD OBSCURES TI THE RELEASE POINT WILL BE

MARKED WITH FLARES RED AND YELLOW STARS.

(D).   MAINFORCE AIRCRAFT ARRIVING EARLY IN THE ATTACK ARE TO AIM THEIR BOMBS AT THE LARGE SALVOS OF MIXED RED AND GREEN TI IF VISIBLE. OTHERWISE ALL MAINFORCE AIRCRAFT ARE TO AIM AT CENTRE OF ALL TI SM RED. CARE MUST BE TAKEN TO AVOID THE WEAKER AND SHORTER BURNING RED DECOYS WHICH MAY BE DROPPED BY THE ENEMY.

(E).   IF CLOUD OBSCURES TI MAIN FORCE AIRCRAFT ARE TO AIM AT CENTRE OF ALL FLARES RED AND YELLOW STARS WHILE HOLDING A HEADING OF 189M ON SKATE AND 217 ON WHITEBAIT. IN THIS CASE BOMBSIGHTS ARE TO BE SET FOR THE TRUE HEIGHT AND AIRSPEED BUT ZERO WIND.

(F).   AIRCRAFT MUST NOT DROP INCENDIARIES BEFORE ZERO HOUR.

(G).   ALL CREWS ARE TO BE WARNED TO LISTEN OUT ON DARKY FREQUENCY WHEN NEAR WHITEBAIT AREA. A MOSQUITO AND LANCASTER WILL ACT AS `MASTER BOMBER' AND WILL BROADCAST COMMENTS AND ADVICE TO ALL CREWS THROUGHOUT THE RAID. THE CALL SIGNS WILL BE AS FOLLOWS:

MOSQUITO: POMMY.

LANCASTER: REDSKIN.

Extracts from the Teleprinter Message Form B from 1 Group to all 1 Group stations including RAF Wickenby on 24th March 1944. Most details of the alternative raid on Braunschweig (Skate) have been deleted. The original with all the detailed instructions is about a yard long and can be seen in The Public Records Office under file AIR 25/11. 1 Group Operational Records. Bomber Command.

There would be a very close look at what the weather would be like en route, at the target and at the time over England when the bombers would be landing. 'Black Thursday', December 16th 1943, was still in the minds of many. The synopsis was collated from various sources. One was from a unit in 8 Group, No.1409 Meteorological Reconnaissance Flight. This was equipped with unarmed Mosquitos with pilots and navigators trained in weather observation, flying all hours of the day and night as and when required. Having no defensive armaments the crews relied purely on the aircraft's superior height and speed to avoid being shot down. Many times they flew deep into Germany in cloudless daylight to gather information about the weather, which demanded not only technical skill but great courage. One such pilot was F/O Currie who had served on 626 Squadron earlier in the Battle.

When everything had been finalised, teleprinter Form B would be sent to all Groups and RAF Stations participating. All target cities were coded by the names of fish. As always, Berlin was called 'Whitebait' but on this night there was an alternative target - Braunschweig and that was coded 'Skate'.

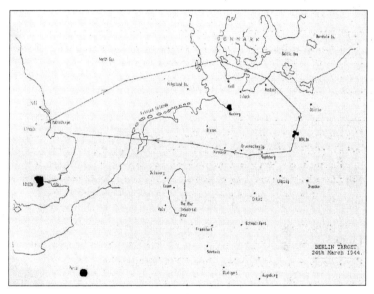

Map 10. Target Berlin, 24.3.44.

Greater details would be given on the route, how the target was to be marked by the Pathfinders and at what time relative to the Zero Hour. There was also the timings when the various waves of aircraft would bomb. This was to not only to avoid collisions but to concentrate the attack in the shortest possible time.

At Wickenby on 24th March the day started cloudy with thick haze all day but clearing by the evening for a take off between six-thirty and seven o'clock. One hour before this time two new crews were aborted the sortie on orders from 14 Base Headquarters at RAF Ludford Magna. Time on target, or Zero Hour, was 2230Hrs with a twenty minute bombing period between 2225Hrs and 2245Hrs.

1 Group aircraft would rendezvous at a point over the North Sea 175 miles north of Texel Island and continue on to cross the enemy coast just north of Sylt, a long thin island easily distinguished on radar and by visual means. Crossing the Jylland Peninsular of Denmark, the bomber stream would carry on over The Baltic to enter Germany twenty-five miles up the coast from Rostock. Flying 105 miles on from there approximately south-east, they would pick up the last turning point before the target, a large lake, the Oberuckersee below the town of Prenzlau. The last leg would turn them to starboard on a heading of 217 degrees magnetic as instructed on the form B.

After bombing, the Force would continue on the same heading for another 30 miles, then turn and go for Den Helder on the Dutch coast with a dogleg track over the top of the Ruhr industrial area. 'Window' was to be dropped on specified stretches of the route.

At the main Wickenby briefing the details of the Berlin raid was given and the route to the alternative target, Braunschweig. It was all according to the weather patterns and at the last moment the Berlin target was chosen – 'The Big City'.

All 626 Squadron's Lancasters were airborne on time taking off in two to four minutes intervals and heading for Mablethorpe and the rendezvous point over the North Sea. Once out over the sea the bomber stream was picked up by the long-range German

Wasserman coastal radar, their speed and direction being passed to the Luftwaffe fighter controllers. LL722 was the only aircraft to abort on 626 Squadron. Some time after take off and gaining height, none of the four superchargers would change into the high S ratio. The problem could have been pneumatic or electrical as electro-pneumatic rams are used to change the superchargers from M to S ratio when flying above 15,000 feet. With Pneumatic or electrical failure the rams would always return the gearing to M ratio permitting low-level flight only. After lightening the load by dumping in the North, Sea pilot P/O Stewart landed LL722 at Wittering at 2125Hrs which must have been fearful as the aircraft had no brake pressure.

Meanwhile, as the bomber stream headed towards the enemy coast an impending disaster was beginning to take shape. Two weather reconnaissance flights had been flown on the 24th March, one in the early hours of the morning and another taking off at 1030Hrs. The weather forecast, among other things, indicated high winds over Europe and fog developing over much of Lincolnshire, The Fens and Norfolk by 0300Hrs in the morning of the 25th. The fog would be problematical but the bombers were due back before 0200Hrs. The navigators were told of nearly fifty miles per hour winds from the north and increasing in strength as the stream flew east. This information was used in their calculations before take off. Over the North Sea it was a different story.

What the bomber stream was flying in is what is now known in meteorological science as a jet stream. Some navigators rightly calculated with the aid of their navigation systems the speed of the wind to be at least 100 miles per hour, double what they had been told and like nothing they had experienced before or heard of in Europe. The outcome was that even experienced Pathfinder navigators began to doubt their calculations. The 'Wind-finder' aircraft navigators downscaled their results and radioed them back to Bomber Command Headquarters who in turn, not believing that wind could blow that speed in Europe, did the same. Command then re-broadcast the wind information to the bomber stream well below the true value. Less experienced navigators, and there were many, used this in their calculations and consequently the tragedy of what was later to be called 'The Night of the Big Winds' started to unfold. Many aircraft were to drift unknowingly south of track into heavily defended areas and this was to be their undoing.

Many crews knew something was wrong when they passed the island of Sylt to the south instead of to the north. After the last turning point before the target the wind was more behind than abeam and the zero-hour was brought forward by five minutes but this was nowhere near the compensation needed. About twenty miles to the target, F/Sgt Mason and his crew in LL829 noted a German decoy site displaying red and green dummy target indicators. In their opinion the give away was that they were not as bright and did not last as long as the real thing that the Pathfinders used. P/O Torrance in JB646, F/Sgt Newton in EE148 and P/O Jackson in ME587 reported the same.

Most captains on 626 Squadron thought that the Pathfinder marking was late and because of the wind overshot the target before it was properly identified. The target indicators could in some areas be seen through the cloud shrouding Berlin but the sky-markers were blown all over the place downwind. EE148 overshot the target to the west but F/Sgt Newton brought the Lancaster round again on to the proper heading as briefed. This made the aircraft a bit late where the bomb load was dropped at 2250Hrs in the centre of the fireglow that was becoming established at the time. F/Sgt Newton saw at lease twenty clusters of red flares drifting east of the Pathfinder target indicators on the ground and on the bomb run two flares to starboard and one to port drifting with the wind. F/Sgt Mason's bomb aimer in LL929 did not see any target indicators at all as the piece of Berlin they were flying over was under 10/10ths cloud. On the run up they came across six sky-markers in a line east to west but at 2250Hrs bombed in the centre of six which seemed a more definite target. Even at this late stage the crew saw only a couple of fire glows but no extensive areas of fire.

The raid this night was being assisted by two Master Bombers, one in a Lancaster and a back-up in a Mosquito. These courageous crews circled over the target area conducting the attack by correcting mistakes and giving encouragement. They had the means in their bomb bays of going in themselves and re-marking a wrongly marked aiming point and sometimes did. Irrespective of flak and night-fighters and all that was going on around them their only concern was to get the Main Force's bombs on the target and of course staying alive. The 'Master of Ceremonies' was what other crews called them. The Master Bomber was always the last to leave the target and consequently, as he was at the tail end of the stream, was very open to attack. This was how W/Cdr. Guy Gibson VC of the Dambusters fame was shot down by a Fw190 after a raid on Munchengladbach later in the year. F/Sgt Bennet, piloting W4967, attacked in one of the early waves, his bomb aimer releasing the bomb load from 22,000 feet at 2234Hrs on four groups of red and yellow flares. At de-briefing after landing he said 'The Master Bomber deserved much praise, having a great physiological effect on crews in a difficult mission'.

In the target area it was reported that there was over a dozen bombers shot down by night-fighters alone. F/Sgt Laidlaw and his bomb aimer of EE623 managed to identify the target although they were late. Luckily it was only 4/10ths cloud below at the time and he bombed some red target indicators even though most were seen to be scattered. This was particularly difficult as the Lancaster's bombsight was not working correctly. At the same time, 2248Hrs and at 21,000 feet, the crew saw another bomber that had been hit and explode in a large fireball. It was all the more distressing not to see any crew parachuting from the stricken aircraft. On leaving Berlin behind the Force was still blown off track when heading for home by the high northerly wind. This put them in real danger as the planed route was meant to guide them north of the industrial cities of Southern Germany and the Ruhr area. LL835, with F/Lt Wright at the controls, was flying so fast over the ground because of the effect of the tailwind that it overshot the primary target. Instead, the bomb aimer dropped the load on the city of Halle, identifying it by its flak defences. Halle was thirty-five miles south of the correct track and ninety miles south-west of Berlin. Like most of the bomber stream at this stage, they were being blown towards that direction anyway.

The first turning point after Berlin was five miles west of the town of Luckenwalde, thirty miles south of the target. LM393 was not far off track, maybe within a few miles of it, and regrettably it was shot down near this town. All the crew were killed. F/Sgt Margetts, the captain, and the other six were posted to 626 Squadron from 1656 Conversion Unit on 30th January 1944. The body of the wireless operator was never found at the crash site or anywhere else and therefore Sgt Probert is remembered on a panel at Runnymede. The six other crew members are buried in the Berlin 1939/1945 War Cemetery.

The bomber stream flew on, flying many miles, in most cases, south of track and encountering the radar predicted flak defences of cities like Leipzig, Kassel and the Ruhr Valley. P/O Jackson, flying ME587, was on time and track to begin with when flying over the Danish coast. In using the inaccurate broadcast winds from Command however, by the time Berlin was reached the Lancaster overshot the target like LL835. In turning back they bombed in a strong headwind at the late time of 2306Hrs. Such was the sense of duty and dedication of a vast majority of bomber crews. To make up for lost time, the Lancaster headed in the direction of 272 degrees after leaving the target area in the hope that it would meet up with the rest of the stream at the last turning point, thirty miles north of Osnabruck. They had a worrying time getting over the Ruhr industrial area but made the enemy coast and the North Sea safely. LL829 avoided trouble by flying north of Dresden, Frankfurt and over the top of the Ruhr Valley, finally going out via Rotterdam and later crossing the Suffolk coast at Southwold.

The navigational problem was that due to the strong northerly wind, the Lancasters and Halifaxes could not point too far- to starboard to counteract it when flying west and 'Crab' across Europe to keep to the planned track. If they did it would have cost too much fuel and the real possibility of a ditching in the North Sea, if they in fact made it as far as the coast. The crews were not only being asked to fight the German night-fighters and flak but also the weather and what every schoolboy knows in physics as the 'Triangle of Forces' when working out the track to be flown against windspeed and direction.

Over fifty bombers were shot down flying the southern route from the target to the Dutch coast. HK539 this night was being piloted by 626 Squadron's Commanding Officer, W/Cdr. Quentin Ross. With one-hundred-and-fifty miles or about an hours flying time to the Dutch coast, his Lancaster was shot down near the town of Warendorf. This place is fifteen miles east of Munster and fifty miles south of the final turning point on the route home.

The grave of Wing Commander Q.W.A.Ross in the Reichwald War Cemetery. W/Cdr Ross's had been 626 Squadron's Commanding Officer for less than seven weeks when his Lancaster was shot down 15 miles east of Munster, only one hour's flying time from the North Sea after participating in the 16th and last raid of the Battle of Berlin on 24th March 1944.

Having been posted in from 11 Base on the 8th February 1944, W/Cdr. Ross took over from W/Cdr. Haines. It will be remembered that it was this officer that formed the Squadron the previous November. The other six of his crew had come from 1662 Conversion Unit the week before. His flying experience with his new Squadron had been very limited, having flown his first sortie with them only a month earlier as 2nd Pilot to W/O. Gallagher in LL772 on the raid to Schweinfurt. The final resting place of HK539's crew is in the Reichwald Forest War Cemetery near the old German town of Kleve, not very far from the Dutch border.

The seven graves of W/Cdr. Ross and his crew of HK539 in the Reichswald War Cemetery: W/Cdr Ross (captain/pilot), P/O J. Gibson (navigator), F/Sgt C. Christie (wireless operator), F/Sgt C. Nathanson (bomb aimer), Sgt H. Watt (flight engineer), Sgt T. Bint (mid-upper gunner), F/Sgt S. Jones (rear gunner). Note the Star of David on the gravestone of Bomb Aimer F/Sgt Nathanson. It took extra courage to fly over enemy occupied Europe knowing that if one were shot down and captured one would almost certainly be shot or interned in a concentration camp.

LM393 and HK539 were the only two Lancasters on 626 Squadron to be lost this night, all the rest landed safely back in England but not at Wickenby. All landed at Seething and other airfields in Norfolk, with barely enough fuel in their tanks to make it across the East Anglian coast.

The Command had taken a terrible toll, seventy-two aircraft missing in action, 392 airmen killed, 131 captured as prisoners of war and four managing to evade and escape. But on this night these four were not the only bomber aircrew on the run. This was the night of 'The Great Escape' where seventy-six airmen, many of them bomber aircrew, tunnelled their way out of the Stalag Luft III POW camp. Three got back to England to fight again, the rest were eventually caught but sadly and brutally, fifty of them were shot by the Gestapo.

And what of Berlin? The aiming point was the eastern end of Tiergarten, right in the centre of the city. Plenty of damage had already been caused in the south and south-west districts from other raids. It was thought that in the normal course of 'creep-back', 800 bombers would devastate the northern areas too. 626 Squadron Lancasters alone were carrying over- four tons of high explosive and incendiaries apiece. Thanks to the unusual high wind and the misinformation about it given to the navigators, it did not turn out that way. Bombs were scattered all over the south-west of Berlin and many outlaying towns and villages. No industrial establishments that contributed to the war effort were destroyed although some were damaged. Housing suffered the most with around 20,000 citizens made homeless. About another 150 lost their lives in the raid.

Unknown to the tired crews scattered over Eastern England in the early hours of 25th March 1944, that was the end of what became known as 'The Battle of Berlin', the biggest offensive against a German target in the World War II. To come next were the preparations for D-Day, the destruction of Germany's syn-thetic oil industry and the support of the Allied armies' advance –

To Strive and Not to Yield

to name only a few campaigns to final victory – but they are
other chapters in the chequered history of 626 Squadron,
Bomber Command and the Royal Air Force.

---

626 SQUADRON OPERATIONAL RECORDS BOOK

25TH MARCH 1944

(Air 27/2145. The Public Records Office)

Cloudy with thick smoke haze all day but fine in the evening. Fog by 2315 at night.
Berlin zero hour 2230. 626 x 16. One hour before take off two new crews withdrawn on
Base instruction.

1 x 626 abort. Cloud most of route out, target 6/10ths. Winds high. Crews reported
blown south of track. Zero hour brought forward five minutes. PFF opened rather later
than revised zero hour. Master bombers indicated that the RP flares should be used but
some bombed on TI, consequently two fires developed. Attack widespread. Many searchlights. Flak heavier than recent attacks. Winds 50 mph greater than Bomber Command
winds on homeward route. Crews reported flying well south of track, many through
Rhur Valley and its flak and searchlights. 626 diverted to Seething due to poor visibility.
No aircraft landed at Wickenby. (12 Squadron to Shipham.)

RAF Form 541: Details of Sortie or Flight.

W4967. F/Sgt. Bennet. Take off 1851. Over target 2234. 22,000 feet. Boozer. 10/10ths
cloud over target tops 6/7000 feet. Bombed centre of four groups of red/yellow flares.
Master bombers deserve much praise and had a great physiological effect on crews in a
difficult mission. Landed Seething 0155. '

LL835. F/Lt. Wright. Take off 1843. Over target 2247. ?1,500 feet. 9/10ths tops
8/10,000 feet. Visability good. Primary abandoned, overshot due to tail wind. Bombed
Halle as last resort. Identified target by DR and flak defences. Landed 0310.

ME587. P/O. Jackson. Take off 1856. Over target 2306. 22,000 feet. 9/10ths. Fire and
smoke. R/P flares seen in the distance on approach. Bombed centre of fires as no PFF
markers seen at time of bombing. Saw decoys. Target burning well at north. PFF was
late. On trip home steered 272 from target in order to meet concentration at 3rd turning point as we overshot target and too late. On time and track over Danish coast on
way out and used broadcast winds from that point and overshot target considerably.
Bombed in strong headwind. Same difficulties caused us to pass over Rhur on way back.
Landed 0240.

EE623. F/Sgt. Laidlow. Take off 1855. Over target 2248. 21,000 feet. GEE. Mandrel.
Monica. 4/10ths cloud below. Identified target with R/G TI bombed on red TI which
appeared scattered particularly incendiaries. Own bombsight partially U/S so BA unable
to hit centre of TI. Saw A/C explode overtarget at 2248 at 21,000 feet. Saw no parachutes. Landed Tuddenham at 0320.

LM393. Sgt. Margetts. Take off 1844. No more heard after take off. Missing.

267

LL829. F/Sgt. Mason. Take off 1849. Over target 2250. 21,500 feet. 10/10ths cloud. Good visibility, identified target by R/Y R/P flares, bombed centre of 6 of them. On run up to target saw string of 6 skymarkers in line from E to W. No TI seen, two fire glows but no extensive fire areas. Obvious decoys N of Berlin in form of red and green TI which were less bright and shorter burning than ours. Rhur defences looked so threatening that we turned sharply north of Frankfurt to skirt and avoid them. Return N of Dresden, N of Frankfurt, Rotterdam, Southwold. Landed Seething at 0243.

HK539. W/Cdr. Ross. Take off 1841. No more heard after take off. Missing.

LL797. W/O. Lone. Take off 1842. Over target 2241. 23,000 feet. Visibility good from above. Identified target and bombed estimated centre of 3 R/Y flares. Big fire glow seen through cloud. PFF scattered. Winds 50 MPH more than broadcast winds. Landed Seething 0255.

EE148. F/Sgt. Newton. Take off 1852. Boozer. Over target 2250. 23,000 feet. Identified target and bombed centre of fire glow. On run up to bomb, saw 3 skymarkers, 2 to sbd, 1 to port and a few re;d TI dead ahead through cloud. Fire glow was extensive. About 20 clusters of red flares each of 3 flares east of PFF marking. Obvious decoys. Overshot target to west and orbited to bomb on track laid down. Landed Seething 0151.

JB646. P/O. Torrance. Take off 1836. Over target 2226 22,000 feet. Identified target and bombed centre of 5 R/P flares which was seen to ignite 3 minutes before. One cluster only of skymarkers with mixed red and green TI underneath cloud. Plain red flares obviously decoys seen on run in above cloud in clusters like bunch of grapes. Monica U/S. Return via N of Kassel, S of Munster, Rotterdam area, Lowestoft. Landed Bungay at 0153.

W4990. F/Sgt. Smith. Saw big explosion at 2229. Landed at Horham at 0153.

LL722. P/O. Stewart. Take off 1840. Mission abandoned, no brake pressure and all superchargers U/S. Landed Wittering at 2125.

268

15. Berlin: Costs & Conclusions

The period that came to be known as the Battle of Berlin was the largest and longest Bomber Command offensive against a single target. Unlike Agincourt, Waterloo or the Battle of Britain there was no clear winner or loser; it has been debated for over fifty years whether Bomber Command won or lost the battle. Certainly Berlin was not 'wrecked from end to end' – as Sir Arthur Harris would have liked – but very large areas were laid waste, including important industrial complexes producing vital war materials (5,427 acres, according to Goebbels' diary). 1,500,000 Berliners were made homeless and many were killed, including workers in the factories, which was just as effective as the destroying the machines they worked on. The Rheinmetall-Borsig arms factory alone employed 18,000 people manufacturing guns, including those installed in night-fighters. Seventy-five per cent of all guns produced by Germany's arms industries were destined the for flak units involved in the defence of Germany's cities. Guns for tanks and artillery to be used on the Russian Front and later in Normandy had to wait.

The Battle of Berlin put Germany on the defensive, which greatly assisted the Allies on the Russian and Mediterranean fronts. Admiral Donitz wanted to recruit 20,000 sailors for his Navy but was told he could not have them, as they were required as flak gun crews, searchlight crews and to swell the ranks of the night-fighter arm of the Luftwaffe. At the time of the Battle, there were over a million employed in manning flak and searchlight units throughout Germany alone, mainly in big cities like Berlin. They were still manning these guns, searchlights and night-fighters when the Allies landed on the Normandy beaches on 6th June 1944, greatly increasing its chances of success.

However, the price paid by the aircrews of Bomber Command was staggering. Not counting raids to other cities during the same period, or the diversions and aircraft that crashed in England, Bomber Command lost 492 bombers on routes to, from and over Berlin on the sixteen raids that made up the Battle of Berlin. Over 3,000 airmen were killed, many of them only in their late teens or early twenties. More airmen lost their lives in the first four raids on Berlin than in the whole of the Battle of Britain.

Nobody disputes the superb design of Roy Chadwick's Lancaster or of the Halifax Mk. III, which although not as good, still did the job. (Stirlings and the other marks of Halifax were taken out of the Battle of Berlin in the early days because they did not). But why so many deaths?

The reasons are believed to be twofold. Firstly, the Luftwaffe mounted an aggressive and efficient campaign with well-armed and well-designed night-fighters, flown by well-trained and experienced aircrew, backed up by excellent command and control and a defencive radar system. The other reason was that, to defend themselves, the Stirling, Halifax and Lancaster had guns that were totally inadequate for the job. A Luftwaffe night-fighter could start firing from 1000 yards with its 20mm cannons, meanwhile the RAF gunners had guns with the same ammunition and calibre as an infantry soldier's rifle. There is also the question of 'hitting power' or how much flying metal it takes to bring down an aircraft. The early marks of Spitfire, equipped with eight .303 machine guns, often failed to shoot down Ju88 A4s and similar bombers in the Battle of Britain in broad daylight, so how were Lancaster crews supposed to defend them-

selves against a Ju88C-6 in the dead of night with half that firepower in the rear turret and only a quarter in each of the other
two?

Larger calibre guns, like the Brownings the Americans had in
B-17s and B-24s, would have saved many aircrew lives, especially
if installed in the rear turret. In the early years of the war, a
20mm Hispano gun turret was being developed, but the work
was cancelled. The RAF proved they could win against the
Germans in the Battle of Britain, the Battle of the Atlantic, the
Ruhr, Hamburg and in many more campaigns, but they stood no
chance against the bureaucracy of the politicians and civil servants of the Ministry of Aircraft Production and Lord Beaver-
brook in particular, who cancelled the Hispano gun turret
project. Whereas Mosquitos were equipped with these guns to
shoot down night-fighters, the Lancasters, Halifaxes and Stirlings
were left almost defenceless.

It was argued that heavier guns and ammunition would mean
that the bombers would need to have their bomb loads reduced.
The Commanders and politicians were obsessed with bomb
loads and that the maximum should be carried. As a conse-
quence, the aircraft, particularly the Lancasters of 1 Group, always flew with the minimum of fuel with not much of a safety
margin. There are many bombers at the bottom of the North Sea
as a result.

Ninety two 626 Squadron aircrew lost their lives during the
Battle. Sixteen have no known grave and are remembered at the
RAF Memorial at Runnymede. Eight survived being shot down
and became prisoners of war.

On 26th November 1943 F/Lt Wood's LM362 crashed while
trying to land in bad weather at Wickenby and nearly took the
WAAF accommodation with it. F/Lt Wood and all his crew sur-

vived, including F/O Wilkinson, flying as second pilot, who was on the first trip of his operational tour. He was later to die as captain of his own Lancaster, ME587, when it was shot down on 30th January 1944. On the same night DV295 crashed while attempting to land at Marham. The captain, F/Sgt Windus and all his crew perished. Earlier on that night DV388 was shot down after bombing Berlin and on the way home with the loss of pilot W/O Kindt and all his crew at Finow, north of Berlin. They were the first losses of the Squadron and all on the same night.

ME577 ditched in the North Sea on 5th January 1944, having run out of fuel on the way back from Stettin. All the crew were picked up by a Royal Navy rescue launch the next day. A few weeks later the same crew were shot down near Koblenz on their way back from bombing Berlin. Only the Navigator, F/Sgt Lee, parachuted to safety, spending the rest of the war as a POW.

ME589 also crashed in the North Sea, somewhere off Schiermonnikog, one of the Dutch West Frisian islands on 19th February 1944. Only the bodies of Sgt Mitton the bomb aimer and Sgt Bodycot the mid-upper gunner were ever found, having been washed up on the shore a few months later. The Dutch people of the islands buried them in their own local cemeteries. The other five crew members have no known grave but have their names on a panel of remembrance at Runnymede. The crew had only been on the Squadron seventeen days.

ME587 'failed to return' from a raid on Berlin on 30th January 1944. The Lancaster did not crash over land so it can be supposed that it lies at the bottom of the Baltic or the North Sea. Having no known graves, F/O. Wilkinson and the names of all his crew are also at Runnymede.

On the same night, F/O Breckenridge's ME584 was actually on the bombing run over Berlin when it was shot up by a night-fighter and badly damaged. Both gunners, P/O Baker and Sgt Schwartz, were wounded and navigator W/O Meek very seriously. Sgt Hall, the wireless operator, was killed. In four attacks by the night-fighter, W/O Meek was hit in the chest and shoulder blade. Despite his wounds and loss of blood, he navigated ME584 back to East Anglia where F/O Breckenridge belly landed it on RAF Docking's runway. W/O Meek was awarded the Conspicuous Gallantry Medal; he and the two gunners recovered from their wounds and ME584 was repaired to fly again. Sgt Hall's body was taken to Scotland, where it was buried at Ardrossan cemetery.

The Runnymede Memorial to Airmen who have no known grave.

On the way back from bombing Berlin on 15th February 1944 and near Erfurt, JB595 was shot down but fortunately the crew managed to get out. It is not clear how the flight engineer, Sgt Phillips, died and when, supposedly from his wounds, but he is buried in the Berlin 1939/1945 War Cemetery. Pilot F/Sgt

Jacques and the rest of his crew spent the remainder of the war in a POW camp.

Eight other Lancasters of 626 Squadron also did not return to Wickenby. JA864, DV190, JB141, ME576, LL797, JB599, LM393 and HK539 were all shot down over enemy occupied Europe. All the crew members were killed except one, navigator Sgt Edwards of DV190, who survived as a prisoner of war.

The last 626 Squadron Lancaster shot down in the Battle was HK539 on 24th March 1944, returning from the last raid on Berlin. It was captained by the Squadron's Commanding Officer, W/Cdr Ross. He had been on the Squadron less than seven weeks, the rest of his crew only a little longer. They all died, with only an hour's flying time to clear the enemy coast, the North Sea and safety.

WAR CEMETERIES IN GERMANY

RHEINBERG WAR CEMETERY

Rheinberg is a town to the north-west of the Ruhr area where so many airmen lost their lives attacking the industrial cities of this part of Germany. The War Cemetery lies about three kilometres to the south-west of it on the road to Kamp-Lintfort and Kerken. Of the 3,335 servicemen who rest here, 2,898 are airmen who died on bombing missions all over Western Germany throughout World War II. 871 came from Canada, Australia, New Zealand, South Africa, Poland and the U.S.A. After they were shot down, most airmen were buried, sometimes unceremoniously, in isolated graves near where their aircraft crashed and at best in local churchyards. After the War and those that could be found, many of these airmen were exhumed and reburied at Rheinberg. Over 450 airmen alone came from Cologne where the Germans had buried them after the many raids on that city. Two sailors from the Royal Navy and fourteen from the Merchant Navy are also buried here. Alongside the airmen and sailors are 417 soldiers who perished fighting in the last months of the War in the Battle of the Rhineland and in the advance to the River Elbe.

REICHSWALD WAR CEMETERY

This cemetery lies in the Rheichswald Forest near the town of Cleves in Germany and a few miles from the Dutch border to the west. Containing 7,654 graves, it is in area the largest cemetery of either world war. Nearly 4,000 airman, many from Bomber Command share their last resting-place with over 3,600 soldiers who lost their lives in the advance into Germany and the fierce fighting for the Rhineland. After the war, thousands of graves of airmen and soldiers were brought to this cemetery from isolated burial sites all over Western Germany by the Commonwealth War Graves Commission to finally rest in the tranquillity of the Forest's trees.

16. After the Battle: 626 Squadron and RAF Wickenby

After the last raid on the German capital in the Battle of Berlin, 626 Squadron continued operations and W/Cdr Rodney took over the leadership. Still more disastrous raids were to come, along with more successful ones. On 30th March, 626 Squadron Lancasters took part in the Nuremburg raid, where bomber Command lost 95 aircraft, the most of any single raid of the war. While preparing the way for the Normandy invasion Bomber Command bombed railways and other communications in France along with concentrations of German Army units that would oppose the landings. One was the fateful raid on the 10,000-man strong German Panzer training and reinforcement barracks at Mailly-le-Camp, eighty miles east of Paris, on the night of 4th May 1944. The reasons why 44 bombers were lost is explained in other publications and has no place here, but it is enough to say that 626 Squadron was there.

On the night of 5th June 1944, the largest invasion fleet the world has ever seen sailed across the English Channel to Normandy, but before the first ramp of the first landing craft fell down onto the sand, Hitler's 'Atlantic Wall' had to be breached. Along with many other bomber squadrons that were smashing the defences that night, 626 Squadron made two attacks on coastal gun batteries. This called for pin-point accuracy, as from the air the batteries did not present a large target and, needless to say, stray bombs dropping on French communities would not be tolerated. Eight 626 Squadron Lancasters attacked the guns at

Crisbecq, while another ten pounded the battery at St Martin Varreville. Although one of the eight that went to Crisbecq was attacked by an Messerschmitt Me109, all came back safely to Wickenby. Twenty-four hours later when the allies had started to move inland, eighteen 626 Squadron Lancasters flew back over Northern France to attack the marshalling yards at Acheres. It was imperative that reinforcements of German tanks, troops and supplies were to be stopped reaching the coast of Normandy. Because the yards were near the town, bombing accuracy was paramount.

In the following months 626 Squadron was to participate in the destruction of Germany's synthetic oil industry, thus curtailing the activities of the Luftwaffe. The direct result of this was that for the first time since the beginning of the war, Bomber Command was conducting raids in daylight. Many targets were chosen now in support the advancing allied armies.

The last bombs dropped in anger by a 626 Squadron Lancaster were released on such a daylight raid. This was to Hitler's mountain retreat at Berchtesgarten and the nearby army barracks in the south-east corner of Germany at 0955 hrs on 25th May 1944. All four Lancasters that went on the raid returned safely, PD287 piloted by W/O Green being the last to land at 1351 hrs.

No.626 Squadron's wartime offensive operational role was now over.

In the winter of 1944/45 the advancing allies, especially Field Marshal Montgomery's 21st Army Group, pushed the Germans out of Holland and back into Germany. As the German Army retreated, they stripped the Dutch countryside of anything that could be eaten, whether it grew in the ground as crops or on it as farm animals. In most parts of Holland the Dutch people were starving, there are even reports of some eating tulip bulbs. Diplomatic channels were opened via the Swiss for Bomber Command and the 8th USAAF aircraft to fly over Holland without hindrance from the remaining Germans. This time bombs did not drop from the bomb bays, it was food. This was known as Operation 'Manna' for the RAF and Operation 'Chow Hound' for the USAAF. 626 Squadron proudly took part in this, their Lancasters loaded with 284 packs of food each and dropping them from 500 feet at 150mph. After many of these mercy missions, the Squadron's last flight on Operation Manna was flown to the Rotterdam area on the 7th May 1945.

Because of Operation Manna and what Bomber Command did to relieve the starving people, the English, and especially the Royal Air Force, have always had a place in the hearts of the Dutch people. Over fifty years on, Dutch schoolchildren are taught in the classroom what the Lancasters, Halifaxes and Stirlings did over Holland in the spring of 1945. Wherever there are graves of Allied airmen in Holland, and there are many, Dutch schoolchildren consider it a duty and an honour to tend and look after them.

As prisoner of war camps in Germany and the occupied countries were liberated by the allied armies, the inmates were fed, medically attended to and shipped back to their home countries or to the West if there own was occupied by the Russians. Many were lucky enough to travel back by Bomber Command aircraft. 626 Squadron Lancasters flew twenty-four ex-POWs back at a time on what was known as Operation 'Exodus'. The last official operational flight of the Squadron was one such sortie, flying back liberated servicemen from Brussels on 11th May 1945.

After VE Day, 626 Squadron still continued to fly, training was still being carried out and the war was still going on in the

Far East against Japan. 626 Squadron bade goodbye to 12 Squadron on 24th July 1945 as they returned to RAF Binbrook. Meanwhile, Bomber Command was putting together a unit to send to the Far East, called 'Tiger Force', but it was never sent, as the war was finally over by mid August.

Although the war was over, there were still some trips that 626 and other squadrons made over German cities, very low and in daylight. These were unofficially known as 'Cook's Tours', the purpose of which was to show the ground crews the devastation that Bomber Command had meted out to the Nazis over the previous five years. The very last sorties made by 626 Squadron Lancasters were when three of them took ground crew to Berlin and back on 7th October 1945.

On 9th October 1945 the day started with fog but as the morning wore on the visibility became better. On this day RAF Wickenby conducted a Disbandment Parade for 626 Squadron, the salute taken by the Air Officer Commanding 1 Group. The last actual day of the Squadron was 14th October 1945. Like so many others, 626 Squadron has not been reformed to this day.

RAF Wickenby became host to 109 Squadron on the 19th October 1945 as they flew in from Woodall Spa with their Mosquitos but in less than a month, on the 26th November, they flew off again to take up residence at Hemswell. RAF Wickenby was disbanded as a bomber station and handed over to No.40 Maintenance Unit (MU). In time it became established as No.93 MU. Most of the accommodation, mainly the old Nissen huts, was handed over the Ministry of Health two years later but the airfield itself, including the hangars, remained with the RAF. In 1952 RAF Wickenby changed hands to become the Headquarters of 92 MU which took on the task of supplying munitions to RAF squadrons and stations throughout Lincolnshire. Bombs of many varieties were stored on the runways including the last of the 24,000, 12,000 and 4,000 pound bombs in the RAF. In 1956 the RAF Wickenby came to an end and the land returned to farming.

The four main huts comprised the Motor Transport Section and its stores. The concrete building to the right was the Parachute Store while the rough ground centre left are all that remains of No.3 Site with its blast shelters. The concrete bases of some of the old Nissen huts still remain.

What remains of the Airmens' Mess, Cookhouse and NAFFI.

The runways, black hangars and the watch office remained however and flying was able to start again in 1963 but this time it was civilian aircraft - Percival Proctors and Austers of the Lincolnshire Air Touring Group. The original hangars were used by the farming community for storing fertilizers and other materials so two new ones were built in 1968. The old watch office was still in good repair and so in 1971 it became the club house of the Wickenby Flying Club, part of the airfield being purchased to use as a civil aerodrome.

The old Watch Office in 1998.

The Miller Aerial Spraying Company was founded in 1967 for crop spraying in Lincolnshire and the surrounding counties. Flying from Wickenby, the company began with Piper Super Cubs and Pawnee aircraft. In the late 1980s when the author visited the aerodrome, the Company had expanded to operate a number of large Schwweizer-Grumman crop sprayers.

The Wickenby Memorial.

Driving round the countryside to the east of the aerodrome, a few of the old Nissen huts can still be seen and the 'White Hart' pub is still there at Lissington (closed on Mondays). Entering the station, as it was from the road on the south side of the airfield, one will notice that the guardroom on the right has gone. Proceeding on one will come to the old watch office on the left of the perimeter track. To go any further it is courtesy to call in the Wickenby Airfield office. On being given permission (maybe) to wander around it will be found that many buildings, like the brick accommodation and the ablution blocks, have been reduced to their concrete slab foundations. What old buildings remain are used for the storage of farm tractors and other machinery as crops now replace grass on a lot of the airfield. The watch office and the black hangars still dominate the flat landscape.

To the south of the watch office one will come across the Wickenby Memorial overlooking the old runways. None of the airmen who died in World War II having taken off from Wickenby have been forgotten.

In 1981 their comrades who survived erected a memorial of solid stone standing ten feet high. Near the top is a bronze figure of Icarus, featured in Greek mythology, plunging to earth. On one side is the badge of 626 Squadron. the other side, the Badge of 12 Squadron. On the front below the figure of Icarus is the inscription:

ROYAL AIR FORCE WICKENBY
No.1 GROUP BOMBER COMMAND
1942 - 1945
IN MEMORY OF
ONE THOUSAND AND EIGHTY MEN
OF 12 AND 626 SQUADRONS
WHO GAVE THEIR LIVES ON
OPERATIONS FROM THIS AIRFIELD
IN THE OFFENSIVE AGAINST GERMANY
AND THE LIBERATION
OF OCCUPIED EUROPE
Per ardua ad astra

On 6th September 1981 the Memorial was dedicated by a service conducted by the Right Reverend Frank W. Cooks, C.B., M.A., former Chaplain-in-Chief, Royal Air Force. The Royal Air- Force provided a Guard of Honour and most fitting, its last Lancaster, PA474, made a flypast in salute.

Every autumn, at their reunion, the members of the Wickenby Register, the 12 and 626 Squadrons Association, return to the old airfield to remember over 1000 of their comrades in arms who did not. As time marches on their number are diminishing but as long as the memorial stands and people hold in gratitude of what they did and sacrificed to keep these Islands free, their memory will live forever.

THE AVRO LANCASTER

MANUFACTURER:	A.V. Roe & Co Ltd, England.
DESIGNER:	Roy Chadwick.
TYPE:	Four engine long range heavy bomber.
FIRST FLIGHT:	1942.
VERSIONS:	Mks I, II, III, X.
ENGINES:	Mks. I, III, X. Rolls Royce Merlin. Mk. II. Bristol Hercules.
CRUISING SPEED:	160 mph (155 mph IAS).
CRUISING ALTITUDE:	20,000 - 24,000 Feet fully loaded.
RANGE:	1660 Miles.
DEFENSIVE ARMAMENT:	Eight .303" Machine guns in 3 turrets.
FUEL:	100 Octane petrol.
MAXIMUM FUEL CARRIED:	2154 Imperial gallons in 6 wing tanks plus 1 or 2400 imp gallon tanks in the bomb bay if required.
LARGEST LOAD CARRIED:	24,000 Pound 'Grand Slam' bomb.
TYPICAL LOAD TO BERLIN (JB595 of 626 Squadron, 22:11:43):	1 x 4000-pound 'cookie', 56 x 30 pound incendiaries, 1140 x 4-pound incendiaries, 90 x 4X (explosive) incendiaries.
CREW:	7.
WINGSPAN:	102 Feet.
LENGTH:	69 feet 7 inches.
MAXIMUM PERMISSIBLE TAKE OFF WEIGHT:	65,000 Pounds.
MAXIMUM PERMISSIBLE LANDING WEIGHT:	55,000 Pounds.

BIBLIOGRAPHY

ADKIN, Fred. *From The Ground Up.*
BLAKE, Ron. *The Airfields of Lincolnshire Since 1912.*
BOYER, Chaz. *Tales From The Bombers.*
BRAMSON, Alan. *Master Airman.*
CAMPBELL, James. *The Bombing of Nuremburg.*
CHARLWOOD, Don. *No Moon Tonight.*
COOPER, Alan. *In Action With The Enemy. Bombers Over Berlin.*
CURRIE, Jack. *Lancaster Target.*
FRANKLIN, Neville. *Lancaster.* Classic Aircraft Nos.
FREEMAN, Roger A. *The British Airman.*
GARBETT, Mike. & GOULDING, Brian. *Lancaster at War 1, 2 & 3.*
GRIEHL, Manfred. *Junkers Ju88: Star of the Luftwaffe.*
HALLAY J.J. *The Lancaster File.*
HASTINGS, Max. *Bomber Command.*
LONGMATE, Norman. *The Bombers.*
MACDONALD, Jim & LEE, Arthur. *The Woods Are Dark.*
McKEE, Alexander. *Dresden 1945.*
MIDDLEBROOK, Martin. *The Bomber Command War Diaries. The Berlin Raids.*
SAWARD, Dudley. *Bomber Harris.*
SEARBY, John. *The Bomber Battle For Berlin. The Everlasting Arms.*
SMITH, Ron. DFC. *Rear Gunner Pathfinders.*
SPEER, Albert. *Inside The Third Reich.*
STREETLY, Martin. *Confound And Destroy.*
SWEETMAN, Bill. *Lancaster.*
TERRAINE, John. *The Right Of The Line.*
THOMSON, Walter. *Lancaster To Berlin.*
WALLACE G.F. *The Guns Of The Royal Air Force.*
WEBSTER, Sir Charles & FRANKLAND, Noble. *The Strategic Offensive Against Germany 1939-1945.*
Wickenby Register Newsletters. AP2062A.

287

Pilots and Engineers Notes. Lancaster Mk I, III & X (AP2062A)
From The Public Records Office:

> AIR27-2145. 626 Squadron Operational Records.
> AIR27-2146. 626 Squadron Appendices 1944.
> AIR28-945. Wickenby Operational Records.
> AIR25-11. 1 Group Bomber Command Operational Records.
> AIR2-9026. Recommendations for Honours and Awards.

Also published by Woodfield...
The following titles are all available in high-quality softback format

RAF HUMOUR

Bawdy Ballads & Dirty Ditties of the RAF – A huge collection of the bawdy songs and rude recitations beloved by RAF personnel in WW2. Certain to amuse any RAF veteran. Uncensored – so strictly adults only! *"Not for the frail, the fraightfully posh or proper gels – but great fun for everyone else!"*　　**£9.95**

Upside Down Nothing on the Clock – Dozens of jokes and anecdotes contributed by RAF personnel from AC2s to the top brass... still one of our best sellers. *"Highly enjoyable."*　　**£6.00**

Upside Down Again! – Our second great collection of RAF jokes, funny stories and anecdotes – a great gift for those with a high-flying sense of humour! *"Very funny indeed."*　　**£6.00**

Was It Like This For You? – A feast of humorous reminiscences & cartoons depicting the more comical aspects of life in the RAF. *"Will bring back many happy memories. Highly recommended."*　　**£6.00**

MILITARY MEMOIRS & HISTORIES – THE POST-WAR PERIOD

Flying the Waves Richard Pike describes his eventful second career as a commercial helicopter pilot, which involved coastguard Air/Sea Rescue operations in the Shetlands and North Sea.　　**£9.95**

From Port T to RAF Gan The history of the RAF's most deserted outpost is comprehensively and entertainingly charted by **Peter Doling**, a former RAF officer who served on Gan in the 1970s. Many photos, some in colour.　**£20.00**

I Have Control... Former RAF Parachute instructor **Edward Cartner** humorously recalls the many mishaps, blunders and faux-pas of his military career. *Superb writing; very amusing indeed.*　　**£9.95**

Korea: We Lived They Died Former soldier with Duke of Wellington's Regt **Alan Carter** reveals the appalling truth of front-line life for British troops in this now forgotten war. *Very funny in places too.*　　**£9.95**

Meteor Eject! Former 257 Sqn pilot [1950s] **Nick Carter** recalls the early days of RAF jets and his many adventures flying Meteors, including one very lucky escape via a Mk.2 Martin-Baker ejector seat...　　**£9.95**

Pluck Under Fire Eventful Korean War experiences of **John Pluck** with the Middlesex Regiment.　　**£9.95**

Return to Gan Michael Butler's light-hearted account of life at RAF Gan in 1960 and the founding of 'Radio Gan'. *Will delight those who also served at this remote RAF outpost in the Indian Ocean.*　　**£12.00**

The Spice of Flight Former RAF pilot **Richard Pike** delivers a fascinating account of flying Lightnings, Phantoms and later helicopters with 56, 43(F) & 19 Sqns in the RAF of the 1960s & 70s.　　**£9.95**

Tread Lightly into Danger Bomb-disposal expert **Anthony Charlwood**'s experiences in some of the world's most dangerous hotspots (Kuwait, Iraq, Lebanon, Somalia, etc) over the last 30 years.　　**£9.95**

Who is in Charge Here...? Former RAF Parachute instructor **Edward Cartner** regales us with more inglorious moments from the latter part of his military career as a senior officer. *Superb writing; very amusing indeed.*　　**£9.95**

MILITARY MEMOIRS & HISTORIES – WORLD WAR 1 & 2

2297: A POW's Story Taken prisoner at Dunkirk, **John Lawrence** spent 5 years as a POW at Lamsdorf, Jagendorf, Posen and elsewhere. *"A very interesting & delightfully illustrated account of his experiences."*　　**£6.00**

A Bird Over Berlin Former Lancaster pilot with 61 Sqn, **Tony Bird DFC** tells a remarkable tale of survival against the odds during raids on the German capital & as a POW. *"An incredible-but-true sequence of events."*　　**£9.95**

A Journey from Blandford The wartime exploits of motorcycle dispatch rider **B.A. Jones** began at Blandford Camp in Dorset but took him to Dunkirk, the Middle East, D-Day and beyond...　　**£9.95**

A Lighter Shade of Blue A former Radar Operator **Reg O'Neil** recalls his WW2 service in Malta and Italy with 16004 AMES – a front-line mobile radar unit. *'Interesting, informative and amusing.'*　　**£9.95**

A Shilling's Worth of Promises Delightfully funny memoirs of **Fred Hitchcock**, recalling his years as an RAF airman during the war and later amusing escapades in the UK and Egypt. *A very entertaining read.*　　**£9.95**

Beaufighters BOAC & Me – WW2 Beaufighter navigator **Sam Wright** served a full tour with 254 Sqn and was later seconded to BOAC on early postwar overseas routes. *'Captures the spirit of the Beaufighter'* **£9.95**

Coastal Command Pilot Former Hudson pilot **Ted Rayner**'s outstanding account of his unusual WW2 Coastal Command experiences, flying in the Arctic from bases in Iceland and Greenland. **£9.95**

Cyril Wild: The Tall Man Who Never Slept – **James Bradley**'s biography of a remarkable Japanese-speaking British Army officer who helped many POWs survive on the infamous Burma railway. **£9.95**

Desert War Diary by **John Walton** Diary and photos recording the activities of the Hurricanes and personnel of 213 Squadron during WW2 in Cyprus and Egypt. *"Informative and entertaining."* **£9.95**

From Fiji to Balkan Skies Spitfire/Mustang pilot **Dennis McCaig** recalls eventful WW2 operations over the Adriatic/Balkans with 249 Sqn in 43/44. *'A rip-roaring real-life adventure, splendidly written.'* **£9.95**

From Horses to Chieftains – Long-serving Army veteran **Richard Napier** recalls an eventful Army career that began with a cavalry regiment in 1935; took in El Alamein & D-Day and ended in the 1960s. **£9.95**

Get Some In! The many wartime adventures of **Mervyn Base**, a WW2 RAF Bomb Disposal expert **£9.95**

Just a Survivor Former Lancaster navigator **Phil Potts** tells his remarkable tale of survival against the odds in the air with 103 Sqn and later as a POW. *'An enlightening and well written account.'* **£9.95**

Memoirs of a 'Goldfish' • The eventful wartime memoirs of former 115 Sqn Wellington pilot **Jim Burtt-Smith**, now president of the Goldfish Club - exclusively for aviators who have force-landed into water. **£9.95**

Nobody Unprepared – The history of No 78 Sqn RAF is told in full for the first time by **Vernon Holland** in this absorbing account of the Whitley/Halifax squadron's World War 2 exploits. Full statistics and roll of honour. **£14.95**

No Brylcreem, No Medals – RAF MT driver **Jack Hambleton** 's splendid account of his wartime escapades in England, Shetlands & Middle East blends comic/tragic aspects of war in uniquely entertaining way. **£9.95**

Nobody's Hero • Former RAF Policeman **Bernard Hart-Hallam**'s extraordinary adventures with 2TAF Security Section on D-Day and beyond in France, Belgium & Germany. *"Unique and frequently surprising."* **£9.95**

Once a Cameron Highlander • This biog of Robert Burns, who, at 104 was the oldest survivor of the Battle of the Somme; takes in his WW1 experiences, later life in showbusiness and celebrity status as a centenarian. **£9.95**

Operation Pharos • **Ken Rosam** tells the story of the RAF's secret bomber base/staging post on the Cocos Keeling islands during WW2 and of many operations from there. *'A fascinating slice of RAF history.'* **£9.95**

Over Hell & High Water • WW2 navigator **Les Parsons** survived 31 ops on Lancasters with 622 Sqn, then went on to fly Liberators in Far East with 99 Sqn. *'An exceptional tale of 'double jeopardy'.* Lancasters Dec 43 **£9.95**

Pacifist to Glider Pilot • The son of Plymouth Brethren parents, **Alec Waldron** renounced their pacifism and went on to pilot gliders with the Glider Pilot Regiment at both Sicily & Arnhem. *Excellent photos.* **£9.95**

Pathfinder Force Balkans • Pathfinder F/Engineer **Geoff Curtis** saw action over Germany & Italy before baling out over Hungary. He was a POW in Komarno, Stalags 17a & 17b. *'An amazing catalogue of adventures.'* **£9.95**

Per Ardua Pro Patria • Humour and tragedy are interwoven in these unassuming autobiographical observations of **Dennis Wiltshire**, a former Lancaster Flight Engineer who later worked for NASA. **£9.95**

Ploughs, Planes & Palliasses • Entertaining recollections of RAF pilot **Percy Carruthers**, who flew Baltimores in Egypt with 223 Squadron and was later a POW at Stalag Luft 1 & 6. **£9.95**

RAF/UXB The Story of RAF Bomb Disposal • Stories contributed by wartime RAF BD veterans that will surprise and educate the uninitiated. *"Amazing stories of very brave men."* **£9.95**

Railway to Runway • Wartime diary & letters of Halifax Observer **Leslie Harris** – killed in action with 76 Sqn in 1943 – poignantly capture the spirit of the wartime RAF in the words of a 20-year-old airman. **£9.95**

Seletar Crowning Glory • The history of the RAF base in Singapore from its earliest beginnings, through the golden era of the flying-boats, its capture in WW2 and on to its closure in the 1970s. **£15.00**

The RAF & Me • Former Stirling navigator **Gordon Frost** recalls ops with 570 Sqn from RAF Harwell, including 'Market-Garden' 'Varsity' and others. *'A salute to the mighty Stirling and its valiant crews.'* **£9.95**

Training for Triumph • **Tom Docherty**'s very thorough account of the amazing achievement of RAF Training Command, who trained over 90,000 aircrew during World War 2. *'An impressively detailed book.'* **£12.00**

To Strive and Not to Yield An inspiring account of the involvement of No 626 Squadron RAF Bomber Command in the 'Battle of Berlin' (1943/44) and a salute to the men and women who served on the squadron. **£14.95**

Un Grand Bordel • Geoffrey French relates air-gunner **Norman Lee**'s amazing real-life adventures with the French Maquis (Secret Army) after being shot down over Europe. *"Frequently funny and highly eventful."* **£9.95**

UXB Vol 2 More unusual and gripping tales of bomb disposal in WW2 and after. **£9.95**

Wot! No Engines? • Alan Cooper tells the story of military gliders in general and the RAF glider pilots who served on Operation Varsity in 1945 in particular. A very large and impressive book with many photos. **£18.00**

While Others Slept • Former Hampden navigator **Eric Woods** tells the story of Bomber Command's early years and how he completed a tour of duty with 144 Squadron. *'Full of valuable historical detail.'* **£9.95**

WOMEN & WORLD WAR TWO

A WAAF at War • Former MT driver **Diana Lindo**'s charming evocation of life in the WAAF will bring back happy memories to all those who also served in World War 2. *"Nostalgic and good-natured."* **£9.95**

Corduroy Days • Warm-hearted and amusing recollections of **Josephine Duggan-Rees**'s wartime years spent as a Land Girl on farms in the New Forest area. *"Funny, nostalgic and very well written."* **£9.95**

Ernie • Celia Savage's quest to discover the truth about the death of her father, an RAF Halifax navigator with 149 Sqn, who died in WW2 when she was just 6 years old. *"A real-life detective story."* **£9.95**

In My Father's Footsteps • **Pat Bienkowski**'s moving account of her trip to Singapore & Thailand to visit the places where her father and uncle were both POW's during WW2. **£9.95**

Lambs in Blue • **Rebecca Barnett's** revealing account of the wartime lives and loves of a group of WAAFs posted to the tropical paradise of Ceylon. *"A highly congenial WW2 chronicle."* **£9.95**

Radar Days • Delightful evocation of life in the wartime WAAF by former Radar Operator **Gwen Arnold**, who served at Bawdsey Manor RDF Station, Suffolk. *"Amusing, charming and affectionate."* **£9.95**

Searching in the Dark The amusing wartime diary of **Peggy Butler** a WAAF radar operator 1942-1946 – written when she was just 19 yrs old and serving at Bawdsey RDF station in Suffolk **£9.95**

MEMOIRS & HISTORIES – NON-MILITARY

20th CenturyFarmers Boy • Sussex farmer **Nick Adames** looks back on a century of rural change and what it has meant to his own family and the county they have farmed in for 400 years. **£9.95**

Call an Ambulance! • former ambulance driver **Alan Crosskill** recalls a number of light-hearted episodes from his eventful career in the 1960s/70s. *'Very amusing and entertaining'.* **£9.95**

Harry – An Evacuee's Story • The misadventures of **Harry Collins** – a young lad evacuated from his home in Stockport UK to Manitoba, Canada in WW2. *'An educational description of the life of an evacuee'* **£9.95**

Just Visiting... • Charming and funny book by former Health Visitor **Molly Corbally**, who brilliantly depicts colourful characters and entertaining incidents from her long career. **£9.95**

Occupation Nurse • **Peter & Mary Birchenall** pay tribute to the achievement of the group of untrained nurses who provided healthcare at Guernsey's only hospital during the German occupation of 1940-45. **£9.95**

FICTION

A Trace of Calcium by **David Barnett** – A commuter comes to the aid of a young woman in trouble, becomes implicated in murder and must use all his resources to clear his name. **£9.95**

Double Time by **David Barnett** – A light-hearted time-travel fantasy in which a bookmaker tries to use a time machine to make his fortune and improve his love-life with hilarious consequences. **£9.95**

Last Sunset by **AA Painter** A nautical thriller set in the world of international yachting. A middle aged yachtsman becomes accidentally embroiled with smugglers, pirates and a very sexy young lady... **£9.95**

The Brats by **Tony Paul** Tony Paul tells the true story of his grandfather, who, as a boy, along with several friends, stowed away on a ship bound for Canada. The youngsters' brutal mistreatment at the hands of the Captain and Mate of the ship caused a scandal that made headlines in Victorian times. *An enthralling real-life seafaring story.* **£9.95**

The Cherkassy Incident by **Hunter Carlyle** A gripping action thriller featuring a terrorist plot to steal nuclear missiles from a sunken Russian nuclear submarine and the efforts of international security agents to stop them. **£9.95**

MISCELLANEOUS SUBJECTS

Just a Butcher's Boy by **Christopher Bolton** Charming account of small town life in the 1950s in the rural Leiston, Suffolk and idyllic summers spent with grandparents who owned the local butcher's shop. **£5.95**

Impress of Eternity by **Paul McNamee** An investigation into the authenticity of the Turin Shroud. A former schoolmaster examines the evidence and comes to a startling conclusion. **£5.95**

Making a Successful Best Man's Speech. An indispensable aid to anyone who feels nervous about making a wedding speech. Tells you what to say and how to remember it. **£5.95**

Near & Yet So Far by **Audrey Truswell** The founder of an animal rescue charity tells charming and heart-warming tales of the rescue and rehabilitation of many four-legged friends in need. **£9.95**

Reputedly Haunted Inns of the Chilterns & Thames Valley by **Roger Long** – A light hearted look at pubs & the paranormal in the Heart of England **£5.95**

BOOKS FEATURING THE SOUTH COAST & THE SOUTH DOWNS REGION

A Portrait of Slindon by **Josephine Duggan Rees** A charming history of this attractive and well-preserved West Sussex village, from its earliest beginnings to the present day, taking in the exploits of its many notable residents over the years. Very informative and entertaining. Illustrated with many photos, some in colour. **£14.95**

Retribution by **Mike Jupp** An outrageous and very funny comedy/fantasy novel for adults and older children, featuring bizarre goings-on in a quiet English seaside town that bears a striking resemblance to Mike's home town of Bognor Regis. Brilliantly illustrated. **£9.95**

Unknown to History and Fame by **Brenda Dixon** – Charming portrait of Victorian life in the West Sussex village of Walberton via the writings of Charles Ayling, a resident of the village, whose reports on local events were a popular feature in *The West Sussex Gazette* over many years during the Victorian era. **£9.95**

A Little School on the Downs The story of Harriet Finlay-Johnson, headmistress of a little school junior in Sompting, West Sussex in the 1890s, whose ideas and classroom techniques began a revolution in education. She also scandalised society at the time by marrying a former pupil, 20 years her junior. *An amazing and inspiring true story.* **£9.95**

The South Coast Beat Scene of the 1960s The South Coast may not have been as famous as Liverpool in the swinging sixties but it was nevertheless a hotbed of musical activity. Broadcaster **Mike Read** traces the complete history of the musicians, the fans and the venues from Brighton to Bognor in this large and lavishly illustrated book. **£24.95**

Boys & Other Animals by **Josephine Duggan Rees**. A charming and delightfully funny account of a mother's many trials and tribulations bringing up a boisterous all-male family on a farm in rural Sussex during the 1950s-70s. **£9.95**